PLANT CONSERVATION

Plant Conservation
Why It Matters and How It Works

Timothy Walker

Timber Press
Portland / London

Frontispiece: *Menyanthes trifoliata*, the beautiful rare bog bean whose lovely image drew extraordinary attention to its plight, also proving that it is easier to protect beautiful plants than dull ones.

I would like to acknowledge the vast amount of field work that goes into plant conservation the world over. Most of this is not done for monetary reward but because those carrying out the work believe that it is The Right Thing To Do.

THIS BOOK IS DEDICATED TO
Bill Potter
Joe Talbot
Gren Lucas
Hugh Dickinson

Copyright © 2013 by Timothy Walker. All rights reserved.
Published in 2013 by Timber Press, Inc.

Illustrations on pages 2, 10, 63 by Sarah C. Rutherford
Illustration on page 30 by Dave Carlson Studios, Carlson-Art.com.
"Water Requirements for Energy Production" on page 193 from Robert F. Service, Another biofuels drawback: the demand for irrigation. *Science*: 326, 516.

Thanks are offered to those who granted permission for use of materials. While every reasonable effort has been made to contact copyright holders and secure permission for all materials reproduced in this work, we offer apologies for any instances in which this was not possible and for any inadvertent omissions.

The Haseltine Building
133 S.W. Second Avenue, Suite 450
Portland, Oregon 97204-3527
timberpress.com

6a Lonsdale Road
London NW6 6RD
timberpress.co.uk

Printed in the United States of America
Book design by Breanna Goodrow

Library of Congress Cataloging-in-Publication Data
Walker, Timothy, 1958-
  Plant conservation : why it matters and how it works / Timothy Walker.
      p. cm.
  Includes bibliographical references and index.
  ISBN 978-1-60469-260-0
  1. Plant conservation. I. Title.
  QK86.W35 2013
  333.95'316—dc23
                          2013008410
A catalogue record for this book is also available from the British Library.

Contents

Preface	A 2020 Vision for Plant Conservation	6
Introduction	What on Earth Have Plants Been Doing for Us? (Everything!)	15
PART ONE	**THE GLOBAL GARDEN LIST**	**45**
1	A World Flora: How on Earth Do We Do It?	46
PART TWO	**OATH OF A PLANT STEWARD: TO CONSERVE AND PROTECT**	**83**
2	Which is Better, Home or Away?	84
3	Conserving Genes: Plants for the Future	122
PART THREE	**AND JUSTICE FOR ALL: DIVERSITY WITHOUT ADVERSITY**	**144**
4	Moving Away from Home: Mobile Plants, Natural or Unnatural?	146
5	Meeting the Needs of Today and All Our Tomorrows	164
6	Pay As You Go: Sustainable Resource Use	186
PART FOUR	**WHAT CAN YOU DO? PARTNERSHIP AND PRACTICE IN PLANT CONSERVATION**	**209**
7	Gardeners Getting Involved	210
The Strategy	So Here It Is—Now You Know	261
Further Reading		281
Organization Websites		284
Conversion Tables		285
Index		286

"Without plants, there is no life. The functioning of the planet, and our survival, depends on plants.... Our vision is of a positive, sustainable future where human activities support the diversity of plant life and where in turn the diversity of plants support and improve our livelihoods and well-being."

—Global Strategy for Plant Conservation 2011–2020, Convention on Biological Diversity

PREFACE

A 2020 Vision for Plant Conservation

Without plants, humans would not exist.

Plants created the world in which our ancestors evolved—and plants have always been, and always will be, the only renewable, sustainable supply of all our needs. The reason they are able to do this is that about 1.2 billion years ago a single-celled organism press-ganged another organism into its service. This unwitting volunteer—a cyanobacterium—had come up with a neat trick. It used the sun's energy to combine the water in which it was living with the carbon dioxide dissolved in that water and made some very useful stuff out of these abundant raw materials.

Since that time, plants crept out of the water, invaded land, and have become complex, multicellular organisms. On the back of their successes arose the animal kingdom—that includes us.

The clear result of this in our lifetime is that the future of *Homo sapiens*, and others, of course, is dependent upon the future of the plants. As important as it is to you to look after your bank accounts and, on the larger scale, support our banking systems, it is as important to look after biological systems. Plants have given us almost everything that we need; they have provided what we need not only to survive on planet Earth, but to do so in comfort. They provide us with food and drinks, their fibres are used to build houses and create cloth, and half of the chemotherapies against cancer are derived from plants. Clearly, there is the sheer beauty of them, as well as our desire to preserve our current standard of living—and our cravings make a considerable contribution this, such as a very pleasing chocolate bar you might have just eaten, in which case your brain would be telling you, in no uncertain terms: plants are *very* important.

To help in the grand strategies and ongoing work to ensure that we *Homo sapiens* survive and that what we cherish is protected, I wrote this book. It is my desire to put the record straight: so much of the news about plant conservation is negative and I wanted to show how much positive and effective activity is taking place around the world. Plant products are very important, are the basis of human civilization; and if we do not look after them our children's future—and, yes, even our future—will be very uncomfortable. I also wanted to show how we can, as individuals, play a part in conservation, preventing the extinction of even one more species. So while so much of conservation work appears to be carried out by government agencies and nongovernmental organizations, when we stop to think about it, these groups are all staffed by individuals playing their parts: field botanists, reserve managers, horticulturists, ecologists, teachers, both professional and backyard garden-variety gardeners, and others—all of whom, in partnership and individual practice, have skills that are at the centre of so much conservation activity. Yet too many gardeners cannot see how essential their work is, and above all how they can partner their skills and involvement.

While we are fortunate to have such a diversity of people caring for and having a strong desire to see plant life continue, it would be easy for some things to be missed. It would be very unfortunate, say, if only the attractive plants were conserved, leaving the dull but ecologically more important species neglected. What has become clear, then, and understood to be necessary, is a coordinated strategy that covers all the bases on the playing field of conservation. This is exactly what we have in the form of the Global Strategy for Plant Conservation (GSPC)—and this, of course, could only happen because of a bunch (surely an apt collective noun for us plant lovers?) of people and several groups made it happen.

In 1999 the Sixteenth International Botanical Congress was held in the United States, in St. Louis, Missouri, the home turf of the Missouri Botanical Garden. At that meeting there was a great deal of horizon scanning with the impending new millennium starting in the following year. Of the many groups at the congress was one comprising the directors of botanic gardens and similar institutions. Together the directors decided that what was needed was some form of coordinated plan that ensured that all aspects of plant conservation were covered—and they had the visionary idea that there should be set targets, and that those targets should be met by 2010. After all, how could we be sure that progress was being made unless there was at least a benchmark against which future activity could be judged?

So, in April 2000, a small group of men and women from all around the world met at the botanical garden on one of Spain's well-known Canary Islands, Gran Canaria. After just a few days at Jardín Botánico Canario Viera y Clavijo, a four-page document was produced, calling upon the countries that signed the Convention on Biological Diversity to agree to support a target-driven strategy for plant conservation. The strategy specified sixteen targets that fell under five broad objectives. This was the beginning of what would be called the Global Strategy for Plant Conservation.

In 2002, slightly revised targets were taken to the meeting of the Conference of the Parties, held in The Hague, Netherlands. This event initiated the biggest, most unique step forward in conservation to date. Never before had the vast majority of the world's governments signed themselves up to a set of measurable targets in the conservation of a major group of organisms. Governments might like setting their departments' targets, but here were self-inflicted targets—and if there are targets, then there is a possibility of failure for all of the participants. There was no precedent and, to date, no global strategy for the conservation of mammals or birds or butterflies. With plants at the bottom of every terrestrial food chain, and at the heart of every food web, this was a very exciting moment for all conservation (not just the conservation of the green stuff).

When 2010 arrived, successes and failures were assessed. This took place at the Tenth Conference of the Parties in Nagoya, Aichi Prefecture,

A food web

A hedge is the base of this food web. Invertebrates live on the hedge, pollinating the flowers when taking nectar. Birds eat the invertebrates and the fruit produced by the hedge. Small mammals such as voles eat the fruit and the invertebrates. Owls eat the small mammals.

Japan, where delegates to the Convention on Biological Diversity adopted an updated version: the Global Strategy for Plant Conservation 2011–2020.

Now, you may be wondering what are these five objectives and sixteen targets? The answer is in the very bones of this book—or, more aptly put, the lignin, the supporting substance providing a woody rigidity to plants. In this book, plant conservation and what you can do are presented in parts and chapters that broadly follow the objectives and targets of the GSPC 2020 vision.

The sixteen targets of the first round of the GSPC under five broad themes were set to be hit by 2010, and these covered all the areas of plant conservation that we must address. As I see it, we hit seven targets; we missed another seven, but by a known amount; two of the targets were missed completely, but this was due to unknown unknowns—which are now known unknowns, and that in itself is progress!

While plants do not grow everywhere, where they do grow they are being regularly harvested more quickly than they can grow. Furthermore, one quarter of the world's land is currently under production, and this normally displaces native biology. These two factors are placing increasing pressure on plant species all over the world; many are having difficulty finding a suitable habitat—and it is predicted that 28 percent of all plant species may no longer exist by 2050.

It would be easy to brush aside international agreements as being so full of hot air that they contribute more to global climate change than they do to action on the ground. Yet this initiative, the vision for 2020, was drawn up by people whose first and foremost interest is their dedicated work with plants. The majority of them work in gardens, and so by definition can be called gardeners of various sorts. It is not surprising, then, that if you are a gardener, you can and are making a significant contribution to almost all of the targets and objectives and may already be involved with the Global Strategy without realizing it. If you are growing *Franklinia alatamaha*, you are contributing to target 8. If you are only growing native species in your garden, then you are supporting target 10. If you are trying to eliminate peat from your garden, then you are supporting target 12. Very few of us are going to be able to contribute to every target, but I think that you may be surprised how much you are already doing.

And urgent action is unequivocally required if we are to prevent the loss of our natural heritage. Clearly the problem is too big for any one person or single institution to solve, and we all know how this can lead

2020 STRATEGY

The Global Strategy for Plant Conservation includes five objectives and sixteen targets for the year 2020:

1. Describe and document plant diversity.
- TARGET 1 Compile an online Flora of all known plants
- TARGET 2 Assess the conservation status of all known plant species
- TARGET 3 Develop and share information, research, and methods needed for implementing this strategy

2. Urgently and effectively conserve plant diversity.
- TARGET 4 Protect at least 15 percent of each ecological region or vegetation type
- TARGET 5 Protect at least 75 percent of the most important ecosystem regions
- TARGET 6 Manage at least 75 percent of production and croplands for sustainability and biodiversity
- TARGET 7 Protect at least 75 percent of known threatened species *in situ*
- TARGET 8 Protect at least 75 percent of threatened species *ex situ* and make at least 20 percent available for recovery and restoration programmes
- TARGET 9 Conserve 70 percent of the genetic diversity of crop plants, their wild relatives, and economically valuable plants while preserving indigenous and local knowledge and practice
- TARGET 10 Prevent biological invasions and manage important areas of plant diversity that are invaded

3. Use plant diversity in a sustainable and equitable manner.
- TARGET 11 Protect wild flora from overcollection
- TARGET 12 Source wild-harvested, plant-based products sustainably; don't manufacture products from wild plants faster than the plants can regrow
- TARGET 13 Maintain and conserve indigenous and local knowledge associated with plant resources

4. Promote education and awareness about plant diversity, its role in sustainable livelihoods, and importance to all life on Earth.
- TARGET 14 Communicate the importance of plant diversity

5. Develop the capacities and public engagement necessary to implement this strategy.
- TARGET 15 Train enough people
- TARGET 16 Establish or strengthen institutions and plant conservation networks to achieve the targets

to a sense of gloom and defeatism. Yet it is possible to break the solution down into smaller actions—ones which individuals *and* agencies can successfully tackle.

This book examines the most crucial areas of plant conservation in order to show the work that each of us can do toward preventing further and greater plant extinctions. It is written for gardeners, plant lovers, nature lovers, biology students, conservationists, backyard activists—all who want to know how to contribute and work toward a 2020 vision of plant conservation.

> **2020 STRATEGY**
> **TARGET 3** Develop and share information, research, and methods needed for implementing this strategy

We need a heroic effort to save the plants—they give us everything. And many people involved in conservation believe there is no technical reason why another plant species should become extinct.

We can all play a part.

Now, to start—and in order to understand how we came to be so dependent upon a bunch of green stuff, and hence how the loss of plants makes us vulnerable to cataclysmic alterations in our well-being—we need to go back to the start of present time.

On a Thursday 13,700,000,000 years ago . . .

INTRODUCTION

Plants have done and continue to do everything for us, harvesting the sun's energy through photosynthesis and using it to produce our daily food and all manner of things we rely on to survive. But without plants, humans would not exist. Plants created the world in which our ancestors evolved, and if we do not look after the 400,000 species of plants growing for many millions of years before *Homo sapiens* emerged, our future on Earth starts to look very insecure.

What on Earth Have Plants Been Doing for Us? (Everything!)

On a Thursday 13,700,000,000 years ago...

Scientists believe that our universe began 13.7 billion years ago. The event is colloquially known as the Big Bang (but whether there was indeed a bang, no one knows). The story goes that as matter flew off in all directions, the laws of physics and chemistry came into play and atoms and molecules began to form and interact. Larger objects began to take shape and interact. Stars formed, emitting energy in the form of light and heat. Planetary systems came together. And about 4.5 billion years ago, Earth was in orbit around our sun, but it was not alone and as a result of a collision with a smaller planet called Theia, which hit Earth at about 10,000 miles per hour, our moon was formed. The implication of which is quite profound—because without the moon, there would be no tides, and the tides are thought by some people to have been very important in the movement of the earliest life forms from sea onto land.

In the beginning, our planet was a different place. Compared to today's benign climate, Earth's earliest temperatures and atmosphere were very inhospitable, and yet it was in such a cauldron that life emerged. Quite how this happened is open to a lot of speculation. Yet one of the biggest questions that science has endeavoured to answer is: where and in what sequence did life emerge?

The word *emerge* is often used in discussions of evolution because, with the incomplete nature of both the fossil record and our knowledge, organisms seem to have appeared without any warning or intermediate stages, and the emergence of plant life is no exception. The oldest fossilized cells were found in 2011 in Australia and are thought to be 3.4 billion years old. These were single-celled organisms that used sulfur instead of water to create energy to live; and it's fascinating to know that such organisms still exist today—they are the purple sulfur bacteria that are often found near hot springs or in stagnant, smelly pools of water. What this shows is that there is room on our planet for many different life-surviving strategies, and that there is never going to be just one species that outcompetes everything else. The natural state of affairs, it seems, is that all this—Earth's diverse biological holdings—increases over time; but what we must keep in mind is that, if diversity is reduced suddenly, biological communities can become unstable and mass extinctions can result. Here, then, is one very good reason (among many you'll learn) for why plant conservation is so important to us and the roughly ten million more species (or, as others claim, roughly thirty million) that currently share Earth with us.

So we know that there were on Earth 3.4 billion years ago microorganisms, but what is so fascinating is that these single-celled organisms were complete organisms—that is, fully functioning, living entities.

From where did they come?

Suggestions that life came from another planet just shift the question to another locality and clearly do not answer it for us. But if we break down a living cell into a number of components—such as the membrane that surrounds every living cell, and the chemistry of life known as metabolism that happens inside the cell, and the genetic information that is passed down from one generation to the next—we can come up with hypotheses about how each of these components came about here on Earth. The problem arises when you try to put all the propositions together, and try to determine which happened first.

It has been shown that the simple lipid membranes, like those found around living cells, formed unaided. Recently, artificial membrane-bound vesicles were created in a laboratory; and the metabolism that takes place inside the cells, chemistry driven by enzymes, was also recreated in a lab. We now can describe the structure of the genetic material in each living cell. We can explain how that information is read and translated into living processes. What we cannot yet explain, however, is which of these three events (the formation of an empty cell or metabolism or self-replicating molecules) came first, how they were brought together, and where this happened.

What we can show is how quite complex molecules can emerge in a broth of chemicals like that which existed on Earth about 4 billion years ago. This means that, without having to introduce material from another planet or introduce the concept of a divine designer, the molecular components of life can be made on Earth. From this experiment came the idea of the organic, primeval soup in which all the building blocks of life existed—so that given enough time, you would get a simple cell that could live, grow, divide, and harvest energy from the environment around it. If this is true about the emergence of life, then its occurrence was inevitable, and therefore should have happened more than once (a similar argument suggests that an infinite number of monkeys at an infinite number of typewriters will eventually write the complete works of Shakespeare). But we believe that the emergence of life did *not* emerge more than once. This is the "soup" hypothesis, and it has been losing ground over the past few decades. Rather, it has been suggested, the concentration of the organic building blocks in that bowl of primeval soup was just too dilute to make the chemistry work. So a new hypothesis was required, and it has been found in an amazing place: the ocean.

If life evolved just once, and most biologists think that this is true, then it was an extraordinary event, requiring extraordinary conditions. Deep ocean thermal vents are where exceptional conditions exist— where life exists at temperatures and pressures that should kill it— yet single-celled organisms live there, in rocks near the vents, and derive their energy from breaking down those rocks. The hypothesis that life emerged at the bottom of the ocean is all speculation and will remain so.

All we can say with some confidence is that 3.4 billion years ago, there were single-celled organisms on Earth. As soon as there were two organisms, there was competition for resources and space. Once there was competition, advantageous innovations would have been selected and propagated in the successful organism; over time, these innovations might have enabled these newer, modified cells to either dominate their environment or move into a new place. Diversity increased.

Now we can name a significant innovation that did emerge, about 2.4 billion years ago: photosynthesis. At its simplest level, photosynthesis is a chemical process whereby light energy is used to make complex molecules from simpler molecules. It is thought that the little organisms that first pulled off this trick were cyanobacteria, also known as blue-green algae or blue-green bacteria. Some people claim that these small, ancient organisms are among the most successful on the planet, not because of their longevity but because of the range of habitats that the species now inhabit. These organisms are still found on Earth, in very cold places and very hot places, in water and in arid areas.

Cyanobacteria's contribution to the story of evolution is twofold. First, it is believed that these living organisms were able to harness the sun's energy by splitting water apart and using the energy released from this process to take the carbon dioxide in the atmosphere and make for itself useful chemicals. This process released oxygen into the atmosphere and is thought to have led, at least in part, to the global oxygenated atmosphere that we breathe today.

Second, and just as important, is that about 1.2 billion years ago one of the cyanobacteria was coerced into helping another, more advanced cell belonging to a big group of organisms known as the eukaryotes. The story is thought to have gone a bit like this.

By 1.2 billion years ago, there was a diverse community of living organisms on Earth. Some of these used the sun's energy to grow; these were the autotrophs, or self-feeders. Some of them derived their energy from either minerals and rocks or from eating other organisms, the heterotrophs. One of these organism-eating, heterotrophic singled-celled eukaryotes engulfed a cyanobacterium with the intention of having it for lunch, but something went wrong. Rather than being digested, the photosynthesizing cyanobacterium took up residence in the predatory eukaryote—and then started to hand over some of the products of its photosynthesis to its would-be killer. Clearly the eukaryote with indigestion had lucked out, because rather than the cyanobacterium being just one meal, it became a meal for life. And, furthermore, the cyanobacterium divided and multiplied and the eukaryote got fatter; and when it divided, the cyanobacterium living inside was split and taken into two "daughter" cells that were produced in the division: the first plants! From them have evolved all the plants that have ever existed, and all those that still exist.

After those first plant cells emerged, the world was never to be the same again. Those engulfed simple symbiotic cyanobacteria, now called chloroplasts, evolved within the plants—and this endosymbiotic event is considered to be one of the most important moments in evolutionary history. This was the beginning of the plants that feed all the organisms—us and most of the other heterotrophs—living on Earth today.

How Many Species Are There on Earth?

The simplest extant organisms that can claim to be plants are the glaucophytes. They live in freshwater, consist of one single cell, and as a group comprise approximately fifteen species. It has to be said that, for many people, glaucophytes hardly qualify to be labeled as plants: some glaucophytes move, which is not a normal behaviour for plants; and some of them do not have a rigid cellulose wall around each cell (another frequently quoted defining characteristic of plants). All considering, however, this odd little group of organisms shares more features with plants—such as land plants and aquatic red and green algae—than they do with any other group of organisms. It might be

The endosymbiotic event

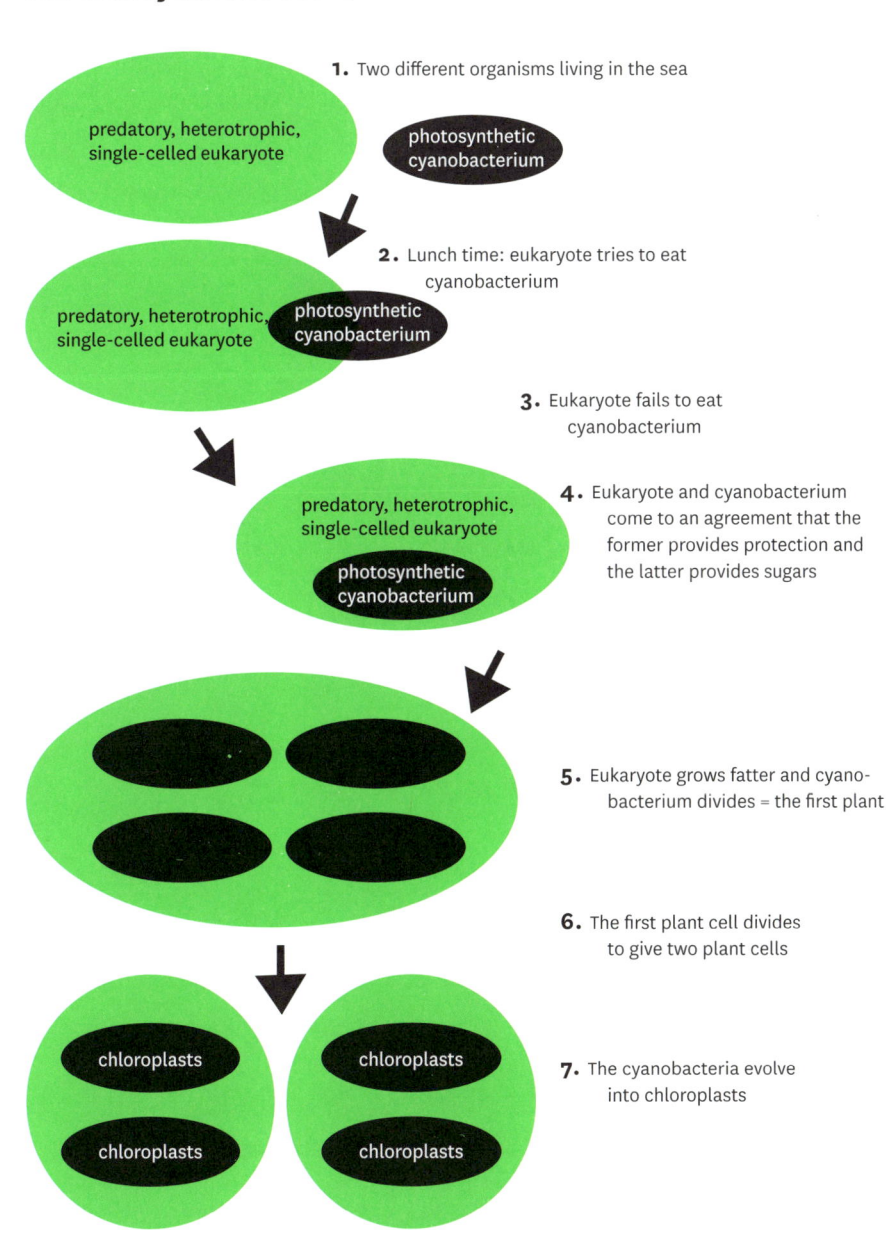

1. Two different organisms living in the sea

predatory, heterotrophic, single-celled eukaryote

photosynthetic cyanobacterium

2. Lunch time: eukaryote tries to eat cyanobacterium

predatory, heterotrophic, single-celled eukaryote

photosynthetic cyanobacterium

3. Eukaryote fails to eat cyanobacterium

4. Eukaryote and cyanobacterium come to an agreement that the former provides protection and the latter provides sugars

predatory, heterotrophic, single-celled eukaryote

photosynthetic cyanobacterium

5. Eukaryote grows fatter and cyanobacterium divides = the first plant

6. The first plant cell divides to give two plant cells

chloroplasts

chloroplasts

chloroplasts

chloroplasts

7. The cyanobacteria evolve into chloroplasts

worth stating that for some people the term *plant* should only be applied to land plants, but I am not one of them because it ignores the ancestry.

While the glaucophytes are not as diverse as, say, the algae, they exist today and are considered to be the closest we have to the original plants that eventually diversified into red and green algae, and ultimately into land plants. There are somewhere between five and ten thousand species of red algae and a similar number of green algae. These numbers may seem vague; and indeed this fuzziness is a small part of a much larger problem in biology: how many species are there on Earth?

Many people have tried to answer this question, and estimates vary from 3 million to 100 million. In 2011, yet another paper was published, with a great deal of razzmatazz. By using a new method of estimations and extrapolations, the authors, Camilo Mora and colleagues, claim that there are 8.7 million species living on Earth, on land and in water. They say that this figure is accurate, give or take 1.3 million species. The irony of this latter figure is that it is generally accepted that we have only described 1.2 million species to date, and that 350,000 of these are

Known Catalogued Plant Species on Earth by Evolutionary Group

Aquatic plants
glaucophytes 15
red algae 6,000
green algae 6,000
charophytes 1,000s

Land plants
liverworts 9,000
hornworts 216
mosses 12,000

Vascular plants
lycopods 1,200
ferns 11,500

Seed plants
conifers and closely related groups 1,000
flowering plants 350,000

flowering plants, which are believed to be among the better described groups (along with mammals, birds, and butterflies).

All this fuzzy ignorance is sometimes described rather colourfully as the taxonomic abyss, but more directly refers to the lack of people trained and, most importantly, employed to describe, catalogue, classify, and name the world's biology, the currency of which is all the species in existence—the global flora. In addition to the 350,000 species of flowering plants that I mentioned, it is estimated that another 50,000 have already been collected, but no one has had the time to look at these yet, to describe, classify, and name them. For now, however, a summary is called for: the list on page 22 shows estimates for plants in their respective evolutionary groups.

It is hopefully clear from what I have written already that we do not know what is "out there." Some countries such as the United Kingdom have been so thoroughly surveyed and explored that we are confident that no more native plants are there to be discovered. The same cannot be said of many countries in the world.

You might be wonder now about how long it would take to catalogue and classify all of the world's land plants. Using the United Kingdom as an example of a country whose plants have been fully documented, it can be extrapolated that it would take 5.25 million people working for a career of forty years for us to have a complete list of the world's plants. (This might seem like a lot, but it would take many times as long to catalogue the world's insects.) This catalogue would then require 1.2 million botanists working for ever to keep the list up to date, which would be an average of 6,486 per country if each country were the same size. It is very difficult for plant conservation to get started without an accurate description of what is "out there," and this is the necessary current work—the first target of our global conservation strategy.

2020 STRATEGY
TARGET 1 Compile an online Flora of all known plants

Compiling the list of the world's plants is not quite as simple as surveying every country and adding the lists together, because many plants grow in more than one country and so you could get many duplicates with different names. The country lists have to be amalgamated very carefully. So without a catalogue of accurate and universal names, there can be no permanent knowledge, and thus the global plant list is a prerequisite of all other work. Once the list has been compiled, then an accurate assessment of regional, national, and international rarity and threatenedness can be carried out.

Making Landfall

As we are here galloping through evolution, and have already reached the algae, we should consider that *algae* is one of those irritating words that has both a scientific meaning and a vernacular meaning that are different. For normal people (that is, non-botanists) algae are probably those green slimy things that grow in fishponds or on shady paths; these same normal people would probably not refer to the plants that grow in the sea and in the intertidal zone as algae, but as seaweeds. To a botanist, though, both the green slimy things and some of the seaweeds would indeed be called algae—but she or he would not then call all of these "plants" because there are seaweeds that are not plants; these are the brown algae. And they are considered to be more closely related to animals than they are to plants. Additionally, the origin of these odd organisms is controversial, probably involving another endosymbiotic event similar to but not nearly as important as the one that introduced plants to Earth 1.2 billion years ago.

Green algae live in salty and freshwater and are very important in the evolutionary story of plants, and in the history of our own species.

These freshwater algae are sometimes known as the charophytes, or stoneworts, and are important because an ancestor of stoneworts is also the ancestor of land plants, which were to become so essential to our species' survival. What this common ancestor looked like is not certain due to the incompleteness of the fossil record, but if you slipped through a wormhole and back 470 million years in time, you would certainly recognize these organisms as plants, some of which managed to spend at least part of their life cycle in the air above dry land.

This was no mean feat. Water is where life emerged. It is a benign environment that is not prone to sudden changes in temperature (and is a very supportive substance, as a beached whale discovers at great cost); and it is wet (not likely to dry out). None of this is true of the land. There were many obstacles to plants getting out of the water and living on the land; multiple innovations do not happen simultaneously in biological evolution. So the first land plants must have acquired the necessary traits separately and over a long period of time that allowed them to survive on dry land and, most particularly, while exposed 24/7 to the air. Among these "pre-adaptations" is the substance sporopollenin, which is almost indestructible and which nowadays protects pollen in its perilous journey from anther to stigma. Another pre-adaptation to life in the air is a thick waterproof cuticle on the aerial parts of the plant.

So the current hypothesis is that a plant similar to modern stoneworts managed to spend some and then all of its time out of the water. Eventually these land-lubber stoneworts had departed so far from the aquatic stoneworts, they belonged to a new group—the liverworts, the closest descendants of the earliest stonewort land plants. The word *wort*, from the middle English period (thirteenth to fifteenth centuries), means simply "plant," so liverworts are plants that look like a piece of liver (but one that is well beyond its sell-by date); and stoneworts are so called because they at times are encrusted in calcium carbonate.

So, for the oldest lineages in the extant groups of land plants, we have the liverworts and the mosses; and in some ways these plants have changed less than any other major group of plants that made it onto land. Their truly vital trait, vital to themselves and to humans, as it turned out, was and still is the ability to grow on bare rock, without soil, while their close relatives, the stoneworts, are restricted to living in water. We see this all around us every day where mosses and liverworts grow on walls. These little plants, 470 million years after plants got out of the water, are still happy in their habitat, a place where most land plants cannot go.

Despite the remarkable evolutionary achievement of land plants, nothing lives for ever. And as they met their death, they started the process of decay and decomposition that is a vital part of the formation of soils. As soils started to accumulate, the plants began to acquire improvements to their root systems that enabled them to hold on to soil, preventing them from blowing away. This role as the green glue that holds life on Earth is critically important.

The land plants, with their roots in soil, became stronger and taller. Woody tissue emerged with proper plumbing, enabling the plants to grow taller, and this increased the volume of air that could be colonized. The invasion of land was about the invasion of the air as well. Woody tissue and good vascular tissue meant that plants could stand up and grow much taller, up to 360 feet in some circumstances.

It is interesting and important to realize that the trees that we see around us, and those that we find in the fossil record, have not all evolved from one ancestral tree—the *prototree* if you like. A tree is just a plant with a stick up the middle, and we find that there are at least four different ways to make a tree today. Tree ferns, conifers, palms, and flowering trees like magnolias are quite different, as different as dragonflies, bees, birds, and bats, which all have wings but are otherwise very different.

The first ferns were different from the ones we know and love—especially in one significant way: some of them were huge! And they fixed a very large amount of carbon dioxide, incorporating it into molecules that enabled them to stand up and grow so tall. When these plants died, many of them did not decay (which would release their carbon dioxide) and were preserved instead, becoming, along with other plants, the coal that we as a species still mine and burn in huge qualities.

If this was not enough, a new evolutionary structure emerged some time in the late Devonian period, 385–359.2 million years ago—the seed—and the details of this plant structure's evolution is still one of the great mysteries of plant science.

Again the fossil record lets us down. There are fossils of plants that look like ferns, from their leaves, but which appear to have seedlike structures. These are known as the seed ferns; and though they look like ferns, they are most definitely not.

A seed is a deceptively simple structure. It consists of three basic parts: an embryo that in the right conditions will develop into a mature plant, a food supply for the embryo, and for the embryo and the food supply, a protective coat. (Any parent who has sent their child off to school will recognize this strategy.) Seed production has survived as a strategy for several hundred million years and this suggests that it is clearly not a daft idea. Still, the majority of seeds that have gotten around have never resulted in mature plants; in fact, many of them end up as dinner for animals. (Fortunately, the same is not true for most school children; though they do love their pumpkin and sunflower seed snacks.)

It should never be forgotten that our species consumes more seeds than any other, and that the survival of *Homo sapiens*, including the whole of human civilization, has been predicated on our domestication of seed plants and our improvement of several species of grasses and legumes.

Domestication

It is clearly safe to say that without plants, *Homo sapiens* would have been up a creek with neither a paddle nor in fact a boat. Conservation of plants is not just a nice idea that fills an otherwise idle moment and gives us a warm glow; it is not an optional extra, but an essential strategy for our future and our children's future. This becomes glaringly obvious if we place close by our considered story of plant evolution, the evolution of our species and, further, the development of human society, whereby plant use evolved—and with it plant domestication.

Eating is a central part of life, and clearly plants are very useful to this end.

The cooking of our food started long before cultivated plants appeared. The evidence of this comes in two forms. First, there are the ash and embers of fires demonstrating that fire had been domesticated by early hominids. Second, there is evidence in the Ngalue caves in Mozambique that 105,000 years ago early humans were grinding grass seeds using stone tools and bowls; the majority of the preserved seeds found look like they were from sorghum, with the rest from palms and bananas. The evidence for cultivated plants is seen in amyloplasts— small compartments in plant cells where the manufacturing and storing of starch happens. Amyloplasts are remarkably resistant to decay and remain behind after the rest of the plant has rotted down. The amyloplasts in cultivated plants are much larger than those of the wild plants from which they are selected and bred. Other caves, in eastern South Africa, have also given up clues of other ways in which *Homo sapiens* domesticated plants, such as bedding made of sedges and grasses and arrowheads stuck on with glue from acacia or wattle.

While these early humans were hunter-gathers and did not grow plants in fields, they did manipulate their surrounding countryside by the judicious use of fire. It seems to modern twenty-first-century humans that fire is mostly a destructive force, but *Homo erectus*, *Homo neanderthalensis*, and *Homo sapiens* all used fire as a means to stimulate

The "Sperms"—from the Greek Word for Seeds
Gymnosperms: We love to live in them
Gradually seed plants dominated land, and many animal species ate the seeds. The first extant group of seed plants to dominate the land were the gymnosperms—conifers. Yet with only 1,000 species left, they are considered to be one of the most important of the seed plants, providing us with the most beautiful and useful materials.

Angiosperms: "An abominable mystery"
There is one more major innovation up evolution's sleeve—flowering plants, the origin of which is still among the greatest of all botanical mysteries. Charles Darwin described the origin of flowering plants as "an abominable mystery" and it still is, one and half centuries later.

Irrespective of whence the flowering plants—angiosperms—came, they have become the most species-rich group of plants currently on Earth, and perhaps ever. They live in a wide range of habitats, perhaps the widest of any extant group of plants. Some have even returned to the water from whence land plants came 470 million years ago. They exist in more different shapes, sizes, and morphologies than any of the other groups. They are more chemically diverse than any of the other groups, and we have been very imaginative in exploiting these chemicals, no more so than in the production of medicines. Worldwide, 80 percent of primary health care is based on plant-derived treatments; and even in clinical western medicine, 25 percent of active ingredients are harvested from plants—in chemotherapy for cancer, this proportion rises to perhaps 70 percent.

soft, young growth from plants. This young growth was more palatable not only to our antecedents, but also to the other animals who came for a nibble—who, while they were taking advantage of the flush of soft growth, would be picked off by the spears of nearby hominids. And likely they were barbecued straightaway.

It is difficult to be sure which plant can claim to be the first to be domesticated by humans, but it happened relatively recently, in approximately the last twelve thousand years. Perhaps unexpectedly, one of the earliest species to fall under the influence of man was figs. Excavations in Jordan have revealed a Neolithic village called Gilgall. Preserved in the ruins are fig fruits, which show clearly that these were not from wild plants but from cultivated plants that made sterile parthenocarpic fruits,

Internal structures of a plant cell

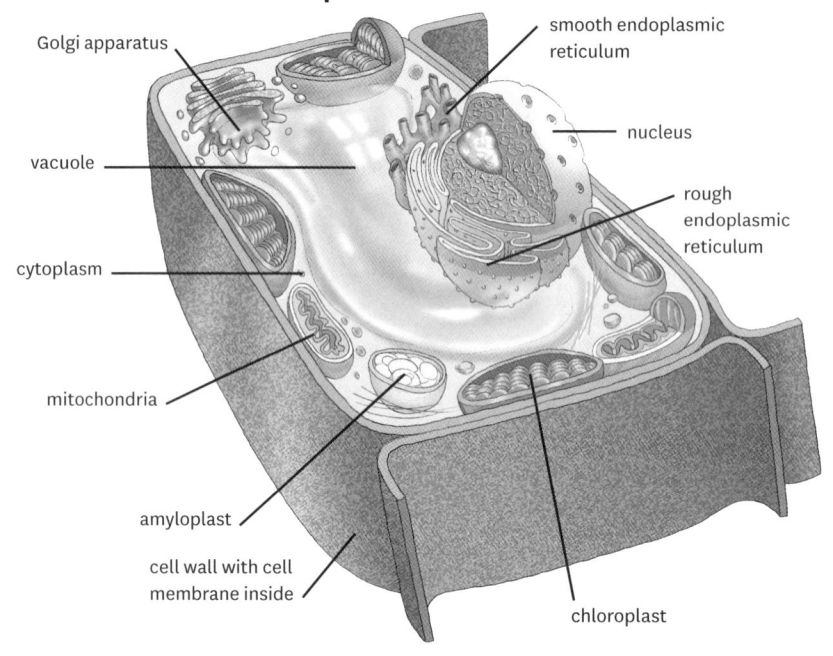

- Golgi apparatus
- vacuole
- cytoplasm
- mitochondria
- amyloplast
- cell wall with cell membrane inside
- smooth endoplasmic reticulum
- nucleus
- rough endoplasmic reticulum
- chloroplast

How Has Domestication Changed Plants?

It is not only seeds of grasses that humans have exploited. Almost every part of a plant has been eaten or otherwise used at some point or other. Roots, tubers, fungi on roots, stems, leaves, flowers, and fruits including nuts. Plants have been domesticated and altered almost beyond recognition. Take, for example, *Brassica oleracea*, an unremarkable member of the brassica family that has been transformed into cabbage, Brussels sprout, broccoli, cauliflower, and kale.

Gigantism Larger fruit or grain

Seed dispersal suppression Seeds remain attached to the plant for longer, allowing the farmer to harvest them all at one time

Simultaneous ripening Fruits can all be harvested in one go

Change in growth form or stature A thinner seed coat facilitates grinding and milling

Change in life form From biennial to annual plants

Change in the breeding system From self-incompatible to self-compatible, to allow faster breeding

Loss of seed dormancy All the seeds sown can germinate quickly and the plants grow together

Changes in biochemistry Loss of toxicity

Changes in the number of chromosomes Doubling, or more, of the chromosomes in each cell of the plant usually resulted in larger, stronger plants

Physiological changes Such as hardiness, thereby extending the growing season and the range of land where plants can be cultivated

Yield per plant The increase results in higher yield be acre

Flavor of the fruit or other parts eaten Fruits can be made sweeter or less bitter, for example

Pest and disease resistance Results in higher yield and fewer pesticide applications

Stress tolerance Such as stress brought on by drought

Maturation Shortening of the time for plants to reach harvesting maturity

> **Really? The Oldest Domesticated Plant?**
> Given their current position as world leaders it is perhaps unexpected that the American continent was the last to be colonized by *Homo sapiens*. It is believed that thirty thousand years ago a group of hunter-gatherers arrived in Beringia (near present day Alaska) from East Asia. They then headed south and sixteen thousand years later they had reached Chile. It is not yet clear which route (coastal or inland) they took, but they clearly had a means of carrying water. They used a member of the cucumber family, *Lagenaria siceraria*, or bottle gourd. The dried shell of the fruits makes a strong, lightweight container that was much prized and valuable before the advent of pottery. The twist in this part of the tale is that *L. siceraria* is an African species with wild populations currently reported from Zimbabwe. The domestication of the plant into a water carrier must have happened before the plant left Africa with the second wave of migrations. This makes bottle gourds a strong candidate for the oldest domesticated plant.

which formed without the need for pollination. It is a safe bet that this plant with parthenocarpic fruit was a random mutation that was spotted by a sharp-eyed person in the same way as a gardener today might eye a new and better colour sport.

―――

And then, on a workday Monday about 10,500 years ago . . .

  . . . *Homo sapiens* began the development of one of the greatest biological achievements in the history of life on Earth: farming. The changes that have resulted from this are as significant as the meteor shower that helped to wipe out the dinosaurs. Through its development, we have been able to increase two-hundred-fold the number of people that the world can support. Without agriculture, the planet can only support about 30 million people (estimates for 2030 global population are calculated to reach 8 billion). No other species has manipulated its habitat quite so successfully.

The driving reasons for the emergence of agriculture are the subject of much speculation, but many researchers believe that it was in part the result of some odd changes in climate after the end of the last ice age. This would certainly help to explain why agriculture emerged independently in several parts of the world. Increases in global temperatures, African drought, sudden falls in global temperatures followed by more rapid warming, a 50 percent increase in carbon dioxide levels, and climate stability would certainly be a plausible backdrop to what came next.

At the Abu Hureyra archeological site in the Euphrates valley in modern Syria, there is evidence of the stone houses in which, judging from the size of the rooms, groups of between approximately fifteen and fifty members of the Natufian people lived. At this site, nine plump seeds of rye have been discovered. These look like seeds from domesticated plants, but some scientists are reluctant to accept that nine seeds is enough evidence to claim that the Natufian people were the first farmers.

The traditional view of the origin of agriculture was that it kicked off about eight thousand years ago in the Fertile Crescent, between the River Tigris and the River Euphrates. Eight crops were domesticated there (einkorn wheat, barley, lentils, peas, flax, bitter vetch, chickpeas, and beans) while simultaneously in China rice was domesticated and in South America potatoes were created out of four other species. This view has now been modified as we bring new techniques to the detective work. These techniques include sophisticated archeological dating, DNA fingerprinting of wild plant species and cultivated varieties, and a better understanding of human evolution and migration.

Agriculture, in Four Stages

The current view is that there were four stages to the adoption of agriculture by the majority of human communities.

continued on page 38

Plant Domestication in Practice I: Human-Made and Human-Used Fibres Derived from Plants

Plant fibres have been used by humans in many different ways. The hard fibres in timber for building is one extreme, while the same fibres are also used in paper manufacture. There are the more flexible fibres of hemp, flax, sisal, jute, and cotton. The first pair of Levi jeans and the first US flag were both made from flax.

Hemp, *Cannabis sativa*, was grown six thousand years ago in China and by AD 105 it was being used in papermaking. The Magna Carta was written on hemp paper in 1215, the original King James bibles were printed on hemp paper in 1611, and more recently hemp has been used in cigarette paper. Hemp is very strong and resistant to the effects of saltwater, so it is good for ships' sails such as those found on HMS *Victory* at the Battle of Trafalgar.

Linen, *Linum usitatissimum*, was originally grown for oil from its seeds ten thousand years ago, but domestication of the species for the production of fibres began nine thousand years ago in Syria, seven thousand years ago in northwest Europe, and five thousand years ago in India. Its use in the manufacture of clothing fabrics declined with the rise of cotton, but it is still used for thread, twine, rope, canvas, sacks, and carpets. Linseed oil, however, is still important, for example, in the manufacture of linoleum.

Sisal, *Agave sisalana*, is a coarse fibre that is added to recycled papers but is also used in the manufacture of cigarette papers, bank notes, tea bags, and filter papers.

Jute, *Corchorus capsularis*, is slightly different from the others in that the fibres are from the phloem, the pipes, that move sugars around the plant. It is used in the manufacture of sacks, twine, carpeting, and paper. Bangladesh exports 350,000 tons of the fibre each year and a further 630,000 tons are used for sacks and hessian (burlap), often with hemp.

Cotton, *Gossypium* species, is the most important plant-derived fibre, for many reasons. The cotton fibres are produced around the seeds. They are hollow and three thousand times longer than wide. In wild species, the hairs are about 6 mm long but this has been increased to 70 mm in cultivated varieties. The function of these hairs is a bit of a mystery. Suggestions include buoyancy in water and to prevent herbivores from digesting the seeds. The hairs are soft and highly absorbent. The fabric is breathable, strong, durable, and a very good insulator. Each fibre has twenty to thirty layers of cellulose molecules coiled in a series of spirals that become entangled when dried. These can then be spun into a strong yarn or thread. Two hundred million hairs are required for 1 kilogram of spun cotton yarn.

Removing the fibres from the seeds creates twice as much waste as fibre, so many people have looked for a use for this waste. Over a thousand uses have been recorded, ranging from concrete plasticizers to food preservatives. Oil from the seeds can be used in cooking and soap powders, but as a culinary oil it has become unpopular following a link to male sterility. The seeds are used to make high-protein animal feed, but this can only be eaten by ruminant herbivores due to the presence of gossypol, which bacteria can break down. Strangely, genetically modified cotton does not have gossypol in its seeds and so it can be eaten by humans.

Of the forty species of cotton, at least four have been domesticated and exploited commercially. It is possible that cotton was cultivated in Egypt twelve thousand years ago, but the oldest direct evidence was found in a cave in Mexico where eight thousand years ago cotton was being woven into textiles. The Mexican species *Gossypium hirsutum* is still the origin of 90 percent of the commercial varieties. Seven thousand years ago, *G. arboreum* was being grown in the Indus Valley in northwest India/Pakistan; and five thousand years ago fibres from *G. barbadense* were being woven in Peru and Ecuador. The final species to be cultivated was *G. herbaceum* in East Africa.

Arab traders brought cotton textiles (calico and muslin) to Europe, and by the ninth century cotton was being grown in Spain by the Moors.

Cotton spread east as well as west from India. In the thirteenth century Marco Polo reported seeing large fields in Iran, and by the fourteenth century cotton was being manufactured in northern Italy. Prior to this, Europeans were largely ignorant of the origin of cotton. The German word for cotton is *baumwolle* meaning "tree wool" because it was assumed that cotton was shorn from lambs that grew on trees whose branches bent down to the ground to enable the lambs to graze. One wonders what these folk had been inhaling to have such imaginative ideas. There is, however, little evidence of cotton in England before the fifteenth century. At that time silk, wool, and flax were the dominant threads. That was to change.

Plant Domestication in Practice II: Three Stooges and Slavery

Three plants have become in a sense the stooges, unwitting accomplices, of some very unpleasant work. Over the past fourteen hundred years, these three plants have altered contemporary human civilization more than any others. Plants have shaped our world's biology during the past 1,200 million years; and over the past 100,000 years, *Homo sapiens* has exploited those plants in a unique way—however, the use of sugarcane, quinine, and cotton tells a story of mankind's exploitive relationship to and with plants that is not comfortable reading. It begins 3,500 years ago with the domestication of *Saccharum officinarum* in New Guinea, and it continues today with the exploitation of children in the cotton industry of several countries.

Sugar The legacy of the sugarcane industry is profound—consider where it is grown. The Amerindians of the Caribbean have been wiped off the face of the earth; the West Indies has a permanent trade deficit where the poor have remained poor due to the absence of a middle class with a conscience and power. And all this has led to migrations to the United Kingdom after World War Two. Additionally, refined sugar remains an addiction in many parts of the world—a completely unnecessary part of a human's diet. Finally, the cultivation of sugarcane established slavery as a means of agricultural production; after it was stopped in the British colonies, it was adopted by America in the first half of the nineteenth century for cotton production.

Quinine Without quinine and its ability to combat malaria, there would have been no British or any other European colonies, and 20,000,000 Africans, who just happen to have protection from malaria from sickle-cell disease, would not have been transported across the Atlantic. This was the only time in history that one race has been taken into slavery selectively.

Cotton The legacy of cotton production lives on. The cotton industry centred in the northwest of England created wealth that enabled Britain to create an empire. That wealth, and military power at sea, enabled Britain to enforce the abolition of the slave trade, but the cotton mills in England deprived the Indians of their livelihoods due to crippling UK tariffs. But the cotton mill workers in England were no more than waged slaves, and from their suffering came the British political party system. The production of cotton in the southern United States in the first half of the nineteenth century cost 4 million slave lives. Many of those slaves were bred for slavery in the first self-supporting, self-breeding, slave-based agrarian country in the history of the world. The Civil War that ended slavery cost 800,000 American lives. It was the worst conflict of the nineteenth century. The British treatment of Egypt during the American Civil War bankrupted Egypt.

Thomas Jefferson described slavery in the South as "a fireball in the night." It is a fireball that still smoulders. Yet out of this ghastly story comes a flame of hope. The factory workers of England did not back the southern states in the Civil War. The nonconformist preachers who had risen out of the extreme poverty had taught the mill workers that there were principles to be followed no matter what. Abraham Lincoln described the support of the English workers as "sublime Christian heroism."

continued from page 33

STAGE 1

Humans were living in caves gathering their food in the countryside and gathering also fibres for clothes and other fabrics. In caves in Georgia, archeologists have discovered fibres of flax that were dyed and woven about 36,000 years ago. This is no mean achievement as flax is notoriously difficult to dye. On the southwest shore of Lake Galilee at the Ohalo II site are ninety thousand plant remnants that have been found from as long as 23,000 years ago. Acorns, pistachios, olives, wheat, and barley have been found, but there is no evidence of cultivation, domestication, or even grinding of flour. So in stage 1, food procurement was from wild plants, and fire was used to manipulate the wild vegetation.

STAGE 2

Cultivation and incipient domestication began alongside a continuing dependence on food procurement from wild plants. It is in stage 2 that we find the earliest direct evidence for the domestication of a farmer's crop, at the Nevali Cori site in Turkey. In order to appreciate the importance of this find, we have to consider briefly a difference between wild plants and crops from the same plants. In the wild, plants drop their seeds when the seed is fully developed—the parent plant lets the seed go, through the development of an abscission layer, a nice clean scar or break. That is, a wild plant lets its seeds go when they are ready. This is not what a farmer wants. He wants to be able to harvest all the seeds in one go, and he wants the seeds to remain on the plant until they are broken off by threshing. Seeds that are detached in this way have a jagged scar where previously there was, in a wild plant, a smooth break. Seeds with jagged scars have been found at Nevali Cori and they have been accurately dated at 10,500 years old. This early incipient domestication involved the exploitation of the local flora. Favoured individuals were protected and undesirables were eliminated. It is believed that there was both conscious and subconscious selection in casual backyard sowings; and that in these backyards there would have been spontaneous hybridization between these selected forms, leading to further improvements.

It should not be imagined that the emergence of agriculture was a smooth progression. The process was not centrally organized, and it progressed unevenly throughout the region. At the el-Hemmeh site in Jordan, people were still relying to a great extent on starch-rich tubers from sedges, ruches, bullrushes, and thistles. Toward the end of stage 2, some 8,200 years ago, there was a 200-year-long cold spell during which time there appears to have been a move away from keeping pigs and toward cattle. You might ask why and I wish we knew; the domestication of animals is less well studied than the domestication of plants.

STAGE 3

There was less hunting and less gathering and more farming. The aforementioned Ohalo II site on the shore of Galilee was inhabited continuously for many years, and this allows researchers to build up a picture of how domesticated varieties took over from wild-type plants. Ten thousand years ago, 10 percent of cultivated plants show domestication syndromes such as bigger seeds or nonshattering seed heads. By 8,500 years ago, the proportion had risen to 36 percent; and by 7,500 years ago, it had risen to 64 percent.

It is clear from other sites that different crops were domesticated at different rates and in different ways. So in China, for example, although rice was being consumed twelve thousand years ago, millet was the staple diet as recently as four thousand years ago. This millet was made into flour, porridge, and beer. The ascendency of rice started slowly; and 6,900 years ago only 8 percent of cultivated plants in China were rice, and of these only 27.4 percent were domesticated. Three hundred years later, 24 percent of the cultivated plants were rice, but only 38.8 percent were domesticated forms.

STAGE 4

The final stage is characterized by the point when the majority of food was grown in fields, when it was being grown away from the original place of domestication, and when people began to live predominantly in villages. This appears to have happened by five thousand years ago. Europe was colonized by these migrant farmers who brought the crops with them. Genetically this was helpful because it isolated the new selected forms from their wild relatives, preventing genetic pollution. This scenario of initial domestication happening in one region, being followed by further, more successful exploitation elsewhere, is found repeatedly in the story of the emergence of agriculture. So for example, squash, peanuts, and manioc were being grown in the Andes ten thousand years ago, but later they were domesticated in tropical lowland forests along with chilli, beans, rubber, tobacco, and coca. We are gradually learning more about the origins of our major crops and they are all different: maize is generally thought to be derived from one species, rice is from two species, potatoes from four, and wheat from six. The genetics of the domestication of these crops is beyond the scope of this

---

Health Care: Medicinal Plants

In discussions of plant-derived treatments, Chinese traditional medicine and the Ayurvedic medicine of the Indian subcontinent are always used as examples, yet for every indigenous population in the world, there is knowledge of their local plants and which can be used in medicine. The conservation of this knowledge is an urgent task. It has been estimated that 25 percent of the medicines prescribed by the National Health Service in the UK contain active ingredients that have been extracted from a plant. Up to another 25 percent are based on molecules that were first found in plants and which are now either exactly replicated in laboratories or have been improved on. To describe plant-derived treatments as "alternative" is obviously nonsense; nor are they complementary. They are the real thing.

book, but it is a fascinating story as it appears that the domestication of the crop plants that underpin civilization is the result of the manipulation of very few genes. This means that we should try to conserve as much genetic diversity as possible in the hope that we conserve the relatively few genes that we need.

Beyond Food

In addition to the grains, pulses, roots, and tubers that give us our staple diets, many other plants play a very important role in our lives. There are crops that give us, directly or indirectly, our major beverages. If you found the origin of wheat complicated, it is nothing compared to the domestication of citrus fruits that is only now being unraveled as a result of DNA studies. Much more simple are the biological histories of coffee and cocoa and tea.

Although starch, a carbohydrate, is the energy storage molecule most commonly found in plants, there are times in the life of a plant when more energy-rich, high-octane compounds, such as fats and oils, are preferable. For example, the plant embryo in a seed wants to get away to a flying start and so fat can be a better way than starch for providing the energy quickly since rapid growth of the young seedling is important for successful establishment. The oils in these seeds have been exploited by humans for cooking but also in industry. Oils are derived from the seeds of a very diverse group of plants including palms, sunflowers, evening primrose, rape, and peanuts. Oils from leaves, flowers, and other parts of plants are also used in perfumery and aromatherapy. The latter is one extreme of the continuum, with clinical medicine at one end and herbal medicine at the other end.

It is not known when hominids first started to appreciate the therapeutic value of plants and plant-derived treatments. There is some circumstantial evidence that as long as seventy thousand years ago *Homo neanderthalensis* was consuming plants for reasons other than food.

The evidence is in the form of pollen grains. Pollen is very useful to archeologists because as we've seen it is coated in sporopollenin which is almost indestructible and very resistant to decay. Many plant species can be identified from their pollen, and 90 percent of the pollen found in some Neanderthal caves is from species of plants still used in those parts of the world for their medicinal properties.

So far a number of events during the evolution of plants have had a fundamental and direct effect on the success of our species:

First, photosynthesizing organisms released so much oxygen into the atmosphere that respiration could become much more energetic by using that oxygen;

Second, the plants that evolved in the oceans and freshwater pools and lakes colonized the land and its air; and

Third, plants contributed to the soil in which domesticated plants, our crops, grow.

And they have contributed to the fossil fuels that power so much of our lives—but this fourth effect has been a destructive one. That the climate has been changing is not seriously disputed; whether we are behind this and can succeed at controlling it is not important here. The world's plants have experienced climate change before, most recently during the shenanigans at the end of the last ice age—and the plants coped, presumably through a combination of migration, adaption, and some traits they had acquired along the way but had yet to put to good, or the best, use. Plants always have been and always will be the only renewable, sustainable supply of all our needs, so we must ensure that we protect them, use them sustainably and wisely, and perhaps the most regenerative, feel the need for them and cherish them.

Starting at the very beginning is a very good place to start. And having started with a concentrated, brief history of plant life on planet Earth, we now have some understanding of the plants that have evolved. The next very good starting place is the compilation of an online world checklist of all the known plant species of the world. This is the first target of the global plant conservation effort to scale back and prevent the extinction of the plants, without which we will not survive, coordinated by England's Royal Botanic Gardens, Kew, and America's Missouri Botanical Garden, which together have the most comprehensive herbarium collections in the world.

There is already a great deal of work being done and accomplished—but there is a great deal more for us to do by 2020 in our worldwide collaboration.

PART ONE

The Global Garden List

Somewhere between 70 and 90 percent of plant species have been recorded and named. Without accurate and universal names there can be no permanent knowledge, and so the global catalogue is a prerequisite of all other work. Once the list has been compiled an accurate assessment of regional, national, and international rarity and threatenedness can be carried out, allowing precious resources to be allocated efficiently.

1 A World Flora: How on Earth Do We Do It?

A great deal of money is spent looking for life on other planets and elsewhere in the universe, yet we do not have a full inventory for life on this planet. We believe that our checklists for mammals and birds of the world are reasonably complete, but for invertebrates we have only just started to scratch at the surface of our ignorance. And it is generally agreed, as indicated by the primacy of the task's position as the first target of the conservation strategy, that a global plan to compile, as comprehensively as possible, a catalogue of all identifiable plant species is the *sine qua non*—without which none of the other objectives and targets will be attainable.

It is believed that we are more than 85 percent of the way toward a full inventory of the plants on Earth. This catalogue would be the global Flora (treatise, capital *F*) and would contain the plants, or flora (the organisms, lowercase *f*), found in a region. A regional Flora is a specialized, technical account of the flora growing in that region. Usually this is a political region, such as a country or county; and sometimes it's a biogeographical region, such as the American West's *Intermountain Flora*, which documents plant diversity existing between the Sierra Nevada and Rocky Mountains. All Floras include keys that enable field biologists and determined gardeners to identify the flora (it will probably not contain many plant pictures!) and can only be written after a great deal of field biology has been done

Many professional botanists express exasperation over how many hours of work need to be done to complete the Flora of Earth, but it is very rare to see a figure. So one evening while waiting for the children to emerge from school (why are they always the last?), I took an old envelope out of my bag and, with the help of the calculator on my phone, I came up with this estimate: for the world Flora to be produced, it would take 5,250,000 people working for a career of forty years for us to have a complete global list of plant species; and that it would then require 1,200,000 botanists working for the whole of eternity to keep the catalogue up to date. Still, if we are going to make any progress with our 2020 goals, we need to know what is out there—and that is the first target of the first objective: to work on generating an inventory of plants.

Fortunately, we have a long history of a classification system for plants that permits new species to be inserted easily. This is because the classification is organized in a hierarchy of ranks; and even if one cannot immediately identify a plant to the level of its most detailed rank—that is, its species—one might be able to put it in a more general context, its genus.

To determine what is "out there," we are basically looking very, very closely, describing what we see (these are the components of our planet's diverse biology—biodiversity); *species* naming is that level in classification that carries the most important, most *specific* information for the task. So, if we are to indeed make any progress, we are going to have to first consider what we understand by the use of the word *species*. It's clearly a word that we all have used and do not question—and yet, there are *at least* twenty different definitions in our biological literature.

If you randomly ask any undergraduate biology student in a prerequisite introductory college course what a species is (as I often do when teaching), more often than not she or he will reply that it is "a group of individuals that can freely interbreed and produce fertile offspring that resemble their parents." (*Parents* is a plural collective noun—so just how many is that, and who are they exactly?) This definition falls to

Species From Latin *species*—appearance, form, kind, sort, beauty; related to Latin *specere*—to look at, to see, behold; see also "spy"
Genus From Latin *genus*—birth, origin, descent, class, kind, type; Greek *genos, gonos*—birth, offspring; see also "kin"

pieces when you try, for example, to group orchids—because one can easily form hybrid orchids between species that are in different genera; and then you can cross these successfully with species from even a third genus. So you can cross two species in *Brassia* and *Laelia* to give a ×*Brassolaelia* hybrid. This could in turn be crossed with a species in the genus *Cattleya* to give a ×*Brassolaeliocattleya* hybrid. The genus ×*Sutingara* has plants from five different genera in its pedigree. (Orchids truly have an extraordinary contempt for rules and, in some cases, for common decency.)

If we consult *The Shorter Oxford English Dictionary*, a species is a group of "things having some common qualities or characteristics." Now, if it stopped there, everything would be fine; but the compilers of that book did not—and next a *biological* definition is given: "a taxonomic grouping ranking next below genus and subgenus, which contains organisms that are uniquely distinguished from others by certain shared characteristics and usually by an inability to interbreed with members of other such groupings."

This may be acceptable to zoologists but as gardeners know, many plants happily hybridize with other species. Our gardens are full of these hybrids and it seems that nature is too; at least 25 percent of wild species are hybrids. So we need another definition in our classification system that does not preclude hybrids.

The definition of a plant species that will be used in this book is this:
A species is a group of individuals that share a unique combination of characteristics that can be reproduced.

Though a lot of work has already begun, our global strategy to compile the world Flora still has far to go. We may believe we know which plants grow where, but that is true only if one has grown up or is a gardener in certain places around the world. Take, for example, Britain and Ireland.

> **"Trying to Define the Undefinable"? (Don't!)**
> "It is really laughable to see what different ideas are prominent in various naturalists' minds, when they speak of 'species'; in some, resemblance is everything and descent of little weight—in some, resemblance seems to go for nothing, and Creation the reigning idea—in some, descent is the key—in some, sterility an unfailing test, with others it is not worth a farthing. It all comes, I believe, from trying to define the undefinable."
> —Charles Darwin in a letter to J. D. Hooker, Director of the Royal Botanic Gardens, Kew, Christmas Eve 1856
>
> This is a lovely quotation from Darwin because it shows that he worked right up to Christmas Day—no extended holiday for him—and it shows that he did sometimes laugh, though perhaps on this occasion dryly. Does it matter that we cannot define a species? Can we say what a dollar or a pound is worth? There are many unquantifiable entities in the world—like love for example—but they still exist. Most of the time we have no problem recognizing species—again like love. Just because sometimes people argue about whether they have two or more species or just one does not matter in the grand scheme of things; and when it does matter, we shall know that our work is done because we have achieved all our other goals. Remember the collective noun for taxonomists is *an argument*.

These small islands are home to about 1,500 species of plants, and the first Flora of an English county was produced over three hundred years ago, with many updates and versions since then. This is also true for the *New Flora of Britain and Ireland* by Clive Stace; the second edition, produced in 1998, lists 4,640 species, whereas 4,800 species of plants are listed in the third edition, published in 2010.

The first accounts of North American species appeared in European works such as those by Robert Morison here in Oxford and John Ray at Cambridge, England. Asa Gray and John Torrey attempted to compile a complete account of the flora of North America in the 1830s, but after that most of the work was at the regional or state level. There is currently a project called Flora of North America, which aims to produce a comprehensive, systematic account of all plant species in North America north of Mexico. To date seventeen of the thirty planned volumes have been published. Unfortunately, not everywhere in the world is as comprehensively botanized; if this were the case, then plant conservation would be much easier. The Royal Botanic Gardens, Kew, in England has just celebrated the completion of *Flora of Tropical East Africa*, which was begun in 1948. It consists of 264 volumes covering 12,104 species. With a global Flora we would then not only know which species grow in specific regions worldwide, we also would have accurate distribution maps and data. So for the areas of the world with no tradition of botany and recording, such as Bolivia and Brunei, one has to start from scratch when creating an inventory. But where to start?

Starting from Scratch: Making a List, Checking It Twice, and Much More

To realize the enormity of the task of creating regional Flora, imagine, if you can, that you are the first European botanist-explorer sent in the seventeenth century to make a inventory of the plants growing on the island of Madagascar, which was part of the French empire at the time.

So you get off the boat and start your work. You walk up the beach and find your first plant. Do you know what it is? Very unlikely because it is estimated that at least 80 percent of the plant species that grow on Madagascar grow nowhere else on Earth. This means that they are endemic to the island. You might think that you have seen something similar elsewhere. For example, it might be a species of palm tree.

Now remembering that this is the seventeenth century, there is no digital camera to record the plant so you have to make notes and perhaps drawings. You would record where you are, what the habitat is like, what the soil looks like, and the altitude. You would need to make a detailed written description of the plant, especially as it is a tree and bringing back a complete plant is not possible. You would also like to bring back a piece if possible.

You would probably make a dried specimen using a plant press. Given that the standard plant press is 18 by 12 inches you are going to be limited to a relatively small piece; at least you could preserve some flowers and parts of leaves.

Once you have done all of this, you can move on to the next plant. One species down and just 14,882 to go. Given that the island of Madagascar is roughly the same size as France, more than twice the size of the United Kingdom, and bigger than all the states in the United States except Texas and Alaska, you can see that the task is daunting, to say the least.

The process will get slower and slower as the days go by because every day you have to change the papers in the press, replacing the moist ones with dry sheets. The work might be quicker if you made friends with the local Malagasy people because the Malagasy people, as is true for all indigenous peoples, will have names for their plants.

When eventually it was time to go home, you would get back on board the boat and sail back to France. You take your samples to the leading botanical institution in France—the Jardin des Plantes in Paris, where there is a herbarium in which previous explorers have deposited their pressed specimens. So you open your press, take out the first plant, and compare it to all the others in the herbarium. If you cannot find a perfect match, then maybe you have a species new to European botany. Before you can be sure that the species is new you need to compare your plant with the specimens in every other herbarium in the world.

Eventually, our botanist will feel overworked and frustrated as she or he tries to produce a catalogue of the plants of Madagascar—because there is less than a 20 percent chance that any of the *species* brought back are comparable to existing plants found in the existing classification system of the time; she or he will have seen some of the genera before, and all but seven families found on Madagascar grow elsewhere on Earth. So there will be a chance to take a stab at naming the family and the genus, and likely not the species.

If no plant match is found anywhere, then a name must be given to that specimen. An existing family will be used, unless nothing suitable exists (recall, seven families are only found on Madagascar). A new genus might need to be created if no similar species have been found before. A species name (the specific epithet, the second part of the Latin name) will need to be made up. This can be a useful term (such as descriptive or geographical origin) or it might be trivial (such as naming it in honor of a much-adored cat).

Then the Latin name and the description of the plant must be published and with the description must be an indication of in which herbarium the original plant can be seen. The herbarium sheet to which this plant is stuck is known as the *type specimen*, and it has a bright red edge all the way around it. This herbarium sheet is then looked after in perpetuity for botanists to consult. If looked after properly, such sheets can survive for hundreds of years.

However, they have added value beyond the purely taxonomic. Every herbarium sheet should have a note saying where and when the specimen was collected. In this way distribution maps can be drawn for now and for the past. These are very important for conservation work since they enable us to analyse how plant distributions change over time in response to other changes.

Over the years, every expedition into the vegetation of Madagascar produces more and more herbarium specimens and more and more species are found, and continue to be found. This work enables botanists to say with confidence that Madagascar is "a hot spot of biological diversity" —a disproportionately large number of endemic species grow there. And not only is it a hot spot, but distribution data held in herbaria can help areas that have suffered most in the past, say, fifty years to benefit from our limited conservation resources because we can target the most important areas for plant diversity in that ecological region so that it can be effectively protected, managed, and conserved.

Today botanists visiting Madagascar can take field guides with them. These contain descriptions and perhaps photographs of the species. A comprehensive field guide for Madagascar does not yet exist. The project started in 1936 in the Natural History Museum in Paris and is more than 80 percent complete with just 45 families to complete out of the 224 found on the island.

Floras lie at the heart of field botany. The first one, published in 1660 by John Ray, was *Catalogus plantarum circa Cantabrigiam nascentium*, or *Flora of Cambridgeshire*. Since the seventeenth century, Floras of many parts of the world have been produced and continue to be produced. We do not yet have a complete Flora for the world, but this is now being developed through the coordinated efforts of the Royal Botanic Gardens, Kew, and the Missouri Botanical Garden in St. Louis.

A drawback with our current system of naming plants is the absence of a central clearing house for names. This means that there is a real danger that species will be named when a perfectly good name already exists. This was more common in the past than it is now, but imagine the situation that you have a French botanist being sent plants from China and an English botanist being sent plants from Japan. The plants may be of the same species, but if the two botanists are not familiar with, and aware of, the other's work, then they may give the plants different names.

The result is that a species has two names and confusion follows. When these mistakes are discovered, the rule is that the older name takes precedent and the second name is called a synonym. On average every species has three names, only one of which should be used. This problem could be avoided if there was just one herbarium in the world. Unfortunately there is never going to be agreement about where this herbarium should be located. However, with the advent of high-quality scanning equipment, it is possible to make very good images available to everyone via the Internet.

The History of Naming Plants, Briefly

In order to understand how we came to have the classification system we use today, one needs to go back more than two thousand years to the Greek philosopher Theophrastus (c. 371–c. 287 BCE) and his framework for grouping plants. In his book entitled *Enquiry into Plants*, he writes of his recognition that some plants share characteristics and look similar. He had no idea why this might be, but here was an intuitive start to naming plants. Taxonomy—the science of placing individuals in groups—had begun.

This European system goes back a long way and, in the interests of impartiality and unbiased reporting, it must be noted that other systems of naming were available before Theophrastus. Here's one example, from about 2700 BCE. Emperor Shennong, often regarded as the founder of Chinese herbal medicine, created the *Shennong pen Ts'ao ching*, or *Great Herbal*. This is considered the first of the great Chinese herbals, and some of the treatments described therein are still used in China.

But getting back to the fourth century BCE in Greece, Theophrastus came to Athens from Lesbos to study under Plato and then Aristotle, from whom he took over as supreme mugwump of the Peripatetic School. Theophrastus's contribution to this story is the ten-volume *Enquiry into Plants*, which was still in print in 1644 (modern authors and publishers can only dream of such longevity). In this book he grouped plants in many different ways, including where they lived, how they lived and reproduced, and to what uses they could be put. Sometimes we can easily see that Theophrastus is describing a group that we still use because the members of the group are all derived from one common ancestor. In Book VI, ii 6–8, he writes about "the class of ferrula-like plants." *Ferrula* is the name we now give to a group of species similar to fennel. Theophrastus describes these plants as having leaves that are arranged in alternating rows up the stem:

> The leaves come alternately—by which I mean that they do not spring from the same part of the joint, but in alternating rows. For a consid-

erable distance they embrace the stalk, like the leaves of the reed, but they turn back from it more owing to their softness and their size; for the leaf is large, soft, and much divided, so that it is almost hair-like; the largest leaves are the lowest ones next to the ground, and so on in proportion. The flower is quince-yellow and inconspicuous, the fruit like dill but larger. The plant divides at the top and has some small branches, on which grow the flower and the fruit.

These plants are clearly those that we now put into the celery family, the Apiaceae, often referred to as the umbellifers because the "small branches, on which grow the flower" are arranged like the spokes of an umbrella. In Book ix, xi 7–9, Theophrastus writes about "various plants called *tithymallos* (spurge)." He records that these plants have shoots, half of which fruit in the present year and half of which will fruit the following year. These are the plants that we now refer to as euphorbias; and species such as *Euphorbia myrsinites* and *Euphorbia characias* do have these biennial shoots that grow vegetatively for one year and then die back to ground level after flowering in the next year.

Another Greek botanist whose works remained in print for more than fifteen centuries was Dioscorides, a Greek physician who worked for the Roman army in the first-century AD. His contribution to the global Flora project is the five-volume *De Materia Medica* in which he describes the plants and other substances that he used in his medical practice. He groups the plants not according to their uses but according to their physical appearance, and so we see the umbellifers and the spurges again being put together. In fact, Dioscorides was first to use the name *Tithymallos characias* for the plant we now know as *Euphorbia characias*.

As the science of grouping and naming plants has one of its origins in ancient Greece, it is fitting that the science of classifying plants should be known as taxonomy from the Greek words *taxis*, meaning arrangement, and *nomia*, meaning method. However, there were also other systems operating elsewhere in the world that independently had come to

> **Taxonomic Ranks**
>
> The process of putting plants into boxes with names on them has intrigued people for many years. However, it was soon discovered that these boxes could then be put into bigger boxes and so on until they all went into a very big box labeled *plants*.
>
> Very often it is easy to see which plants go into the smallest boxes and how these then go together into the next size up. These boxes are referred to by classifiers as *ranks* and they can be the subject of a great deal of heated discussion among taxonomic rankers. The system we use at the moment has eight basic ranks:
>
> 1. Domain
> 2. Kingdom
> 3. Phylum
> 4. Class
> 5. Order
> 6. Family
> 7. Genus
> 8. Species
>
> There are many mnemonics for remembering this, most of them unprintable but highly memorable by students.

similar conclusions about groups—particularly groups of species, which we now call genera; and groups of genera, which we call families. For example, when European botanists arrived in China they found that the plants they knew as magnolias were all in the same group: *Magnolia denudate* was Yu-lan and *Magnolia liliflora* was Mu-lan. In South America, however, the magnolias were known as *Eloxochitl*, meaning the flower with the green husk.

The fact that European *taxa*, the terms used in taxonomy, have come to be adopted as the international system is in part an accident of history. It does mean that there is—as pointed out by the well-known British botanist, curator, and director of Cambridge Botanic Garden, Max Walters—a Eurocentric bias when it comes to the internationally accepted names for plants. So take the iris family, the Iridaceae.

Sometimes it is possible to see more than five ranks between species and kingdom and so other ranks are invented. Sometimes these are just sub- or super- or sometimes a new rank, such as *tribe*. Some taxonomists have become so frustrated by the ranking system that they want a rankless classification known as the PhyloCode. So far it has not caught on.

One area that worries gardeners a great deal is the ranks below species, and frankly these are a nightmare but a few are worth knowing about. A variety (abbreviated to var.) is a form of a species that exists within a community of plants. For example, there are bluebells with white flowers. This is a variety. A subspecies (abbreviated to ssp.) is a form of a species that lives in a particular region of the world and is different enough from the same species growing elsewhere to be worth recognizing with a subspecies name. A cultivated variety (abbreviated to cultivar) is a form of a species that is only kept going by gardeners propagating it by cutting or divisions.

It is important to keep this all in perspective. Family, genus, and species are the really useful ranks and the really important ones.

This a family familiar to gardeners and the European botanists who created the family, choosing to use the genus *Iris* to be typical of the family. However, when you look at the other genera such as crocuses and gladioli and freesias, you realize that irises are far from typical. Take, for example, *Mahonia fortunei*, a Chinese species where the genus commemorates a Pennsylvania nurseryman and the species commemorates a Scottish plant hunter.

The accident of history to which I refer was the fall of Constantinople in 1453, which catalyzed the Renaissance that was already underway in Italy. In sixteenth-century Italy, many botanists were trying to reveal the pattern of nature, and thus reveal God's plan. Three of the most important Italians were Luca Ghini (1490–1556), Piers Andrea Mattiola (1501–1577), and Andrea Cesalpino (1519–1603). These men built upon the legacy of Dioscorides and in some cases were simply picking up where Dioscorides had left off, in particular Mattiola, who updated the plant names that Dioscorides had used in *De Materia Medica*.

One botanist in particular was going in the right direction and he was not Italian but Swiss. Conrad Gesner (1516–1565) is celebrated in the naming of the plant family Gesneriaceae, which contains many familiar houseplants such as African violet (*Saintpaulia*) and Cape primrose (*Streptocarpus*) and the wonderful rock garden plants Pyrenean violet (*Ramonda myconii*) and *Haberlea ferdinandii-coburgii*. Gesner corresponded regularly with both Mattiola and the German botanist Leonhart Fuchs (1501–1566)—as in *Fuchsia*—and both Fuchs and Mattiola recognized that Gesner was a genius. Although this was before the easy communication of e-mail, these botanists were prodigious writers, and, unlike e-mails, their work survives them.

Gesner's life work was not completed when he died of plague at the age of forty-nine; however, in the fifteen hundred annotated drawings he left behind, we can see a man who had realized that flowers, fruits, and the seeds therein were more important in classification than leaves alone. Gesner had also observed that if you collected seeds from a plant and sowed them you would get a range of plants in terms of flower colour, size, habit, and other characteristics. However, if you grew the same number of plants from a cutting taken from the same plant, you would get very little variation between the plants.

Gesner was also not satisfied with a classification system that put all trees together in one group and all herbs together in another. (*Herb* here means a soft herbaceous plant that does not form perennial woody structures above ground; it does not mean culinary herb, many of which are woody.) This was because Gesner realized, for example, that an apple tree has far more in common with a strawberry than an apple tree has in common with a palm tree or a pine tree. Gesner's belief that classifications should be based on many (if not all) observable characters was to lie dormant until it germinated a century later in the mind of the second greatest English natural historian of all time, John Ray (1627–1705).

Two other Swiss botanists (of French extraction) should be mentioned here: the Bauhin brothers—Johann (1541–1613) and Gaspard (1560–1624)—honoured by Linnaeus in the genus *Bauhinia*, whose butterfly-like pairs of leaflets represent the filial partnership. The elder brother Johann (a.k.a. Jean like his father) travelled with Gesner, and like Gesner, Johann died before his *Historia Plantarum Universalis* could be published. *Historia Plantarum* (literally translated as a narration of what has been learned about plants through research) was a common goal for many botanists at that time. In these *magna opera*, they set out to describe, name, and classify all the plants known to European science. Despite there being far fewer plants known to botanists then, many *historiae plantarum* went unfinished and unpublished or were finished and published posthumously. For example, Robert Morison (1620–1683), the first professor of botany at the University of Oxford, was involved in a road traffic accident in the Strand in London in 1683, leaving his *historia plantarum* to be finished by Jacob Bobart the Younger (1641–1719), the second Horti Praefectus at the fledgling botanic garden in Oxford. This was eventually one of the first and most expensive books to be published by Oxford University Press, and it very nearly bankrupt the embryonic publisher. The OUP is now publishing *Flora of North America* and hopefully history will not repeat itself!

Unlike his hero Conrad Gesner, Gaspard Bauhin did not consider every character equally and so amalgamated grasses and beans—clearly unsupportable. Sadly, Gaspard does not get the credit for something that we take completely for granted today—the binomial system of nomenclature. Until this time botanists had used as many words in the name of a plant as were necessary to distinguish it from other species. These names began with the grouping that we would regard now as the genus—*Rosa*, *Euphorbia*, or *Magnolia*—but this would be followed by a descriptive phrase. Together, these became clumsy polynomials, so Gaspard Bauhin sought to reduce the name to as few words as possible, and preferably to just one. So he suggested, for example, that rather than the name *Tithymalus umbella multifida dichotoma involucellis subcordatis ramis sterilibus foliis setaceis caulinis lanceolatis*, it would be more convenient to say *Tithymalus cyparissius*. It seems like a good idea to me.

His life work was *Pinax Theatri Botanici*, published in 1623, just one year before he died. This is an illustrated account of plants in which he described six thousand plants, giving each of them a binomial name. He introduced a number of new names for genera that we still use. He also proposed many specific epithets (species names) that were adopted more than a century later by Linnaeus in his landmark *Species Plantarum* published in 1753; some ideas are slow to catch on. For example, the plant still known in 1738 to Linnaeus as *Euphorbia inermis, foliis confertis linearibus, umbella universali multifida, partialibus dichotomis: foliolis subrotundis*, Gaspard Bauhin had already reduced in 1623 to *Tithymalus cyparissius*.

So by the time that England was tearing itself apart with a civil war, there was already a substantial body of work classifying and naming the world's plants. What was lacking was any consensus as to how it should be carried out (and the size of some of the egos involved was always going to prevent universal agreement). Against this maelstrom of social turmoil and academic arrogance dragging down progress came John Ray, surely one of the most modest geniuses of all time.

Much was written and said about John Ray in the first decade of the twenty-first century. Anna Pavord's scholarly but eminently readable work *Naming of Names* goes a long way to setting the record straight as to Ray's rightful place as the father of modern taxonomy, in the same way that Gaspard Bauhin should be seen as the father of modern nomenclature. What concerns us here is not Ray's heroic struggle against principle, poverty, and feelings of inadequacy. Of greater significance is that, with hindsight, Ray was paving the way for the work of Charles Darwin. Chapter 13 of *Origin of Species* makes sense because of the work done earlier by Ray. It would be presumptuous of anyone to try to guess what

Ray would have made of Darwin's ideas, but if ever there were two scientists who should have met, it was Ray and Darwin. It is comforting to hope that maybe somewhere they are deep in conversation; it would be a meeting of minds that would result in so much more than the sum of the constituent parts.

John Ray's Lasting Legacy

So why is John Ray important? Ray has left us with six legacies.

First, Ray's definition of a species is still taught in introductory biology courses and works for most plants and animals. He considered that a species is a group of similar organisms that can freely interbreed and produce fertile offspring that resemble their parents. This has been refined but it is still fine if you don't worry that some plants break the rules. (If you are worried about biology's predilection for breaking rules and for never being black or white, then I would suggest that you change your hobby and start collecting stamps.)

Second, following on from this, Ray realized that between the individual members of a species there are variations. This was not completely new. Conrad Gesner had observed the same fact. Both men realized that the variation within a species could only be preserved and propagated if you grew a new plant from seeds rather than by taking a cutting, in which case you get identical plants. By realizing this, Ray was predicting the discovery of genetics and gene variation, which eluded both him and Darwin, yet neither man was put off by their inability to explain what they saw.

It is also comforting to hope that maybe somewhere they are deep in conversation together with Gregor Mendel, who was the first to demonstrate the existence of genes, and Francis Crick, who with James Watson was the first to propose the correct structure of the DNA in those genes. By recognzing the variation within a species, Ray was also laying down the rationale behind artificial seed banks, where large amounts of natural genetic diversity can be stored in a very small space. These banks are a pivotal part of twenty-first-century plant conservation. Here again he was centuries ahead of the academic pack.

The **third** way in which Ray set the method for the classification of plants was to insist that taxonomists should use every characteristic that they can see and measure or quantify them in some way. It was not good enough to select which characteristics you were going to use in advance and then try to force the plants into the boxes.

The common sense of this is easy to see. For example, when you are arranging books on a shelf, it is a wretched nuisance when the shelf is not tall enough or not deep enough to take the books in the arrangement that you want. Ray believed that you can only use the data that you can see and let your classification follow from what is in front of you, without any preconceptions. Ray was working with his eyes, hand lenses, and microscopes that enabled him to look at the plant in great detail—but essentially from the outside in.

In 1931 the first electron microscope was designed and patented. Eventually these machines were able to show details never seen before. Then in April 1953, Watson and Crick proposed the structure of DNA in the journal *Nature*. Sixty years later we can now sequence the DNA of plants overnight and compare the sequence of the bases in the genes that are so important for the control of plant development. The use of electron microscopes and DNA sequencers has enabled us to look differently at plants—now from the inside out—thus revealing more characters that were not visible to Ray but which, it is sure, he would have used.

Ray realized his **fourth** major contribution to plant classification as a result of his insistence on using all characters—that all flowering plants fall into two big groups: the monocots and the dicots.

The plants in the monocots, which is a numerically smaller group, share all or most of the following characters:

- They grow a new set of feeding roots each year from the base of their stems. Gardeners exploit this fact when they lift and move dormant

Monocots tend to have

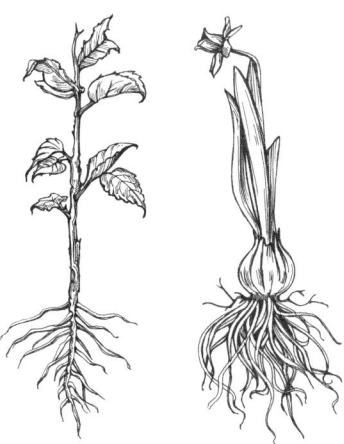

Dicots tend to have

seeds where the seedling produces one seed leaf

roots that regrow each year from the base of the stem

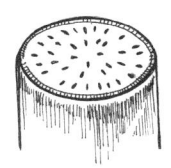

seeds where the seedling produces two seed leaves

roots that grow longer and fatter each year forming a permanent structure

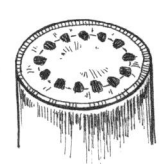

stems with the vascular tissue grouped in bundles of pipes scattered through the stems

stems with the vascular tissue grouped in a ring around the outside of the stems

leaves with veins that are parallel

flowers with parts in multiples of three

leaves with veins that grow out from a central vein and lateral veins to form a netlike arrangement

flowers with parts in multiples of two, four, or more commonly five

bulbs that have no roots. The gardener knows that the bulb will grow new roots at the start of the next growing season.
- If you cut through the stems of the plants, you will find that pipes in the plumbing (or the phloem and xylem in the vascular tissue, to be more precise) are arranged in bundles scattered though the stem. This can be seen very clearly if you cut though a palm tree or if you slice up some stem ginger in the kitchen. The veins in the leaves of these plants are parallel. This can be seen very clearly in the leaves of grasses, irises, and hostas.
- Flower parts (the sepals, petals, stamens, and carpels) are in multiples of three for each. This is very clearly seen in tulips and daylilies.
- Ray noticed that when the seeds of these plants germinated, such as a maize or onion seed, on a vegetable plot, there was initially just one leaf (the seed leaf or cotyledon), unlike the two seed leaves that emerged when growing a broad bean.

Because he had to give these two groups names, he chose to call the smaller group monocotyledonous plants and the larger group dicotyledonous plants. These are too long to say on a day-to-day basis, so they are shortened to monocots and dicots.

This seemingly esoteric distinction is of great practical value to farmers and gardeners because they regularly use weed killers that will kill dicots but not monocots. This is useful in fields of wheat, maize (corn), barley, and other crops, or on your lawn at home, where no one really likes seeing daisies and dandelions. It should be noted that the monocots are still regarded as a good group despite everything that we have learned in the past three hundred years about plants. It should also be noted that the dicots have not fared so well. There were a number of plants that always looked uncomfortable in the dicots; plants like water lilies, magnolias, and bay trees always seemed to be nonconformists that had gone down evolutionary pathways independent from the monocots and dicots. It was not until the very end of the twentieth century that the true dicots (eudicots) were finally recognized, and the independents were recognized in their own right as neither monocots nor true dicots.

Ray's **fifth** lasting contribution to the taxonomy of plants resulted from his thorough method which used every characteristic that could be seen: he grouped plants into many of the botanical families that we still use. For example, he saw that a bunch of species have hairy stems and leaves, their leaves are arranged alternately up the stem (as opposed to in opposite pairs like in maples), they have blue or pink flowers, and in the centre of their flowers are four small nutlets arranged like a hot cross bun. He placed these in a group now called the borage family, or Boraginaceae. Ray did not use the botanical term "family" (an eighteenth-century invention), preferring instead *genera summum*.

The only one of Ray's rules for classification that is not always easy to follow today is rule number 3 because sometimes DNA sequencers are not available to botanists working in the field. This may of course change as the science of conservation progresses. DNA-analyzing equipment may well soon be in the working hands of protective plant stewards and conservationists worldwide.

Ray's Six Rules for Classification
1. Plant names should be changed as little a possible since this would reduce mistakes and confusion.
2. The differences between members of groups should be qualitative rather than quantitative.
3. Diagnostic features should be easily seen and obvious.
4. Consensus among botanists should be used as a principle for deciding which groups to recognize.
5. Related plants should be grouped together.
6. Groups should be defined by the least number of characteristics possible to make them distinct (even though they may share many).

The Science of Good Conservation

"Good conservation needs more than good hearts: it needs good science too." Thus wrote British ornithologist Simon Barnes in 2012. He used the restoration of skylark populations in the United Kingdom as a good example of where only science could explain how to develop a successful strategy for this iconic species. There are many areas within plant conservation where the scientific method has unequivocally provided answers to problems and the technology required to find the solutions. Take, for example, the need to know how many plant species are out there, what they are, where they grow, and whether they are declining and therefore in need of some protection. One of the holy grails of field botany is the idea of replacing written identification keys and hand lenses to identify species by, for example, exploiting differences in the DNA of different species. Put simply, you would take a piece of plant tissue such as a bit of leaf and place it in a chamber of a hand-held device. You would close the lid, switch it on, and in an hour or two the name of the species to which the plant belongs would appear on the screen.

This technique, known as DNA barcoding, is based around the hope that within the tens of thousands of genes in a plant species, there is a stretch of DNA that varies very little between members of the same species but varies significantly between the members of different species. At the present moment a gene known as matK found in the chloroplasts of plants is the most widely used. Thus each species would be characterized by a different stretch of DNA in the same way as items in shops are defined by the black-and-white stripes of the Universal Product Code better known as the barcode. In an ideal world you would have just one length of DNA that could be compared across all 400,000 species of plants. So far it appears that three different parts of the genes are required.

Once there is a global agreement on which stretch of DNA you are going to use, every plant species has to be analysed and the DNA barcode has to be stored on a database somewhere, in the same way that the police have a collection of fingerprints. A not insignificant amount of work is being overseen by the Consortium for the Barcode of Life (CBOL) and the International Barcode of Life (iBol) project. Once all the barcodes are on the database, then all your handheld gizmo has to do is extract the bit of DNA, analyse it, and send that analysis (the DNA barcode) to the database via a phone link or something similar. The database would quickly recognize the barcode and send the name back to the botanist in the field.

This may sound like science fiction, but such devices already exist for varieties of major crops. For the system to wrok, every species needs to be in the database; otherwise you will be told that you have discovered a species new to botany. An advantage of DNA barcoding is that it works at any time of the year because you do not need flowers and/or fruits, which most written plant keys require. Species will be identified by any part containing DNA—from pollen grains to seeds or bits of leaf or root. The first country to complete the DNA barcode library for its entire flora was Wales, in 2012. The team took samples from plants of all the 1,143 species collected in Wales and stored in the National Museum of Wales herbarium. Testing of the barcodes showed that they were 75 percent accurate when the locality of the plant is anywhere in Wales, which is a very good start; if you could give the locality of the plant to within two kilometres, then the accuracy rose to 93 percent.

The ability to identify plants from pollen grains or even bits of wood has a wide range of applications, some of which are very important to conservation biology. First, it can be carried out quickly which is not always the case. Second, pollen grains or seeds from soil samples can reveal former distributions of plants. This can then be used to show how plants respond to changes in their habitats, whether climate change or changes in land use such as transformation into arable land. Should you wish to know which plants an animal has been eating, then study of the plant debris in their faeces could tell you. Less disgusting would be the study of which plants are visited by which pollinators. The pollen would tell you and so you could decide if the decline of a plant was due to the lack of visits from pollinators.

One of the first major studies carried out using the DNA barcode was led by Vincent Savolainen from Imperial College London and the Royal Botanic Gardens, Kew, funded by the UK government's Darwin Initiative that was established following the first Earth Summit in Rio in 1992. This initiative helps countries that are rich in biological diversity but poor in resources or expertise. The project resulted in DNA barcodes for orchids in the forests of Costa Rica and for the woody plants of Kruger National Park. Woody plants when not in flower are notoriously tricky to identify, and orchids are almost impossible to identify without flowers.

However, DNA barcodes also have other uses. Imagine that you are a customs officer and you are inspecting a consignment of orchids. How can you tell which species you are looking at? Already identification of orchids in the genus *Phragmipedium* by barcoding is accepted as legal evidence in court cases. The ability to identify a processed plant product back to its origin would be a major breakthrough in the control of trade in endangered species. Plants in herbal medicines and foods could be identified, and the purity or otherwise of the plants could be confirmed. How can you tell if a piece of furniture is made from the timber named on the importation document or whether it is from a species the international trade of which is prohibited? DNA barcoding could provide the answer.

It would be nice to be able to say that once Ray's work was published, everyone fell into place behind it. Sadly, it was not to be—and the completely artificial system proposed by Carl Linnaeus was adopted, preventing progress for about a century. Linnaeus believed that reproduction was at the centre of plant life and that the male and female parts of a plant were all you needed to look at and then to count in order to group species. While flowers are important, there is no reason why the number of male stamens or the number of ovaries is particularly important.

It has to be acknowledged that although Linnaeus's classification was a backwards step, what he did achieve was standardization of names along the lines proposed by Gaspard Bauhin. Linnaeus's *Species Plantarum* of 1753 marks the starting point for legitimate species names. By the same token and logic, the publication in 1789 by Antoine de Jussieu of a complete set of botanical family names marks the starting point for legitimate family names.

And by the start of the nineteenth century, a hierarchy of taxonomic ranks had been accepted and established by the botanical community: individuals are grouped into a species; species are then grouped into a genus. These genera were then grouped into a family, families then grouped into orders. Orders are grouped into a class. Classes are grouped into a phylum; and finally, the phyla are grouped into a kingdom—in this case the plant kingdom.

With the publication of *On the Origin of Species* by Charles Darwin in November 1859, many scientists believed they had the reason why it was possible to create such a hierarchy. As Darwin so beautifully put it:

> From the first dawn of life, all organic beings are found to resemble each other in descending degrees, so that they can be classified in groups under groups.... This classification is not arbitrary like the grouping of the stars in the constellations.... I believe that propinquity of descent is the bond that is partially revealed to us by our classifications.

Classification Today: The Natural System

Now you might be reading this and thinking that it is all very sensible (and hopefully interesting), but in a world with all kinds of pressing problems, is it really important or is it just a job-creation scheme for vegetable "train spotters"? Well, the answer is yes—it is important, and Darwin said so when he wrote that "Naturalists try to arrange species, genera, families in each order and class, in what is called 'The Natural System'—and the ingenuity and utility of this system are indisputable."

The natural system referred to here is the evolutionary system used by almost all biologists today. In it evolutionary relationships are reflected by the arrangement of the taxa; and the relationships are illustrated in evolutionary trees created for every plant: leaves represent species; the twigs, the genera; the branches indicate the families, orders, classes, phyla; and the main trunk, the kingdom. Like real trees, these taxonomic trees (or phylogenies to give them their proper name) are not even or symmetrical with some branches supporting few twigs and leaves while others have many.

The practical utility of this natural system is manifold, but here are three examples.

First, field work and conservation start with a determination of the species present. After all, species are the currency of biology; and naming and identifying species in the field is of primary importance for conservation. It involves the use of identification keys, which in stages will identify the plant by assignment into smaller and smaller groups, until it is in a species group. The biological key was first devised by French biologist Jean Baptiste Lamarck. It is a beautifully simple idea, and keys are great fun to make.

If you have to make a key to identify four plants, get a piece of each plant in front of you and look for a characteristic that will be able to split the four plants into two groups of two. In our example, the "piece" of each plant here is the flower, and the characteristic that can differentiate them is the colour: two of the plants have white flowers and the other two have flowers that are not white. A key to identify these plants would start to look like this:

1a	Flowers white: go to 2		
1b	Flowers not white: go to 3		
	2a	Leaves opposite pairs = species 1	
	2b	Leaves spirally arranged = species 2	
		3a	Flowers red = species 3
		3b	Flowers yellow = species 4

You then concentrate on the ones with white flowers: you might be able to divide them into those that have leaves that are in opposite pairs and those that have spirally arranged leaves. Of the plants that have flowers that are not white, one may have red flowers and the other yellow flowers. Keys are normally much more complicated than this example, but it is a lovely, simple device.

When we are out in the field identifying plants, our brains work so fast that we are unaware of what they are doing. For example, when you look at a plant, within a few nanoseconds you will have decided that you are looking at either a moss, a fern, a conifer, or a flowering plant. (OK this *may* not be simple sometimes, but stay with me!) Once you have decided into which of these big groups your plant falls, the next thing to decide is to which family the plant belongs.

If you have decided that it is a flowering plant, there will then be a key to the families of flowering plants through which you will work. There are (currently) a maximum of 431 possibilities and in many parts of the world fewer than half that number. Many families can be identified, with a bit of practice, without the need for a key. However, once the family has been nailed, then the plant is put in a genus, which can happen quickly if it belongs to a monogeneric family. Once you have identified the genus, then the identity of the species is just one key away.

The second practical application of evolutionary classification is in the search for drugs. It has been known for a long time that some families of flowering plants are very imaginative when it comes to making molecules. For example, plants in the potato family, the Solanaceae, have given us atropine and hyoscyamine, both of which are very useful in medicine. Unfortunately, the same family has given us nicotine. A recent example of the value of understanding the evolutionary tree came when it was discovered that snowdrops make galantamine that can be used to delay effectively the development of Alzheimer's disease. Unfortunately snowdrops do not make much galantamine and they do not multiple quickly, and so they were never going to be a commercially productive plant. The taxonomists were able to guide the pharmaceutical industry quickly to another galantamine-producing genus in the same family—*Narcissus* or daffodil. Professor Steve Blackmore, Regius Keeper of the Royal Botanic Garden Edinburgh, has likened looking for drugs without an evolutionary tree to looking for a house in London without the A–Z street guide.

A third value for the evolutionary tree is when we are trying to compare the biological diversity of two different areas of the world. You could simply identify all the plants, make a list of the species, and count how many different species you have in each area. However, there is a logic that suggests that this is rather crude. For example, if you have a field that contains four species and all are in the grass family, there is less biological diversity in that field than in the field next door, which also contains four species all in different families, such as a grass, a bluebell, an oak tree, and a gorse bush. This is a very odd field and exists only in the mind of the author, but hopefully you see his point.

Now if we return to the evolutionary tree analogy—the species are the leaves, the twigs are the genera, the branches the families, the large boughs that support the branches are the orders, the few biggest boughs are the classes, the first divisions of the trunk the phyla, and the one main stem is the kingdom. Our sketch is very diagrammatic; evolution does not produce lovely, even trees like this because boughs and branches become extinct and the sizes of the families and genera vary greatly, but the basic idea is sound.

A phylogeny or evolutionary tree of taxonomic ranks

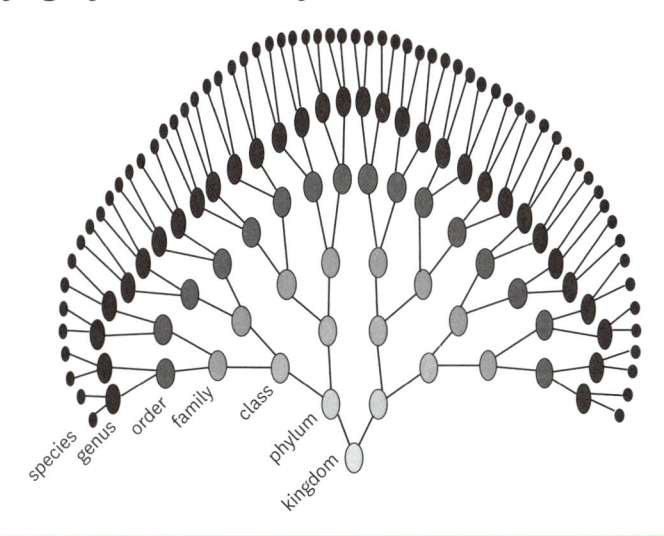

Phylogenetic Diversity

Imagine having four species that are in the same genus—these will represent less of the evolutionary tree, or less phylogenetic diversity, than if those four species were in different classes. A phylogeny is a branching diagram that represents evolutionary relationships. So the more of the evolutionary tree we have in a habitat, the more valuable that habitat is in evolutionary potential, and therefore that habitat will be higher up on the conservation priority list for protection and management.

Eventually we would like to have a phylogeny with 400,000 leaves—that is, species—showing how all the species of flowering plants are related to each other. This is a huge challenge. There are still some parts of the evolutionary tree where we do not know how the families are related to each other. However, *Origin of Species* offers some words of comfort. Darwin concludes that "we shall never, probably, disentangle, the inextricable web of affinities between the members of any one class; but when we have a distant object to view, and do not look to some unknown plan or creation, we may hope to make sure but slow progress."

There is one more way today to catalogue the world's plant species: by writing monographs. A monograph lists all the species in a genus. For each species there is a description and a distribution map. In an ideal world we would have a monograph for each of the 12,962 genera of flowering plants that are currently recognized. Some of these would not take very long because many genera (perhaps one third of them) contain just one species. Some like *Astragalus* and *Euphorbia* have more than two thousand species and are much more difficult to write.

However many species there are in the world flora inventory, it is vitally important that we know whether our species are coping well and maintaining their numbers—or if they are struggling to keep up in a world that is changing, often as a result of the actions of *Homo sapiens*.

2020 STRATEGY

TARGET 1 Compile an online Flora of all known plants
TARGET 2 Assess the conservation status of all known plant species

Species Assessment: The Red List

It is rarely questioned today that the future of many plant species is threatened. The number of species facing that threat and how quickly they will succumb to that threat are debated widely. Our knowledge is not uniformly distributed. Some regions, such as the United Kingdom and the US state of Washington, are very well surveyed; others, such as India and Bolivia, are less well documented. Likewise, the current distribution of some groups of plants, like maples and rhododendrons, is well studied; whereas other plants such as the magnolia family and oaks are less well studied. There is neither rhyme nor reason to this (even though

Cutting-Edge Developments for Plant Documentation
Digital and satellite imaging

The use of digital imaging is helpful at two different scales. I have already written about the role of herbaria in cataloguing the world's plant species. Some herbaria are very large. The Royal Botanic Gardens, Kew, has more than seven million specimens. Kew has plant specimens from all over the world. The herbarium in the Department of Plant Sciences, Oxford University, has 800,000 specimens and as at Kew these are not just of UK species. The herbarium staff can spend a lot of their time loaning specimens to other herbaria in other countries. It would be much simpler if there were high resolution digital images that could be sent around the world or just freely available on websites. The other scale is satellite imaging of vegetation that is then fed into geographical information systems better known as GIS. This brings together maps, computer-aided analysis, and huge quantities of data to identify patterns and changes.

Bioquality

However, sometimes there is absolutely no substitute for good, old-fashioned fieldwork. A good example of this is the rapid botanical surveys (RBS) technique developed by William Hawthorne from the Department of Plant Sciences in Oxford and the Ghana Forestry Department. William has used the concept of bioquality, whereby you do not just count the number of species at a site but you give extra points to the species that are endemic to a region. Species that are widespread score lower. RBS has been used in many parts of the world, in Asia, Central and South America, and in Africa. It not only collects distribution data but also ethnobotanical information and herbarium specimens. All the data is then entered into the BRAHMS (Botanical Research and Herbarium Management System) database developed by Denis Filer also in Oxford. This makes the data available around the world for analysis by anyone from mining companies to PhD students.

Monographs

In 2012 it was believed by many botanists that there were 352,828 legitimate plant species accurately named and described, though some put the figure lower at 271,500. These numbers were arrived at by counting how many species names have been published and then estimating how many of them are synonyms. For example, if there are one million names, but on average each species has been named twice, then there are only 500,000 species. Some believed, though, that there were 50,000 specimens in herbarium cabinets that belonged to species yet to be legitimately named. Luckily, a project at the University of Oxford is trying to step up the pace of this important work of producing monographs. Remember these are books that describe all the known species in a genus. They are notoriously difficult to produce if there are more than twenty-five species spread over a large part of the world. Monographs are the gold standard because they aim to record every species, which involves vast quantities of fieldwork and is so time-consuming that they rarely get completed. A team led by Robert Scotland, Reader in Plant Systematics at Oxford and including people from the Natural History Museum London and the Royal Botanic Gardens at Kew and in Edinburgh, is trying to find a way to produce monographs on *Convolvulus* (two hundred species) and *Ipomoea* (six hundred species) in just three years. They will do this entirely from herbarium specimens and will aim to

1. Describe each species briefly.
2. Sort out any confusions in the names such as many names referring to the same species.
3. Write identification keys and provide a DNA barcode.
4. Give brief distribution data.
5. Draw an evolutionary tree for the group.

Once a monograph is out there it can be viewed as work in progress and as new species are discovered they can be slotted in.

Atlases

The use of the data held in herbaria and vegetation atlases has enabled many people to draw maps of the world showing the concentration of plant species. What is immediately clear is that generally speaking, and Charles Darwin was one of many people who observed this, the number of plant species in a region declines the further you get from the equator. Second, the distribution of plant species diversity is very uneven. For example, 10 percent of the world's plants live in Indonesia, and Borneo alone is home to fifteen thousand species, a third of which are only found in Borneo. The reasons for the concentration of plant diversity are not always clear and can be very controversial. Ecologists are constantly trying to explain the processes taking place in habitats because this will enable us to manage those habitats properly to protect and to promote the diversity.

magnolias are a very popular bunch of plants, but it would appear that being a popular garden plant does not guarantee understanding).

There is an assessment system that categorizes the threatened status of a plant species: the Red Data system of the International Union for Conservation of Nature (IUCN). The organization is one of the oldest and best-respected conservation organizations on Earth; it was formed in 1948 with the vision of creating a just world in which nature is valued and conserved. The IUCN has hundreds of members ranging from governmental and nongovernmental organizations to thousands of volunteer experts drawn from more than 160 countries, and it is probably best known for the production of the Red List, which gives details of the threatened species of either geographical regions or of particular groups of plants. The IUCN Red List of Threatened Species began in 1963 and is the major tool for achieving target 2—identifying plants and mapping species distributions for those species that are threatened with extinction. From here, conservation guidelines can then be addressed.

In this programme, species can be listed as anything from extinct (completely disappeared and not seen for fifty years) down to of least concern (those plants whose status is fine for the time being), with seven categories between these two extremes. While this is a wonderful system, it does have the drawback that it takes too long to accumulate the data necessary to categorize 400,000 species. Instead there is the heuristic, rough and ready RapidList tool, which allows for a preliminary assessment to be registered by botanists working on monographs and Floras. This reduced the categories from ten to just three: threatened, not threatened, and don't know. Data is being accumulated much more quickly now. The data in the accompanying table may suggest a number of questions concerning the actual meaning of the categories of conservation status as defined by the IUCN.

EXTINCTION

How do we know if a species is extinct? If a plant has not been recorded for more than at least fifty years, then it is put on the presumed-extinct

IUCN Categories and RapidList Comparison

IUCN CATEGORIES		MAPLES	RHODODENDRON SPECIES
EXTINCT	completely	0	2
	in the wild	0	0
THREATENED	critically endangered	7	36
	endangered	19	39
	vulnerable	28	241
NEAR THREATENED		8	66
LEAST CONCERN		108	483
DATA DEFICIENT		21	290
NOT EVALUATED		0	0

Data from Fauna & Flora International and Botanic Gardens Conservation International list. This will be easier to ascertain for species with narrow distribution than for a cosmopolitan species, one that grows in many places all over the world. Alternatively, a species might only be known from a fossil such as *Archaeanthus linnenbergeri*, a preserved flower discovered in Kansas in rocks that have been dated at over 100 million years old.

There is a cliché that extinction is for ever. In plant conservation there may be two stages to extinction. If the plant is one that we have brought into our gardens, the species may disappear from its habitat in the wild but it may be happy in gardens. Such a plant is said to be "extinct in the wild." It would be much clearer if the term was "known only in gardens," but we are now stuck with the former. Plants that are extinct in the wild but growing in gardens include the following.

Franklinia alatamaha, a member of the tea family, is similar to its relative, camellia. It was first observed in 1765 by botanists John Bartram and his son William. The Bartrams were farming botanists who are credited with establishing the first botanic garden in North America in the backyard of their farmhouse just outside of Philadelphia, Pennsylvania.

SPECIES IN THE MAGNOLIA FAMILY	OAKS	RAPIDLIST CATEGORY	OAKS IN RAPIDLIST
0	0	EXTINCT	0
0	0		
31	13	THREATENED	78
58	16		
23	27		
9	22		
20	97	NOT THREATENED	97
10	33	DON'T KNOW	333
94	300		

William Bartram collected seeds during a trip to Georgia, and the seeds were sown in 1777, flowering four years later. The species has not been recorded in its habitat since 1803, but it is grown widely enough in American gardens for it to be safe from extinction.

Why *Franklinia* died out is not known for sure. Some people think that it was simply at its "best before" date and that it was collected just before natural extinction caught up with it; other people think that it died out as a result of overcollection by gardeners. This might have been the final nail in its coffin, but it is hard to see how, for this species at least, this alone could have done the deed. However, the same cannot be said for *Eucommia ulmoides*. This small tree, one of the more important plants in traditional Chinese medicine, is now near threatened as a result of overcollection. This plant, too, was formerly much more widespread, which we know from fossils found elsewhere in the Northern Hemisphere.

THREATENED

The IUCN has three categories of "threatenedness" (if such a word existed before I wrote it down): critically endangered, endangered, and vulnerable, with a fourth category of near-threatened. The basic difference among these categories concerns how much longer the species will survive unless something is done to reverse its decline. I am not going to bore you with the calculations that are carried out to classify a species into one of these groups because they are freely available on the IUCN website. It is sufficient for us to know that if a species is in one of these four categories, then there is a good chance that it will not be around to celebrate this author's hundredth birthday in 2058, unless something is done (for the plant not the author).

Of the other categories, "least concern" is a euphemism for no concern at this point in time. "Not evaluated" means that an evaluation was not carried out for any reason, including lack of time, while "data deficient" means that an evaluation was not carried out because of lack of data for the classification exercise, so in effect the evaluation is inconclusive.

What can be seen from our very small sample of just four groups of plants (maples, rhododendrons, oaks, and members of the magnolia family), there is a lot a variation in the numbers of threatened species. In 1994 a comprehensive survey carried out by the World Conservation Monitoring Centre proposed that 13.6 percent of plants species worldwide were threatened with extinction. In 2008 another report put the figure at 28 percent of the 400,000 species of land plants being extinct by 2058. Yet another extrapolation came up with a figure of 44 percent. The expression "fiddling while Rome burns" comes to mind at this stage. I think that the best summary for the present is that if all currently threatened species became extinct in the next one hundred years and if that rate continues unabated, then by 2552 this period will be known as the sixth mass extinction event.

Fortunately it is not too late to do something to avert this disaster.

"An Inordinate Fondness for Beetles"

We do not yet fully understand why some families are bigger than others and why some genera are huge while others have just one species. There are evolutionary reasons, ecological reasons, genetic reasons, or perhaps other reasons. It is an often quoted fact that there are three native species of beetles in the United Kingdom for each native species of plant. There is an equally often quoted, perhaps apocryphal, story of J. B. S. Haldane, an English evolutionary biologist who died in 1964. When asked what he could deduce of the character of God from his study of the creation, Haldane is said to have replied, "An inordinate fondness for beetles."

Perhaps Haldane should be better known for his comment "My own suspicion is that the universe is not only queerer than we suppose, but queerer than we can suppose."

What is undeniably true, though, is that we cannot wait until we have fully understood how queer biology is before we start to help it to survive on an Earth that is changing as fast as it ever has in the past 4,000 million years.

PART TWO

Oath of a Plant Steward: To Conserve and Protect

There is a lot of work to do if we want to stop plant species from becoming extinct. There is a lot to do to keep the planet fit for *Homo sapiens*. If we learn from our mistakes, realize that small is beautiful and that every contribution helps, then we will be able to turn cents into dollars and pennies into pounds—because the value of our work is far greater than the price.

2 Which Is Better, Home or Away?

What is clear by now is that for a variety of reasons, some plant species are declining, and it has often been assumed that the best place to conserve a threatened plant is at home in its natural habitat. There are three problems with this idea. First, trying to protect a plant in the same place it is dying out is akin to giving underwater resuscitation to a drowning man: unless the cause of the problem is removed, the solution will fail. Second, what do we mean by "natural"? In a world where climate is changing, the wisdom of corralling threatened species in fixed endemic nature reserves is being challenged. Third, if we're intent on protecting threatened species by growing them *in situ*, keeping them in their normal habitat, what do we do when that habitat is endangered or has been destroyed? Cultivating elsewhere, or removing surviving plants from their natural, wild ecology and restoring them *ex situ* (away) seems to be a good idea. It is crucial, though, to recognize and preferably remove the reasons for the plants' threatened status, their decline or disappearance and extinction. Sometimes this is easy, sometimes it is impossible—and between these two extreme circumstances different strategies will be required.

> **2020 STRATEGY**
>
> **TARGET 7** Protect at least 75 percent of known threatened species *in situ*

At Home: *In Situ* Conservation

Sometimes there is a simple, straightforward approach to protecting a plant on its home turf: remove the threat. In cases of overcollection, that threat is us—fueled by our sweet predilections for gifts of poesy, filling our beautiful vases, and decorating our holiday dinner tables.

One example of this simple elimination type of conservation can be seen a few miles south of the Oxford Botanic Garden, where I am sitting writing this page. On the south side of Oxford city there is a village called Iffley, situated on the eastern bank of the River Thames. On the other side of the river are water meadows that take water when the river is in flood. Through the nonwinter months, the meadows are grazed by cattle, and this management regime is perfect for the snake's head fritillary or *Fritillaria meleagris*: here it grows in profusion, so much so that, despite its dietary benefit to the cows, it was profuse enough at one time to be harvested in large numbers for the cut-flower trade. Additionally, on Fritillary Sunday, the local children would come out of Sunday school and collect a poesy of flowers for their mothers and grandmothers. The fritillary grows from a bulb, and so it was believed that removing the flowers would not harm the parent plant.

Sadly, bulbs, like all of us, are not immortal. Over the years the number of flowering bulbs fell to the point that, over many acres, fewer than a thousand flowering bulbs remained in the meadow. At this point the local wildlife trust purchased the field and began a campaign to reduce the collection of its flowers. One option was to put up a tall fence topped with razor wire and a big sign saying Keep Out or something stronger. Happily the wise people at the wildlife trust decided to try option two, which was to impress the local people that these are "special flowers"—the county flower, indeed. Now, rather than taking flowers home to granny, granny was put in a wheelbarrow and taken to the flowers. The result was that, in less than three decades, the number of flowering bulbs has risen from fewer than one thousand to more than eighty thousand. Removing the threat can remove the problem.

The fate of *Cypripedium calceolus*, a lady's slipper orchid, is a classic English example of the decline of a species because of human overcollection. While there is still a relatively large population of this species in mainland Europe, in the UK it became reduced to just one plant in North Yorkshire. Famously, the location of this sole survivor was kept a secret and guarded around the clock. This extraordinary commitment was not enough to prevent a slug from eating that flower's stem one year. It would be fair to say, however, that although loss of this species has been attributed to overcollection, clearance of woodland and the introduction of grazing sheep had helped to reduce the potential areas in which the plant could grow. The story for *Cypripedium calceolus* in England has a happy ending, though, because of the work conducted in botanic gardens. As a result of a long research programme at the Royal Botanic Gardens, Kew, this lady's slipper is now growing and flowering again at eleven sites around the country.

In the case of the snake's head fritillary, a simple type of human intervention worked; and for the lady's slipper, a straightforward solution was applied, calling on the science of conservation typically conducted at botanic gardens. But sometimes the threat cannot be removed easily and so a more complex solution is required.

This was the situation in Oxfordshire when the sole remaining population of *Apium repens*, or creeping marshwort, on Port Meadow was found to be declining rapidly. The reasons for this were complex and difficult to unravel totally, but changes in the management of the River Thames to prevent flooding appear to have contributed to the problem. No one in their right mind is going to suggest that we should allow people's homes to be flooded, with all the misery that this brings, in order to save a very small plant, so a compromise solution had to be found. A group of knowledgeable volunteers formed the Oxfordshire Rare Plants Group, and with the aid of a wide range of organizations including Natural England, the University of Oxford Botanic Garden and Herbarium, and the Millennium Seed Bank Project at Royal Botanic Gardens, Kew, the population on Port Meadow was propagated from seeds carefully collected on Port Meadow and a new population of marshwort was established two miles away on a site belonging to the Oxford Preservation Trust. This project shows that, at the stewardship and conservation level, species recovery projects are rarely the work of just one concerned

Translocation: One Type of *In Situ* Conservation

The *Apium repens* story is a nice example of an *in situ* project that translocates a plant population to protect it. The migration of plants may need to be assisted in some way, and the *Apium* effort is an uncontroversial example because the plants were moved just a few miles—to a very similar place—where there was considered to be ecological room for *Apium* to fit in and become another member of the community. In effect this species has been given a new home where it can look after itself.

Clearly, though, the concept of translocated populations can be controversial, and assisted colonization such as this should only be planned if there is a high risk of local extinction. There are a number of potential risks with translocation: the incoming species might bring diseases with it; the newcomer might hybridize with other plants to create new species that might run amuck and lead to the decline of the natives; the incoming plant might alter other aspects of the ecology of the region, such as the water table. And it is complicated but very important to constantly monitor the new site to ensure that none of the preexisting members of the community lose out.

The concept of translocated populations was applied early on in Western Australia, where Corrigin grevillea (*Grevillea scapigera*) was thought to be extinct in 1989. Following extensive search by amateur and professional botanists, forty-seven plants were eventually found; but all on their own there was no chance of cross-pollination with other individuals, so new plants were made using vegetative propagation from those found. There is often a point in a species recovery programme when local backyard gardeners get involved; and it is a pivotal moment because, if they cannot grow it, the future can look very bleak—for the humans and the plant species. Fortunately the gardeners delivered. In 1996 the first plantings were done, and by 2001 there were 648 plants, flowering and producing viable seeds, established at three sites. Now thirty thousand seeds have been collected and are available for more conservation and restoration work.

A similar project aims to save the crimson spider orchid (*Caladenia concolor*) from extinction. There was a suspicion that this species had become extinct until an amateur orchid enthusiast found a wild population of the crimson spider orchid while on his holidays. Various groups got involved: the National Parks and Wildlife Service, Australian National Herbarium, Albury Botanic Gardens, Department of Land and Water Conservation, and nongovernmental community site managers, who could be volunteers or workers from charities or not-for-profits. A new site was found that had the conditions required by the orchid and which was secure from changes in the future. The original site was given extra protection. Rabbits, cats, and humans on mountain bikes and four-wheel drive vehicles were excluded or shot; and the invasive European grass *Briza minor* was destroyed by hand pulling, because if left unchecked the grass would have swamped the orchid. New orchid plants were raised, which is often tricky as they need a symbiotic fungus. Fortunately its codependent had been cultured in Kings Park and Botanic Garden in Perth Western Australia, then some new orchids were grown *in situ* following hand pollination, and some were grown *ex situ* prior to planting out in its new habitat.

group or individual; and that to conserve and protect plants over a long period of time, many different agencies, and agents, need to be involved, each bringing a particular skill to the project.

It should be stated that there are threats faced by plants that are not the result of overcollection and other human activities. These include climate change such as that which happened just 11,500 years ago, when the temperature of the planet rose by 7°C in just fifty years; or the much earlier Azolla Event about 49 million years ago, when the temperature in the Arctic slowly fell from 13°C to -9°C (55°F to 15°F) over a period of 800,000 years. Other examples of threats include disease, mass migrations of other species, fire, floods and storm surges, glaciers, hurricanes, and volcanoes. These natural disasters are threats to some species but present opportunities to others. They are part of life's rich tapestry, and organisms have responded in a variety of ways including adaptation, migration, tolerance, or if nothing else works, extinction.

> **2020 STRATEGY**
>
> **TARGET 4** Protect at least 15 percent of each ecological region or vegetation type

ECOSYSTEMS: INTERACTIVE POPULATIONS AND SAFEGUARDING SPECIES

The conservation of individual threatened species can be successful when the problem is perceived as solvable by one person or group of people; it is conservation on a human scale. For example, the survival of the last UK populations of *Stachys germanica*, or downy woundwort, is the result of pioneering work by Jo Dunn and now other members of the Cotswold Wildlife Group. It is true that iconic species can be the hook on which conservation projects can be hung, as this has been especially true for animal threats.

It is currently popular in some circles to take swipes at conservation projects such as the giant pandas in China. The armchair conservationists are unable to see that conserving pandas in their habitat means conserving that habitat and the countless other organisms that make up that habitat including the soil. Take, for example, the bittern in the United Kingdom; this bird species had almost disappeared from the UK because of hunting and habitat destruction. However, as result of careful management of existing reed beds at Minsmere in Suffolk, and the creation of new areas at Lakenheath Fen also in Suffolk, this wonderful creature can be seen in several places in England including in central London at the Barnes Reserve of the Wildfowl and Wetlands Trust. However, all three of these sites are not just about bitterns—they are about integrated populations of plants, animals, and fungi all

HIPPO and the Killarney Fern

The problems facing one threatened plant, the Killarney fern (*Trichomanes speciosum*), are so diverse that this species could be used to demonstrate all the major conservation threats: the acronym, a mnemonic of choice for students of conservation, is HIPPO—Habitat destruction (or transformation), Invasive species, Pollution, (human) Population growth, and Overexploitation.

Trichomanes speciosum is a strange plant. It has flimsy thin leaves with almost no waterproofing layer (or cuticle), which means that it can only live where the relative humidity approaches 100 percent year-round; where it does grow, it is found in very shaded places, and it is frost sensitive. Given these constraints, its distribution is limited—to Cornwall, Wales, and the Atlantic Coast of Ireland and Scotland, though there is an odd population in North Yorkshire. Add to these specialized, limiting needs are the categorical threats of HIPPO, all of which exist where the Killarney fern is found: accidental trampling in its habitat by hill walkers and botanists, animals grazing, woodland clearances; an invasive, non-native plant, *Rhododendron ponticum*; because of the delicate feature of its flimsy leaf structure, a sensitivity to water pollution in the form of sewage or fertilizer runoff; and collector exploitation, which is considered still so serious that the remaining sites in Wales are secret. Not least of all, threatening contributions are also presented by changes in water flow as a result of hydroelectric projects and natural fluctuations in climate changes in rainfall and winter temperatures. So to HIPPO is normally added climate change. Yet this is a complex and difficult area for conservation for these two reasons: we do not know for sure how climate will change from one point in time to the other; and as was pointed out by Charles Darwin, it is often very difficult to predict how tolerant plants will be in conditions different from those in which they are currently growing. It has been suggested that for the Killarney fern, climate change could be a good thing: if the climate becomes a bit warmer and a bit wetter, then this species range would be able to expand.

HIPPO conservation categories can also relate to a multitude of different situations with very complex conditions to resolve. For example, habitat destruction or transformation can involve use of land for agriculture or some other form of production, for which conservation possibilities may involve compromises or land sharing. In the pollution category, the threat is often too difficult to remove altogether such as in Tasmania, where an area downriver from a copper mine can grow very little if anything. Sadly in many cases mining for natural resources has damaged local flora, yet there have been some good, responsible stories where the pre-mining plant community was reestablished following extractions.

And perhaps most complex of all is human population growth. We humans are faced with ourselves and all that goes along with how our decisions and actions impact not only plants but our home planet and the whole complex range of ecological systems that operate on Earth. The reasons for population growth or decline are not only complex but are often affected by unexpected factors such as war or economics or earthquakes.

contributing to a complex ecological system. In the case of the iconic snake's head fritillary, this conservation programme has certainly also led to the protection of the water meadows in the Thames Valley.

Another icon of the English spring is the English bluebell, currently known as *Hyacinthoides non-scripta* (and also answering to *Endymion non-scriptus*, *Hyacinthus non-scriptus*, *Scilla nutans*, and many other synonyms—a good example of how many more names there can be than species). It is hard to believe that the English bluebell is under threat if one sees the millions of flowering bulbs carpeting woodland, but the decline of this deciduous habitat intersects with the bluebell's survival. So, given that perhaps half the world population of English bluebells lives in the United Kingdom, it is a species that has been, by law, well protected. Since 1981 it has been illegal for any UK landowner to dig up bluebells, and since 1998, illegal to conduct trade in wild-collected bulbs. As a result not only has the English bluebell been protected but so has its habitat.

There is, however, another threat to English bluebells in their habitat of deciduous woodlands which may be impossible to halt—from a very close relative, the Spanish bluebell or *Hyacinthoides hispanica*. These two species are so closely related that they readily form fertile hybrids, know as *Hyacinthoides ×massartiana*. In England there is extreme antagonism towards the southern relatives for more than just jingoistic reasons. The English bluebells are a deeper blue than the Spanish species which are more pinkish; the English plants have the most delicate scent and they hang their flowers modestly with the tips of their petals bent back gracefully; the Spanish plants do not. Put the two together and you end up with a hybrid swarm because the bumblebees happily visit both species. The resulting plants have neither the colour nor the scent of an English spring. Does this matter? It is up to you—but do we want our countryside to become as homogenized as our high streets and main streets where the same shops and franchises dominate?

It has been proposed that these two species are recent creations, their ancestral species having been separated geographically at some point during the past three million years of ice ages. They are clearly morphologically distinct. (The colour of the anthers is the best way to separate them; blue anther, Spanish; cream-coloured pollen, English.) However, for all their morphological differences, they can still interbreed freely and produce fertile offspring. To some biologists this means that they are the same species and the distinction of Spanish and English is meaningless, and so they should all be combined into a species known as the European bluebell.

There is a ten-acre English bluebell wood at the Harcourt Arboretum at Nuneham Courtenay in Oxfordshire. This is part of the University of Oxford Botanic Garden and as I write this text, the phone is regularly ringing with people asking if the bluebells are out yet. As they walk through the wood (keeping to the paths because bluebells have zero tolerance of trampling, and one foot is enough to kill them), many visitors express the opinion that this is England as God intended it. Far be it from me to suggest what God had in mind, but it seems to me that He has left some of the decisions to humans because our English bluebell wood only looks as it does because one of my colleagues spends three days at the beginning of December each year flailing down the bracken to a fine mulch up through which the bluebells grow a few months later. The bluebell wood is much more than bluebells. It is home to at least forty-five other plant species, several species of bats, many fungi, birds, moths, beetles, and frankly we know not what. Like Lakenheath Fen and Minsmere elsewhere in the UK, this is a community of interacting populations of plants, animals, and fungi all contributing to a functioning ecosystem.

There is another concern here because bluebells can propagate themselves vegetatively, and so a large population could be just one clone. However, undergraduate studies of our bluebell wood at the arboretum have revealed three important facts. First, our bluebells are genetically diverse and thus well prepared for adaptation to changes (that is, evolution) that may occur in the future. Second, they are breeding with each other enthusiastically rather than self-fertilizing which can only end in weaker plants and inbreeding depression. Third, there is very little infiltration by Spanish genes so far.

This bluebell story shows that gardeners need to be careful when they choose what to grow in their gardens. If an exotic (or non-native) species is brought into our gardens, is there a risk that it will hybridize with local native species and create a problem? And it clearly demonstrates that the preservation of one iconic species in its habitat conserves that species and all the other species who share that habitat. My mother-in-law has a wise mantra—if you educate a woman you will be educating a family. In that same way, if you conserve a species you will be conserving a habitat. However, habitats are not just for the individual species

Diversity Is the Sacred Cow of Biology

A reduction in diversity is perceived as a Bad Thing almost unquestioningly. Recent scientific studies have shown that we are right to revere biological diversity: the functioning of an ecosystem and the services provided by that ecosystem are harmed if diversity falls. For example, it has been clearly demonstrated that plant biodiversity is crucial to buffer the negative effects of climate change and desertification in dry lands. However, the further an *animal* is up the food chain, the less the effect of the loss of a *plant* species. Hence humans are often the last to notice that a plant has gone. It has also been shown that the resilience of a plant community to the normal fluctuations experienced from year to year is proportional to the diversity of the plants. In some years a plant species may be of little importance, but every few years it has a good year. As gardeners we know that every year the herbaceous border looks different, but the more different plants that you grow in that border the greater the chance that you will have a good display every year, albeit a different display. This is true at every level and may be even more important at a small scale of a few acres. This is very significant because it means that local extinctions matter.

A good example of a local extinction is the loss of meadow clary (*Salvia pratensis*) from Wales. During my lifetime (that is, since 1958) the number of populations of meadow clary in the United Kingdom have declined from more than one hundred to fewer than twenty-four in 2012. In Wales the last population petered out in 2004. However, all was not lost because in 2003 Trevor Dines, a member of the staff at Plantlife (a UK charity that conserves plants), had taken a few seeds to Treborth Botanic Garden, near Bangor, Wales, where one mature plant was raised.

This species produces both bisexual flowers and female flowers and there is a risk that you might get a plant that is wholly female, in which case seeds are unlikely unless you can find a pollen donor. In a large population, having a few all-female plants is a good way of ensuring that at least a few plants do not run the risk of self pollination. If you are the only plant, then being bisexual and therefore being able to pollinate yourself is a good insurance policy—Darwin's "reproductive assurance" principle. The Treborth plant had bisexual flowers and the horticulturists there have successfully raised more plants. In order to introduce a bit more diversity into the gene pool (or puddle in this case), plants from Gloucestershire, England, have been crossed by hand with the plants from Wales. The seeds are maturing as I write.

A similar problem exists for *Campanula patula* or spreading bellflower. Before 1930 there were more than one hundred sites in the UK. By 2009 this had reduced to just seven sites with more than forty plants in the UK, and in Wales this species had declined to just one population of nineteen plants. All may not be lost—there might be a lot of genetic diversity in the soil seed bank, because this species can reappear after soil is disturbed. The records of the British flora in UK herbaria are being subjected to DNA analysis to look for a historical pattern in the distribution of the species, to see how this plant has spread in the past.

It is not just the rare stuff that must be investigated and understood. Common or locally abundant species need to be studied, as we've seen in the example of English bluebells.

therein. We need to maintain functioning communities and habitats as much as we do the individuals that make up those assemblages because ecological systems provide us with ecological services. These ecosystem services may or may not be dependent on the presence of particular species. However, focusing on the conservation of individual species within habitats and ecosystems is still important because research has confirmed Darwin's principle of divergence, which predicts that the loss of species from a community, often referred to as local extinctions, will alter and harm the functioning of that ecosystem.

Changes on your doorstep are important because local extinctions, such as those of *Apium repens*, *Stachys germanica*, or *Fritillaria meleagris* described here, are much more common than global extinctions. Thus conservation on a local scale is important and we do not have to be involved in global projects in order to make a difference. This is a very important point because a problem for anyone involved in plant conservation is that the moaning minnies will always be happy to say that there are still problems needing to be solved. Well, yes, of course there are—but there will be one fewer for every gardener who gets involved. The scientific research is clearly showing that small projects are important as well as large projects.

When one looks at a habitat and the communities of organisms contained therein, it is often difficult to see what they are all contributing. Could a species be lost and no one and nothing would notice? It seems that at least one other species would notice if a species is lost, but not every species would be affected. It also seems to be true that the more removed you are in the food chain from the species that goes missing, the less likely you are to notice. This means that carnivores and omnivores are the last to be affected by and therefore notice the loss of a plant species; humans are in this biological group.

At any one time it might be possible to show that a particular species is functionally redundant and unimportant to the functioning of a community. However, at another time it might have an important role to play. So diversity is good for the stability of an ecosystem in the long term. A more diverse community has more ecological resilience to change and so the more variable the conditions are in an ecosystem from year to year or from season to season, the more diverse the plants have to be to maintain the level of ecosystem services. This has been put succinctly thus: many species are needed to maintain multiple functions at multiple times and places in a changing world. It is also becoming clear that a species may have different functions at the same time in different communities as well as different functions in the same community at different times.

continued on page 103

Ecosystem Services

Traditionally ecosystem services are broken down into four groups.

1. Regulating services

These are features of an ecosystem that keep Earth in a state that we can exist in without changing our way of life. The plant life on this planet has a large influence on weather patterns. The water cycle, for example, depends on the transpiration of plants. At a time when we are releasing large amounts of carbon dioxide into the atmosphere, the role of plants in the sequestration and locking away of that carbon cannot be ignored. This is a simple concept. Trees grow by their leaves taking in carbon dioxide and using the carbon to make many molecules including things like cellulose and lignin. These are resilient molecules—think of all that timber in your home. While those carbon atoms are locked away in your tables and chairs, they cannot contribute to climate change.

2. Supporting services

There is, for example, the fundamental way in which the roots of plants hold onto the soil and prevent erosion. When plants first colonized dry land approximately 470 million years ago, there was no soil. Now 470 million years later there is lots of the stuff, so much in fact that many people take it for granted, not gardeners, of course, because every gardener knows that the soil is the most important part of his or her garden. In some parts of the world, soil is being eroded a hundred times faster than it is being deposited. This has serious implications for both farming and the conservation of habitats. It is now becoming apparent that our understanding of the biology of soil is woefully inadequate. Soil science was never the most popular part of any course that I have attended, but we need to learn more about soil and quickly. We now know that globally soil contains three times the amount of carbon as either the atmosphere or terrestrial vegetation. Loss of soil therefore has serious implications for the sequestration of carbon dioxide.

Included in supporting services are the products of photosynthesis that we and every other animal consume. However, photosynthesis does much more than just making raw materials. The 400,000 species of plants with which we currently share this planet provide us with our habitat. Everything comes back to photosynthesis in the end.

3. Provisioning services

These include food, fibres, and medicines that *Homo sapiens* will continue to depend upon until it is replaced by another species or self-destructs; but even more importantly than these are the ecosystems protecting the fresh water supplies that our species is using at a rate that is rapidly approaching unsustainable. Roots tenaciously hold onto soil. This is clearly demonstrated if you find yourself in a tropical woodland after the ubiquitous afternoon storm. The streams run very fast but the water is clear of particles of soil. If the vegetation is removed the clear streams turn to mud.

4. Cultural services

These are the recreational, aesthetic, and spiritual attributes of Nature that are often dismissed as inconsequential compared to the other services or just overlooked. This is a mistake because if you are trying to promote conservation, the sheer beauty of nature is one of the most persuasive arguments.

Value or price?

So there are ecosystem services—which might tempt you to ask: do they have a monetary value? And if so, how does one determine their price?

It has been calculated that ecosystem services are worth £33 trillion (that is £33,000,000,000,000 or $52.3 trillion) per annum to the world. This is approximately twice the value of global domestic product. Do these figures mean anything? Probably not because there is no retailer in the universe from whom we could purchase them. So protecting ecosystems is a Good Idea and currently the world's governments have given themselves the target of protecting 15 percent of all types of ecosystem by 2020. You might think that this is optimistic but not so. The previous target was 10 percent protected by 2010 and we reached 11.7 percent.

However, when setting targets for conservation one has to realize that there are priority areas for two reasons. First, plant species are not distributed evenly over the planet and so protecting 100 square miles in one area might conserve far more species than 100 square miles elsewhere. Second, we know that vegetation and ecosystems in some parts of the world are more threatened than elsewhere.

On 24 February 2000 the scientific journal *Nature* published a very important paper written by Oxford University biologist Norman Myers and co-workers that has become a classic in its field and beyond. Myers and his collaborators proposed a system for identifying biodiversity hotspots for conservation priorities. Their motivation for this huge data-crunching exercise was that there is never going to be enough money to protect everywhere at once. They decided to look for those parts of the world that both enjoyed high levels of biological uniqueness and suffered from high levels of habitat loss. Biological uniqueness is called endemism and the opposite of endemic is widespread or cosmopolitan. They discovered that 44 percent of plants and 35 percent of vertebrates were confined to twenty-five areas that occupied just 1.4 percent of the land on Earth.

Interestingly not all of these twenty-five regions were tropical. All five of the regions that experience a Mediterranean-type climate were in the top twenty-five: the Mediterranean basin, central California, central Chile, the Cape Peninsula of South Africa, and southwest Western Australia. New Zealand and the Caucasus also made the top twenty-five. Although the tropical Andes and the Mediterranean basin came out as the priority areas based on numbers of endemic plant species, Madagascar "won" the prize for the most deserving recipient of conservation investment.

Case in Point: *In Situ* Conservation in Madagascar

Madagascar is undeniably special. It was the original home of *Catharanthus roseus*, or rosy periwinkle, which produces vincristine, a molecule that is now used to save the lives of eight out of ten children born with infantile leukemia. The extraordinary baobab trees are a must-see for any botanist, but they are just one of the twelve thousand species that grow on the island, and 80 percent of these species grow nowhere else. Sadly, since 1970 one third of the humid forests have been cleared with the result that Madagascar has the highest soil erosion in the world at 20,000 to 40,000 tons per square kilometre per annum.

At the 2003 IUCN World Parks Congress held in Durban, South Africa, the president of Madagascar announced the intention to create the 57,000-square-kilometre Systeme d'Aires Proteges de Madagascar in order to increase the area of Madagascar wherein biology is protected from 2.9 percent in 2002 to 10 percent by 2010 (and by 2012, 10.2 percent of the island was protected). Following the announcement that more of the land on Madagascar was to be protected, work began on deciding where that land should be. On 11 April 2008 the journal *Science* published a paper by University of California Berkeley ecologist Claire Kremen and colleagues. What made this study exceptional was the level of detail and the variety of species assessed.

Madagascar is about twice the area of the UK and similar in area to France. Kremen and her many collaborators divided the island into more than half a million squares and for each square they recorded the presence or absence of 2,315 different species. Normally these species would all be from the same taxonomic group, and the most common surrogate groups used are plants or birds. Plants are used because they are the basis for all animal life, and if the plants are diverse and healthy then the animals will come along too. Birds are used because they require a number of different organisms to be present in the ecosystem, and so healthy bird populations are symptomatic of a healthy community and ecosystem. Furthermore good data is often available for both of these groups, plants because they are immobile and relatively easy to survey and birds because they are relatively big and not too numerous.

Even so, conserving plants at home in their habitat, *in situ*, is not straightforward, as every species will be different. Leaving Madagascar for just a moment, in the Philippines it was decided to compare the current locations of the protected areas such as national parks with the important plant areas. The lack of overlap was disappointing but important to know. It was then decided to look at the conservation of palms, which are particularly important economically as well as ecologically. Sixteen hotspots were identified for species in the palm family, the Arecaceae. Only thirteen were in the newly identified important plant areas, though this was better than the fact that only five were in the existing protected areas. This highlights the need for accurate data for all species.

Back on Madagascar, Claire Kremen chose not to use birds but instead used data for plants, and lemurs, and ants, and butterflies, and geckos, and frogs. For each of the 2,315 species, they either mapped the actual distribution of the species or a theoretical distribution based on known habitat preferences. They then calculated the best 10 percent of the island to protect for each of the six groups of organisms. It would have been wonderful if the six 10 percents of each of the six groups had overlapped perfectly but this is biology and perfect is not an option (after all this is not physics). When all six different 10 percents for each group were added together, the area covered 26.5 percent of the island. Not surprisingly if the plants' 10 percent had been chosen, more of the other species would have been protected than if any of the other five taxa had been used as a surrogate, but an unacceptable number would have still been missed. This illustrates an important point of conservation: compromises will always have to be made.

In order to reduce the 26.5 percent to just 10 percent, rejection of areas had to begin with the understanding that no species was to be omitted entirely. Slowly the area was whittled down to 10 percent. Reassuringly much of it was where the reserves are already situated.

There were, however, a few surprises when areas previously not protected came out as winners. Still this was not the end of the story because Kremen and her colleagues faced two dilemmas. Firstly, should they recommend abandoning areas already protected in favour of theoretically better regions? In the end they produced both a solution constrained by the existing parks and a second solution that assumed no areas had already been protected. Secondly, they tried to reduce the number of small areas. It is widely agreed that a few large reserves will be better than lots of fragments. The point at which the size of the fragment becomes biologically too small varies with species, introducing another variable to be considered. Fragmentation is a particular problem in Madagascar and on many other islands with a high percentage of human-transformed area.

One such island is Great Britain where in some parts of the country well over 90 percent of the land is agricultural. This is no bad thing because English farms are some of the most productive in the world. In central England, on the border between Buckinghamshire and Oxfordshire, there is a terrific project led jointly by the Berkshire, Buckinghamshire and Oxfordshire Wildlife Trust (BBOWT) and the Royal Society for the Protection of Birds (RSPB). The idea is to create a large area (73 square km or 28 square miles) of wetlands that will support a wide variety of animals. In addition to joining up reserves already owned by the two organizations, land belonging to local farmers will be included in the project. It is the inclusion of the local community that makes this a very good long-term prospect. In addition to providing a habitat for the true fox sedge (*Carex vulpina*), water voles ("Ratty" from *The Wind in the Willows*), otters, and wading birds such as snipe and curlews, the reserve will significantly improve water quality. The value of this should not be underestimated because 50 percent of public water in the UK has to be treated because of agricultural run-off costing £200 million each year.

continued from page 96

If you are beginning to feel a bit bamboozled and wondering if ecology is full of complicated interactions, variable variables, feedback loops, and chicken-and-eggs situations, then you are dead right! Charles Darwin used the term "entangled bank" in the final paragraph of *Origin of Species*:

> It is interesting to contemplate an entangled bank, clothed with many plants of many kinds, with birds singing on the bushes, with various insects flitting about, and with worms crawling through the damp earth, and to reflect that these elaborately constructed forms, so different from each other, and dependent on each other in so complex a manner, have all been produced by laws acting around us.

We are slightly closer to understanding the laws to which Darwin alludes, but we are not there yet.

2020 STRATEGY
TARGET 5 Protect at least 75 percent of the most important ecosystem regions

What are the home advantages of *in situ* plant conservation?

When species are conserved *in situ*, the scale tends to be bigger than in the conservation of species in gardens, and so there is probably more genetic diversity being conserved at the same time. Additionally, intact communities are conserved along with all the other aspects of the local ecology that are required for the reproduction and health of the population, such as pollinators and mycorrhizal fungi. And wider ecological services are preserved and maintained. Finally, there is a practical reason for *in situ* conservation: the appeal to funding bodies and private donors of the conservation of iconic species such as orchids or even birds.

Sadly, inevitably, there are going to be problems associated with *in situ* conservation. It is more expensive to establish: site security is vital, and if the ownership of the land is not fixed, then any further investment could be wasteful and better used elsewhere; endless monitoring, often requiring 24/7 attendance, is expensive, with estimates varying widely. At the top end, in 2008 the cost of adequately and continuously mapping the distribution of all 400,000 plant species was calculated at US $773 million per annum, while in 2001 the much lower figure of US $10 million was proposed. The difference was that in the latter plan, local communities were involved in the work, which meant that the conservation programme was more accurately targeted and implemented, driven by local interest and knowledge which all had an impact on how much expenditure was necessary (volunteers workers, for example, are more inspired and committed when the environment has personal value). If this monitoring indicates that the ecosystem is changing in undesirable ways, then some degree of intervention and management will be required, possibly for a very long time. Threats such as the soil seed banks of non-native invasive species can be difficult and expensive to remove.

The final question mark over *in situ* conservation is whether containing species in a fixed nature reserve is the best policy in a world where the climate is changing quickly. Many people have noticed that spring flowering has been creeping earlier over the past thirty years. In 2004, for example, wood anemones (*Anemone nemorosa*) and meadow buttercups (*Ranunculus acris*) flowered fourteen days earlier than the hundred-year historical average. Snowdrops (*Galanthus nivalis*) flowered twenty-one days earlier and sloe, also known as blackthorn (*Prunus spinosa*), flowered an extraordinary thirty-nine days earlier than would be expected. This study, carried out by World Wildlife Fund, asked the question: can nature keep up?

To answer this question we need to know how fast the climate is changing. A study in 2009 showed that the velocity of climate change was lowest in mountainous regions and highest in deserts and flooded grasslands, and so yet again biology refuses to be consistent. Small protected areas will be more at risk than large areas, which makes sense because plants will be able to migrate within the larger reserves and parks. The conclusion of this study was that in one hundred years' time, it is possible that only 8 percent of present-protected areas will be in the "right place" for the species that currently live there.

Another concern about climate change is that the various components of a community will get out of sync. A study at Wytham Woods near Oxford has shown that this might not always be the case. This area of a thousand acres of ancient and mixed woodland has been extensively surveyed and monitored for several decades. It is home to many breeding pairs of the common English bird *Parus major* (known to the delight of small boys as the great tit). The date of their first brood hatching has been recorded along with flowering times of the plants in the woods and the emergence of the invertebrates that feed on the plants and which in turn feed the great tits. The research has shown that, in fact, all the players in this food chain respond in the same way to the weather, and everything appears to be fine. However, the problems might be severe for migrating birds, which might turn up after all the food has been eaten.

So, is the best way to protect plants *in situ*, in their natural homes? While not wishing to be accused of being pedantic, I must reply that the answer does rather depend on what you mean by natural—or, since this is my book, what I mean by natural.

In 1783, Goethe wrote, "Nature is ever shaping new forms: what is, has never yet been; what has been, comes not again." If this is true, then the aims and objectives for nature reserves are for us to define as we see fit. It is now generally accepted that there is no default setting for how the world should look. Natural means different things to different people. For some research workers, natural states are those that existed before the Europeans turned up and started clearing land, farming, grazing, and controlling wildfires. This definition is being revised now by other researchers because humans have been altering the world for much longer than the Europeans have been colonizing the world. Furthermore, some human-induced changes are impossible to change.

In addition, we must realize that environmental and ecological changes are normal; the world is in permanent flux and few of our present major ecosystems are more than twelve thousand years old. Records from paleoecological studies seem to indicate that for any given place, over time there are many alternative, very different "natural" states.

Away from Home: *Ex Situ* Conservation

> **2020 STRATEGY**
>
> **TARGET 8** Protect at least 75 percent of threatened species *ex situ* and make at least 20 percent available for recovery and restoration programmes

If plants cannot be safely managed in their natural habitats, then the species must be moved to safety. If the conservation of a species involves moving it to a new location of any kind, then the conservation may be described as *ex situ*. However, the new location can be one of several very different options. One extreme location is a seed bank, where desiccated seeds are stored for many years at −18°C (0°F). Less extreme is a self-sustaining population of an endangered species in a garden.

This second approach is often regarded as second best, but for some species the value may lie in what they can do for us rather than what they contribute to their community. While this is perhaps not a popular view, it is a real one—because different plants require different strategies; and to conserve, say, a tree species that takes thirty years to hit puberty is obviously going require different techniques from those used to save an annual species.

So there is no one-size-fits-all solution in conservation biology, and *ex situ* conservation will not be the perfect solution but will have both advantages and disadvantages.

continued on page 110

Climate Change, Changing Conservation

This is no place to discuss exactly what is happening to the climate and how fast it is changing. What we must remember is that climate change is the default setting for planet Earth. Climate has always changed and will always change. There have been times in the past 4 billion years when the climate has changed dramatically. The climate seems to be in one of those periods of rapid change at the moment. To describe it as global warming is a gross and misleading simplification. New weather patterns will emerge, some of which will be like nothing currently present on Earth.

How this will affect plants, be they currently common or rare, no one knows Tiddly Pom, but the wise words of Charles Darwin are important here: "The degree to which an organism is adapted to its present locality is often overestimated." Plants live where they do and can, and not necessarily where they would be most comfortable. In fact, because the default setting for life is uncomfortable, it is often *tolerance* of the limiting factors in a habitat that determines the winners and losers in the struggle for survival (which plants are the least uncomfortable, which is different from those that are most comfortable).

There is no evidence at present that climate changes will render all current protected areas unsuitable. Fences on wheels is a nice metaphor for the idea of moving the location of a nature reserve, but it may not be practical to always assume that we will know in which direction to push the fences.

However, the uncertainty surrounding climate change is one of the forces behind a major shift in strategies away from black-and-white *in situ* versus *ex situ* conservation. It seems to many of us that two things need to be conserved: one, the ecological services; and the other, individual species and the genes contained therein. The former must be done at home, *in situ*, and the latter must be done away from home, *ex situ*. There will be times when they can be done together, but this is a bonus and cannot be the default setting.

Ex Situ: Advantages of Conservation Away from Home

1. It's the only option for conservation when the habitat of the threatened species has been completely destroyed.
2. A threatened species can be entirely separated from the threats to its survival.
3. New populations can be protected from random, stochastic events and climate change, which will threaten even the best-managed *in situ* populations of threatened species.
4. Monitoring of *ex situ* populations is easier than wild populations because they are always near the people who are running the programmes.
5. Protecting one-species-at-a-time is conservation on a human scale—and, lame as this might sound, people have to feel that they can make a difference in their lifetime if they are going to be able to make a difference. *Ex situ* programmes are well suited to people's backyards or gardens.
6. *Ex situ* conservation cases for *Franklinia alatamaha* and *Apium repens* show that it works, and it works for centuries.

Ex Situ: Disadvantages of Conservation Away from Home

1. *Ex situ* conservation programmes are not a permanent solution because other aspects of the plant's biology are not automatically conserved. These include pollinators (though plants do not necessarily care who pollinates then so long as someone does), animals that disperse their seeds (though at least four in five species do not use any form of animal-based dispersal), and beneficial fungi.

2. The population of the endangered species that is propagated in the *ex situ* location will have a low genetic diversity. As in the case of *Franklinia*, which was already rare and thus limited in genetic diversity, the one remaining population itself was not genetically diverse either.
3. Many gardeners growing threatened species are well known for favouring "good garden plants"—that is, plants that may be robust and with particularly appealing yet unusually coloured flowers. While these may be best for our borders, they may not be the best plants for a wild population. This can be easily avoided by careful, random selection of plants when the new population is being established.
4. A threatened species might become so happy in its new home that it could escape and become a non-native invasive species. This has been claimed for *Gladiolus caryophyllaceous*. Originally from South Africa, this attractive species has escaped from gardens in Western Australia and is now naturalized in the area. However, it is not now on the South African Red List of threatened species. I can find no example of an invasive non-native species that is threatened in its homeland.
5. The threatened species will meet closely related species, from a completely different part of the world, and will form hybrids. Hybrids formed in cultivation are loathed and even feared by many conservation workers. They are loathed because they are not the "real thing" genetically, and they are feared because of "hybrid vigor," a biological phenomenon the origin of which is still a mystery. But whatever the cause of this vigor—manifested generally by growing faster and bigger, and producing more seeds (in the bigger fruits)—it makes the hybrid potentially dangerous if it escapes from our gardens.

continued from page 106

Without realizing it, gardeners have been the custodians of the world's plants for centuries. Trying to search history to determine which plant species was first recued by gardeners from the extinction vortex, and when plant conservation may have initially taken hold in any culture, will never be possible, but *Ginkgo biloba* is a strong candidate because this species has survived for at least 200 million years and it is rarely found in the wild outside of cultivation.

Ginkgo biloba is a loner. It is the only species in its genus, family, order, and even class in some classifications (and has thereby single-handedly proved the arbitrary nature of taxonomic ranks). *Ginkgo* is as closely related to the rest of the plant kingdom as humans are related to starfish and sea urchins. Like several other species of gymnosperm, *Ginkgo* was formerly much more widespread and, two million years ago, grew far beyond present-day China to which it is now confined. Its characteristic oddities (leaves different from any other seed plant and sperm with motile tails) may have been its saving grace, and why it was widely planted by Buddhist monks in China (some specimens are believed to be more than 1,500 years old). It is also held in great esteem by the followers of Confucius, who is reputed to have liked sitting under a ginkgo tree when pondering the meaning of life, truth, and everything. Ginkgo is credited with many powers, in particular as a promoter of good memory and delayer of the onset of dementia (and it certainly appeared to work for my old mother for a number of years).

Of ecological interest, the bark and leaves of ginkgo contain a fire retardant and, similar to redwoods, possess a genetically determined feature that is not currently required for its survival. There are reports that following the fires after the 1923 earthquake in Tokyo, ginkgoes came through it better than any other species. Perhaps most extraordinary is the claim that ginkgo trees were not killed by the atomic bomb blast at Hiroshima. Of particular interest to gardeners is the extraordinary tolerance *Ginkgo biloba* has to shade and poor air quality, especially in cities dominated by high buildings and motor vehicles. There

"Greatest Natural Historian in the World"

If *Ginkgo biloba* is the oldest example of a species saved from extinction by cultivation, the best documented example has to be *Franklinia alatamaha* from the US state of Georgia, and it is to farmers-turned-botanical gardeners John Bartram and son William that we owe a debt of gratitude.

The Bartrams are as important as the Tradescants in the history of world gardening. Originally farmers just outside what is now the Philadelphia, Pennsylvania, the Bartrams can claim to be not only the fathers of American botany but also the fathers of American gardening. Linnaeus described John as "the greatest natural historian in the world." A visit to the Bartram homestead is a pilgrimage that all gardeners should make. This is the nursery where so many great garden plants were brought into cultivation, as well as oddities such as the Venus flytrap (*Dionaea muscipula*). It is often thought of as the first botanic garden in North America, and like many botanic gardens around the world, it was the recipient of many plants from other gardens. Philip Miller sent many seeds of plants from the Chelsea Physic Garden in west London. Sadly one of these was the Norway maple (*Acer platanoides*) which has subsequently become a real nuisance as it invades the Delaware Valley and more of the United States and Canada each year.

The Bartrams traded with many gardens and gardeners in America as well as Europe. They exported their seeds in what were known as Five Guinea Boxes in England and as Bartram's Boxes in America. The five guineas refers to the cost of five pounds and five schillings, £5.25 or $8.15 in modern money (plus inflation of course!). One of these boxes arrived here in Oxford in the early 1740s when J. J. Dillenius was professor of botany and keeper of the Botanic Garden.

Among the plants whose seeds were included in some of the boxes was *Franklinia alatamaha*, a small, deciduous tree that can grow up to 30 feet high though it is often seen as a large multi-stemmed shrub. At first sight it appears to be related to camellias, and so it is, being in the same family—the Theaceae. *Franklinia alatamaha*, like *Ginkgo biloba*, is the only species in its genus. The flowers are thought by some to smell like honeysuckle which is slightly odd because they have a very different structure. The flowers of *Franklinia* are dish shaped and look superficially like *Cistus* flowers, which are classic beetle-pollinated flowers; whereas honeysuckle flowers are tubular and pollinated by night-flying moths, which I mention because an understanding of the pollinator requirements of plants is essential if a species is to be conserved. If the plant is growing away from its natural habitat, hand pollination may be required if a new pollinator does not come along.

Franklinia was discovered and recorded by the Bartrams in 1765 along the banks of the Alatamaha River in Georgia. Years later William collected seeds between 1773 and 1776 on a long collecting trip subsidized by John Fothergill, for whom *Fothergilla* is named. Fothergill was a prodigious plant collector and yet another Quaker in this story. *Franklinia alatamaha* was already a rare plant before Bartram started collecting seeds. He recorded in 1791 that he only saw it growing in a few acres. The last verified account of it growing in the wild is from the writing of another plant collector, John Lyon, in 1803, but by this time it was already safe in cultivation, where it remains over two centuries later.

are now many more plants growing in human-made environments than there are in the "wild." It is possible that even the "natural," seemingly wild populations of *Ginkgo* in central China near the Yangtze River are the remnants of cultivation, deliberate plantings. This thought is based on genetic analysis which has revealed that the species' genetic diversity is less than one would have expected to find in a randomly outbreeding group of wild individuals.

Why *Franklinia* disappeared is the subject of much debate. It was already very restricted in its distribution and so to blame overcollection by Bartram, Lyon, and others is harsh and unjustified. If anything, gardeners reached into the extinction vortex and pulled it back from the brink because all the existing plants of *Franklinia* are descended from the Bartram collections. Flooding of the Alatamaha River has been blamed, as has fire, perhaps clearing land for agriculture. A fungus introduced by cotton growers may have put the final nail in the coffin of this species. However, Keith Thomson, formerly director of the University of Oxford Natural History Museum, believed that this species was the victim of natural climate change and it was neither able to migrate fast enough to find a new habitat nor able to compete with the other plants in North America.

So like many other plants, including *Ginkgo biloba*, *Franklinia* has been saved from extinction. But there is no evidence that the Bartrams were setting out to conserve rare plants—rather, they sought to find good plants with commercial potential. A well-documented example of deliberate, conscious conservation of a critically endangered species is the ambitious project to establish a self-propagating population of dawn redwood or *Metasequoia glyptostroboides* (perhaps the most tuneful Latin binomial) in North Carolina. The planting began in 1995.

This is a good example of an *ex situ* species recovery programme where, to insure the survival of a species, it is removed from its natural habitat and placed outside its normal circumstance—in this case, from China to the United States. The dawn redwood had only been known as a fossil from central China until 1941, when living plants were discovered in Hubei Province there. Seeds were sent in 1947 to the Arnold Arboretum in Boston, Massachusetts, and from there distributed to many other gardens, including Oxford—our tree is now over 50 feet tall (though the pigeons keep damaging the leading shoot). It is thought that only one natural population remains, about five thousand trees in the Lichuan County in Hubei Province. If the plants in this population are genetically distinct and freely interbreeding, then all is not lost; five thousand individuals is a good starting point. Sadly, such is the demand for seeds of this species that the natural regeneration has halted because of the overcollection of female cones.

continued on page 116

The *Ex Situ* Species Recovery Programmes

A species recovery programme aims to establish a self-propagating population of the threatened species. There are five basic elements.

1. Understand the habitat from which the plant comes.

During this stage of the process the possibility of restoring the habitat is assessed; and in addition to understanding the habitat in terms of its soils and other organisms present, especially the animals and fungi, the pollination requirements of the species must be studied. It is also important to know if there are any seeds of the species being recovered in the soil seed bank.

2. Examine the genetics of the species.

Small populations have a lower than ideal level of genetic diversity. Measuring the genetic diversity of a population is work for laboratory scientists at present. However, the 50/500 rule is useful as a rule-of-thumb. Put simply, if you have 50 unrelated individuals, there will be sufficient genetic diversity for the population to avoid the problems of inbreeding in the short term. Random crossing between 50 unrelated organisms will result in an inbreeding rate of about 1 percent, which is half the rate of inbreeding tolerated by breeder of domesticated animals.

The 500 figure relates to the number of unrelated individuals that you need to guarantee that the rate of the appearance of new beneficial mutations balances the loss of variation due to random genetic drift. So, initially, to protect a species from the problems of inbreeding, you only need to grow 50 plants. In the longer term 500 should be grown.

3. Establish the provenance of the plant.

The provenance of the plants being grown in the conservation programme is vitally important. The conservationists must be sure that their plants are the Real Thing, just like a newly discovered painting by an Old Master must be confirmed by an expert as the Real Thing.

So the plants must be correctly identified—but more than that, they must belong to the home side, the native population. So if you want to conserve the last remaining population of a North American species you do not use plants raised from seeds of European or Asian plants of the same species.

4. Learn how to propagate it and how it reproduces in the wild.
This is the next logical stage in the understanding of the biology of our target species. Since in the first stage we investigated the pollination requirements of the plant and whether there are any viable seeds in the soil seed bank, we now need to make sure that we can germinate those seeds and grow the seedlings into flowering-sized adult plants. If there are no seeds available then the gardeners are really needed because we shall have to employ other familiar techniques such as cuttings and air layering. If none of these work, or if the plant is something odd like an orchid, then micropropagation (sowing on sterile agar jelly) might be required. The latter was needed to propagate lady's slipper orchid.

When we have learned all we need to know about the propagation of the plant, we need to know how to store the plant safely. For many plants this will involve an artificial seed bank, where the seeds are dried and then frozen. While this works well for about 70 percent of plant species, the so-called orthodox species, it does not work for the other 30 percent, the recalcitrant species.

5. The people: the final element of any species recovery programme.
The people who are going to either carry out the work or support it in other ways will involve not only biologists but politicians plus their electorate, funding bodies, land owners, and school children. The full list of the people involved in plant conservation appears in the final chapter.

continued from page 113

Often species that are threatened with extinction are also suffering from a genetic bottleneck, where a healthy gene pool has been reduced to a gene puddle. This can lead to inbreeding which can further reduce their chances of long-term survival. If you have a threatened species that hybridizes with a closely related species, the resultant plant with its renewed vigor might be able to survive in the original habitat and fulfill the same ecological roles as the original threatened species. I acknowledge that this is a big *might*, but by dismissing all hybrids as unacceptable we are risking throwing away the baby with the bathwater and shooting the goose that has laid the golden egg.

I have obviously nailed my colours firmly to the mast of *ex situ* species recovery programmes. This is because I am repeatedly told that it is second best to *in situ* conservation and someone needs to point out forcibly that *ex situ* conservation has a vital role to play. *If* all *in situ* programs are successful, then perhaps *ex situ* would be superfluous—but they are not. Many *ex situ* programs have worked so well because gardeners are so very good at growing plants.

This argument for or against *ex situ* programmes will not be settled here, but it can be continued. And advanced. Hybridization happens; it happens in our gardens and it happens in our meadows and woods. When it happens in our gardens it is called playing God and creating monsters, but when it happens in meadows and woods it is called evolution. It is currently believed that somewhere between 25 and 85 percent of all wild species are of hybrid origin.

The one problem we did *not* have with *Euphorbia stygiana* was the need for a specific pollinator. This was not true for *Encephalartos ferox*, an attractive plant if you are careful when handling it and you can tolerate the occasional perforation of your skin by the ferocious spines on the tough, unforgiving leaves. *Encephalartos* is a cycad, a modern-day representative of a group of plants whose heyday was about 150 million years ago. Today the majority of cycads are rare; and the trade in all species of cycad is controlled by the Convention on International Trade in

Endangered Species (or CITES) because it's just not practical to rely on the ability of customs officials to distinguish a threatened species from the minority of species that are not threatened.

And *ex situ* cultivation and conservation of cycads has led to a downgrading of the threatened conservation status of many of the species. Like all cycads, the plants of *Encephalartos ferox* are either male or female. In Oxford we only have a female. At the Royal Botanic Gardens, Kew, they have both male and female. When our female produced a huge, bright red, female cone we begged Kew for some pollen from their old male who was fortuitously coning at the same time. Kew most generously provided the pollen but this was just the start of the adventure because we had to find a vector for the pollen, or to put this into English, we had to find a pollinator. Unfortunately the weevil that should do the job is not here. Stewart Henchie, a senior member of staff at Kew, came up with an ingenious substitute—his bicycle pump. A solution of water and pollen was sucked up into the pump and this was then forcibly propelled between the scales of the female cone. The result was a good rate of fertilization, and many viable seeds were produced. Since Stewart's pioneering work with his bicycle pump, the technique has been much refined and the pollinator of choice for *Encephalartos ferox* is now a turkey baster. The female cone at Oxford was successfully pollinated, and dozens of its seedlings have been raised. These have now been distributed among other major European botanic gardens and similar institutions.

Pressure on wild populations to produce seeds and new offspring on their own, and on the human collection of seeds for cultivation, has been reduced by *ex situ* programs such as those mentioned in this chapter. But conservation through seed production and collection, especially for rare species, can create problems of overcollection, as illustrated in the case of the cones of the dawn redwood, *Metasequoia glyptostroboides*. Yet seeds provide a wonderful opportunity for *ex situ* conservation and preservation of not just endangered species, but currently common species and also varieties of the crops upon which we depend for our future prosperity. This is where the artificial seed bank steps in. They are and have already been crucially important in the success of species recovery conservation programs.

Case in Point: *Ex Situ* Risks in Botanic Gardens—Hybridization and the Dangers of Playing Away from Home

When we embarked on a species recovery programme for *Euphorbia stygiana* we had assumed that the risk of hybridization would not be a problem. Perhaps making assumptions was the first risk.

We believed that only two potential perpetrators of interbreeding with *Euphorbia stygiana* existed. *Euphorbia dendroides*, from Crete, is not reliably hardy in Oxford and so is not grown outdoors and rarely flowers with us. *Euphorbia mellifera*, from the Canary Islands, does happily grow outside and flowers well, giving off the most wonderful heady smell of rich honey. *Euphorbia mellifera* flowers in March and *E. stygiana* flowers in May, making the risk of hybridization and genetic contamination acceptably low.

But in the spring of 1999, two seedlings popped up in the Botanic Garden under *Euphorbia stygiana*, and two similar seedlings appeared in the gravel garden that is part of the garden kept by my wife, Jill. While these seedlings initially resembled *Euphorbia stygiana*, they grew with the unmistakable vigor of hybrids. These were given the working name of *Euphorbia* 'Devil's Honey' by way of a simple allusion to the putative parentage.

What I had not previously noticed was that in April the last male flowers of *Euphorbia mellifera* were produced just as the stigmatic surfaces of the first female flowers of the *Euphorbia stygiana* emerged.

The sleuthing had to begin. We needed to confirm the parentage of the hybrids we found. A biology undergraduate, George Pasteur, supervised by Stephen Harris (the remarkable curator of the University of Oxford Herbarium), took up the challenge for his project. The methodology began with George taking all of the morphological measurements that he could find on the two parents and the hybrids. These showed that in every way the hybrid was intermediate between the parents, including flowering in April. However, there was another method available to George and Stephen. Because we thought that we knew both of the actual parent plants for the hybrids in both the Botanic Garden and in Jill's garden, George was able to compare the DNA of the pairs of parents with the suspected hybrids. In both cases the DNA evidence confirmed the morphological data.

The big picture for plant naming here is that when the hybrids began to flower and produce viable seeds that gave rise to fertile offspring, they resembled the parent hybrid plants. It was decided that these hybrids should be named formally so that the story could be recorded and fixed in the literature. So 'Devil's Honey' should no longer be used. I decided that George's exacting work should be recognized and the new hybrid was given the name *Euphorbia* ×*pasteurii* (though this may confuse people in the future since it might be assumed that this plant was named after a French milkman and not an English student.) And 'Devil's Honey' should never have been used in the first place. Unbeknown to me at the time, the styx referred to in the specific epithet *stygiana* is not the river on the way to the next world (perhaps to meet the devil); the styx referred to is actually the *Styx*, a ship on which botanist Hewett Cotterell (H. C.) Watson sailed to the Azores in 1842. During his three months of botanizing on the four major islands of the Azores, Watson first encountered the shrubby euphorbias of the Azores. His familiarity with the flora of the Canary Islands led him to record these plants as *Euphorbia mellifera*. It was only later, when he compared his collections with herbarium specimens of Canary Island *Euphorbia mellifera* that he decided that the Azorian plants were a distinct species that he called *Euphorbia stygiana*.

The fact that *Euphorbia stygiana* and *Euphorbia mellifera* can freely interbreed to produce fertile offspring might tempt you to think that H. C. Watson was right in his first conclusions and that the Azorian plants are just a form of *Euphorbia mellifera*. It is not unreasonable to propose that the original colonizing seed (or seeds) on the Azores was brought from one of the Canary Islands (or other parts of western Europe where *Euphorbia mellifera* formerly grew). This is therefore an example of evolution in action. Darwin said that there is no fundamental difference between species and varieties. He described varieties as incipient species, or species about to exist or appear. In this proposed scenario the plants that grew in the Canary Islands produced seeds that migrated to the Azores and hence the species became split between the Canaries and the Azores. With the passage of time the different ecological conditions on the Canaries and the Azores selected plants of *Euphorbia mellifera* that looked different from each other and thus a new species—*Euphorbia stygiana*—was created. (I have assumed that *Euphorbia mellifera* came first because the Canary Islands are older than the Azores but it could have happened the other way round.)

By bringing *Euphorbia stygiana* and *E. mellifera* back together we could be said to be reversing speciation and thus reversing evolution. We are remixing the gene pools from the two archipelagos. The hybrids are fertile with both of the parents. If you brought all the Macaronesian Islands together in one land mass I suspect that there would be just one species. Until that happens, however, we have two natural species (*Euphorbia stygiana* and *E. mellifera*) and one artificial hybrid species (*Euphorbia* ×*pasteurii*). If either *Euphorbia mellifera* or *E. stygiana* were ever to be peering over the rim of the extinction vortex then expanding the gene pool of the failing species by crossing it with the other should be considered. That is my view. It is not a widely accepted view. It does not represent the views of the majority, and I would not recommend saying so to anyone until you know them well.

3 Conserving Genes: Plants for the Future

Every day you eat many seeds or foods made from them. The toast or cereals that you had for breakfast were made from seeds. Perhaps you had a sandwich for lunch and a bar of chocolate—more seeds. For your evening meal you might have had beans or nuts in some form, or maybe a pie—yet more seeds. Seeds, as an important food supply, did not evolve for our benefit or for the benefit of a specific animal. Their evolutionary directive arose as a plant's survival capsule, carrying its most precious cargo: an embryo containing the plant-to-be's genetic material. A seed's genes, of which there are thousands, provide the instructions for the embryo, controlling its development into a young plant and then, when matured, also its day-to-day behaviour, its flowering and fruiting. At this point it might be helpful if I give a simple overview of a seed's structure and function—please see the accompanying box.

Like all species, humans need some plants more than others for their everyday activities. Food, clothing, shelter, medicines, and fuels are all derived from plants. We have manipulated a few species to provide us with most of our basic needs. However, we need to be continually updating the cultivated, man-made varieties of these plants to produce more food and to resist the pests and diseases that see these fields as theirs to eat and devour. While the genes of cereals are easily stored as seeds, which is why seed banks are so useful, this is less easy for crops such as potatoes and fruit trees.

Seed Banks

Clearly, a "natural" seed bank already exists in nature—in the soil—and in this environment seeds can be a pain in the neck. My father believed that preventing weeds from producing seeds was very important: "one year's seeding means seven years of weeding" was his mantra.

Structure and Function of a Seed

A basic seed structure consist of three parts:

Embryo This part of the seed will grow into a mature plant with roots, shoots, leaves, and other elements.

Endosperm Food for the embryo is very important because before the young plant has rooted and developed green leaves that photosynthesize sugars, energy is required for the embryo. The embryo may appear to be doing nothing in the seed but it is alive and therefore it is respiring. The embryo will therefore be using up the food albeit very slowly. The colder it is the slower will be the respiration. The known record is thirty thousand years for a seed to survive frozen in soil.

Seed coat The protective coat is provided by the maternal plant in this plant marriage. The seeds may be enclosed in a fruit of various sizes and shapes and textures but the coat is always there on each seed.

Seed structure simplified

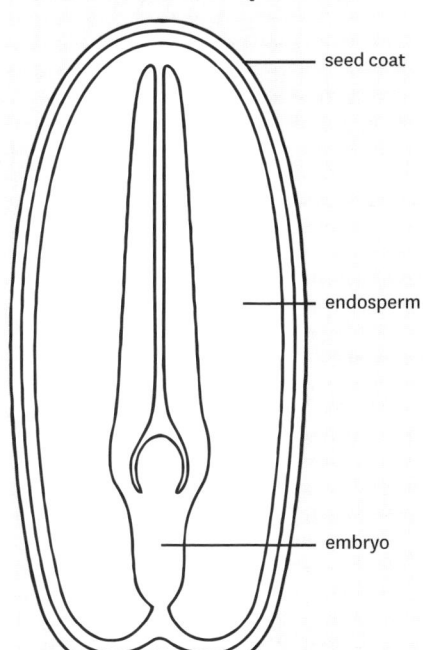

A seed's function is to transport the embryo from the flower to the ground and to protect it until the conditions are right for germination and growth of a new plant. By way of its embryo, it provides the safe haven for the genetic material that its parent plants provide. Sometimes there are also features in the seed that assist the embryo in "sensing" the right conditions for its germination. It also can protect the embryo from animals, fire, or any of the other dangers that seeds encounter.

Soil is a reservoir for plants waiting for the right conditions. Species that make cones, such as pines and banksias, hold their seed "banks" in the cones in the tree canopy. Ever since humans have cultivated plants, for economic or amenity reasons, they have stored seeds. If the species is an annual, then this is the only way of ensuring that you have that plant next year; if it is a perennial, then it is a way to guarantee you can grow new plants if they were lost in the winter. These types of seed stores are normally in paper envelopes in a gardener's dry shed or in the fridge. One thing that must never be forgotten is that seeds are alive, and so infinite storage is very unlikely, because the seed's food supply will eventually run out. That being said, in 2012 some 30,000-year-old frozen seeds of *Silene stenophylla* began to germinate in a laboratory in Russia. The record for the germination of a seed after many years without freezing is 1,300 years for a seed of *Nelumbo nucifera* that was buried in mud. In the UK, seeds of wood spurge, *Euphorbia amygdaloides*, have remained alive in the soil for 125 years, waiting for a clearing in the tree canopy to provide suitable conditions for the plants and to break the dormancy of the seeds.

It is not a big leap of reasoning to think that if a seed can survive in the soil for many years, then seeds might be stored in artificial seed banks—in drawers, boxes, cupboards, or even fridges and freezers. In fact, many artificial seed banks have been set up. For example, in Western Australia there is the Threatened Flora Seed Centre (TFSC), where more than 70 percent of Western Australia's plants are stored. We have already considered the Millennium Seed Bank Project in the UK, with more than twenty-five thousand species in storage. In the United States the Rae Selling Berry Seed Bank for the rare and endangered plants of the Pacific Northwest holds more than fourteen thousand collections of more than three hundred species of rare and vulnerable plants.

Seed banks can be found around the world. The Millennium Seed Bank in England is one example of a working seed bank; it alone has supplied seeds to more than 4,600 research projects in many parts of the world. From Burkina Faso in Sub-Saharan western Africa, a thousand species have been collected and stored both at the msbp and in the cnsf (Centre National de Semences Forestieres) in Burkina Faso. This represents 50 percent of the species in the country. The seeds are being used in community-based projects that are restoring habitats and developing new agricultural methods. To the east and south of Burkina Faso is Malawi where the msbp have collected over a thousand species, which is more than a quarter of all of the species in the country. Many of these are narrow-range endemics.

The UK Royal Botanic Gardens, Kew, is heavily involved in the conservation of the flora of Madagascar and with good reason. This is one of the hottest biodiversity hotspots on Earth in terms of the number of species in the area and the very high proportion of endemic species—perhaps more that 80 percent of the species are found nowhere else. Kew and the Madagascan government have established the Silo National des Graines Forestières. The goal is that by 2020 this will contain 25 percent of the native species concentrating on five groups of plants. Endemic species, trees for restoration projects, culturally important plants, economically important plants, and endangered species from outside protected areas.

Slovakia is a country with three times the number of species found in the UK and 747 of these species are threatened. Furthermore 488 species are endemic to Slovakia and thus found nowhere else. The msbp and the Slovak Seed Bank now have 198 species. Pressures from human encroachment and uncontrollable fires make seed banking very important. For example, *Erica greyi* was rediscovered after a gap of over a century, but this last population has now been wiped out by fire, in South Africa.

How a Seed Bank Works

How do seed banks function? Following are a set of questions that every seed bank director needs to ask when considering setting up and collecting seeds for a seed bank.

continued on page 129

Case in Point: Banks and Brown's *Banksia brownii*

Most of gardening starts with a seed, and so do many biology courses. Just over 250 years ago an undergraduate called Joseph Banks arrived in Oxford with a greater interest in natural history than in the more classical Oxford syllabus of theology, Latin, and ancient Greek. Unfortunately, the story goes, the Oxford botany professor at that time, Humphrey Sibthorp, while giving his first lecture in the Botanic Garden, had an unfortunate accident. Speaking of the differences between the mint family (the Lamiaceae) and the stinging nettle family (the Urticaceae), Professor Sibthorp took his eyes off the undergraduates, turning and facing away from his students—a foolish professorial act at any time. Seeing the specimens from both families laid out on the demonstration bench, a young man in the front row swapped over the specimens. When the professor returned to the bench, rather than grasping the dead nettle he picked up the stinging nettle. This was the end of formal botanical instruction for decades.

Such was Joseph Banks's determination to learn about botany that out of his pocket he paid Cambridge University lecturer Israel Lyons to come over to Oxford to teach. Thus Joseph Banks went on to become one of the greats of botany, pivotal to the foundation of the Royal Botanic Gardens, Kew, president of the Royal Society of London, and a trustee of the British Museum. Despite this, Sir Joseph Banks is probably best known for being the botanist on the *Endeavour* with Captain James Cook. Cook led the joint Royal Navy–Royal Society expedition that explored the southern parts of the Pacific Ocean and especially Australia between 1768 and 1771. Banks developed an interest in all matters Australian and appropriately the Australian genus *Banksia* was named in his honor. He collected botanical specimens far and wide and amassed a library and herbarium that was curated by a line of men who were also to be remembered in the names of many plant species: Daniel Solander, Jonas Carlsson Dryander, and Robert Brown. The latter of these was an extraordinary scientist who deserves to be more widely known.

Robert Brown inherited Banks's library and herbarium, and most appropriately both men are celebrated in the Western Australian species *Banksia brownii* or feathered-leaved banksia. (There is also *Banksia solandri*, and Brown named a genus after Dryander *Dryandra*; and the genus *Brunonia* is named for Brown himself.) *Banksia brownii* is of interest to us because it is critically endangered under the International Union for Conservation of Nature (IUCN) criteria. This means that according to calculations, in the next three generations this species will decline by more that 80 percent. Given that there were fewer than twenty-thousand plants left in fewer than twenty populations in 2005, the species is obviously in need of help.

Banksia brownii is an important component of the threatened Montane Thicket and Heath community of the South West Botanical Province, Australia. The threat is an introduced disease *Phytophthora cinnamomi*, or bush die-back. The problem is made worse by the fact that *Banksia brownii* is an obligate seeder—a plant species that survives fires by regenerating from seed. The adult plants are killed by bush fires, which are a normal part of life in this part of the world, but the seeds in the soil or in cones from the canopy are not cooked and germinate after the fire has passed. The seeds of banksias are held in the cone-like fruits on living and dead plants, though the living plants are more important. Following fire the seeds are released within three months. The shed seeds are very vulnerable to being eaten by animals and the percentage lost in this way can be very high if the seeds lie on the surface of the soil for any time. If they can be buried, then their chances of survival are much higher. The seeds that do survive will germinate, but at this stage they seem to be particularly susceptible to *Phytophthora*.

There is a further threat, which is the mismanagement of the fire regime. If the fires become too frequent, then the new plants do not have enough time to grow to flowering size between incinerations. *Banksia brownii* needs between four and six years to reach flowering size. If the fires are only three years apart, the reserves of seeds of *Banksia* in the soil and in the cones dwindle to nothing. These are obviously parlous times for *Banksia brownii* and the animals that pollinate it. The Australian government has drawn up a five-year recovery plan for this species, identifying every remaining population. The plan has fourteen action points, including trying to control *Phytophthora* and by managing the fire regime.

However, when the threat is so ubiquitous, it seems that a good place to start is to remove some plants far away from that threat—and for that you need seeds. So included in the plan are the collection of seeds and their long-term storage while suitable new sites are found where disease-free plants can be planted. It has been reported that the seeds of *Banksia brownii* can be stored successfully at room temperature for up to seven years without serious loss of viability. However, this is not true for all species of plants. For the majority of plant species drying to as low as 5 percent of the moisture content and then freezing at -20°C (-4°F) is currently the best option for long-term storage. Limited evidence indicates that this might be suitable storage for banksias, but *Banksia brownii* was not one of the species for which there was data.

In April 2007 it was decided that seeds should be sent from Kings Park and Botanic Garden in Perth, Western Australia, to England's Millennium Seed Bank Project (MSBP) in Wakehurst Place, West Sussex. The MSBP is a department of the Royal Botanic Gardens, Kew, which Sir Joseph Banks had founded almost two and a half centuries earlier. (Now, that's long-term planning!) The Millennium Seed Bank is not only a repository for seeds for long-term storage, it has become a world-leading research institute. When one considers the importance of seeds to our survival as well as the survival of plants, our ignorance of their biology is remarkable. In fact, the little that we know about seeds has been described to me by one researcher as "bright stars of facts in a dark sky of ignorance."

The germination techniques and staff skills at the MSBP meant that by September 2007 there were 165 healthy seedlings in the nursery at Wakehurst Place. Healthy here means free from the dreaded *Phytophthora cinnamomi*, but the plants could of course have picked up something else during their stay in the United Kingdom. So when the plants were returned to Perth in September 2007 where they were held in quarantine until May 2008 to ensure that they were free from disease. Then they were planted out in two disease-free sites near Albany, Western Australia. This was the first-ever repatriation of an Australian endangered species. There is a long way to go before we can state that this species is safe, but the experience does show that we are starting to learn how to rescue declining species.

continued from page 125

How do you decide which species to collect and from whom do you have to get permission?

The first decision has to be which species should be targeted. Central to the initial funding of the Millennium Seed Bank was to have all the native species in the UK successfully stored by midnight on 31 December 1999. This was a great idea as it made the initial project very attractive to the initial, major funding body, namely the National Lottery–funded UK Millennium Commission set up to fund big projects to mark the start of a new millennium. If you were being uncharitable you could say that this sort of target is only practical in countries like the UK which are rich in terms of GDP but poor in terms of plant species. The great thing about this target was that it got the ball rolling and the infrastructure in place and the Millennium Seed Bank Project is a world-leading establishment. The MSBP is now concentrating on other groups of plants beyond the borders of the UK, such as plants from the semi-arid tropics. Now they are concentrating on species that are most at risk and those which are potentially or already the most useful. By 2020 the MSBP hopes to have seed from 25 percent of the world's plants species safely in the store. They hit their first goal of 10 percent by 2010; in September 2011 there were 30,885 species in the store and an eye-watering 1,866,543,099 seeds.

Different seed banks concentrate on different groups or geographical regions, normally the geographical region near to the bank. So the Threatened Flora Seed Centre in Western Australia collects species that are highly threatened, that are declining rapidly, and that are only present in a small number of sites or across a narrow range, and particularly it collects species endemic (unique) to Western Australia. They also give priority to species which are on their own branch on the evolutionary tree. These species (like *Ginkgo biloba*) are very useful to our study of the evolution of plants over the past 470 million years and beyond. This might seem like a piece of esoteric research of limited academic interest, but if we can understand how plants have coped in the past during periods of rapid change then we might be able to get through the present period of rapid change more successfully.

How do you find and identify the plants that you seek?
Having decided upon which species your seed bank is going to concentrate, you have to find them. This is where local knowledge comes in for the first time. In almost every aspect of plant conservation in general and seed banking in particular, participation of the indigenous population is essential if the project is to succeed and continue to succeed for any length of time. Having found the plants, then you must obtain permission to collect seeds. If you own the land then there is no problem. but you need to get permission from the land owner if you do not. There may be further restrictions if the species is covered by the Convention on International Trade in Endangered Species (CITES). At the same time as getting permission to collect the seeds you must get permission to export the seeds from the country of origin and permission to import the seeds into your country.

Finding the plants can be easy in some countries like the UK where there is very accurate data going back many centuries. Data is variable for other countries. A huge amount of historical information about plant distribution exists in herbaria around the world, and this is a good place to start to draw up priority lists and distribution maps. Once these are in place then it is essential to go "into the field" to have a look and make accurate up-to-date maps. At this stage you will have to identify the plants, which will be much easier if they are in flower. They will not be in flower when you go to collect the seeds. In most cases this will mean a reconnoiter twelve months before the seed-collecting trip and in the spring of the same year to look for flowering plants. The complexity of planning is compounded by the fact that not all plants flower at the same time and so do not fruit at the same time. The same plant is unlikely to flower on the same day each year. As gardeners we know this because no matter how much time you spend planning the herbaceous border, each year is different and you get surprises, some of which are lovely and make you look like a skillful gardener!

How do you know when the seeds are ready to be collected?
So when planning a collecting trip you have to try to guess when the seeds will be mature and ready for collection. While collection of immature fruits is not ideal, it is not always a disaster. Following research at the MSBP, it is now known how to look after immature fruits and seeds to increase the chance of their germinating when they are brought out of the store. An example familiar to gardeners is the wood anemone, *Anemone nemorosa*, in the buttercup family (the Ranunculaceae). It is well known that you should sow seeds from plants in this family fresh, so hellebores, aconites, clematis, and aquilegia seed should be sown when they come off the plant. This might be connected with the fact that the embryo still has some growing to do after it comes off the plant, and if it dries out in an envelope, rather than being kept at high humidity in the soil, the embryo cannot fully develop and cannot tolerate desiccation prior to being put in the freezer.

continued on page 134

Seed Bank Maintenance: Viability, Germination, and Dormancy

There are a number of ways to check whether seeds in a seed bank are still alive and capable of germination.

Perhaps the simplest way is to sow a small sample, and if they germinate they were viable. You do now have to decide what you are going to do with the seedlings. If it is a common species for which the seed bank is only an insurance against disastrous stochastic events, then you might be happy to pop them on the compost heap. If the seedlings are of an endangered species, then this is an unpalatable option so they might be used in further experiments or distributed to other living collections.

If the seeds do not germinate, then it is possible to test whether the embryo is respiring and therefore alive. This is called the tetrazolium test, and it is very simple. You carefully open up the seed and reveal the embryo. You then cover it with a diluted solution of 2, 3, 5-triphenyltetrazolium chloride (or tetrazolium!). If the embryo is alive the otherwise clear tetrazolium turns red, and the redder it turns the more metabolically active is the embryo. Unfortunately the embryo is now dead, but you only need a small sample for the first test.

If the embryo stains very pale pink or not at all, then you have a problem because the seeds are dead. If, however, the seeds are alive according to the test, but they are not germinating after thirty days, then the seeds might be dormant. The term *dormancy* is often misapplied. If you have a packet of seeds from a good commercial seed company, the seeds do not germinate in the packet because they are not in moist soil at the correct depth and temperature. In this case the seeds are said to be quiescent. If the seeds do not germinate after thirty days in moist soil at the correct depth and temperature, then the seeds are said to be dormant (always assuming that they are not dead). If the seeds are dormant then there is something actively inhibiting the growth of the embryo and thus the germination of the seed.

Dormancy can be imposed on a seed in a number of different ways. Perhaps the simplest is the physical inhibition of germination by a very hard seed coat that prevents the absorption of water. This type of dormancy can be removed by heat cracking the seed coat, slow decay over time, chemical erosion such as travelling through the gut of an animal (quickly hopefully and without being bitten first), or physical erosion by particles of soil. The next category of dormancy involves the use of a chemical inhibitor that has to be removed or inactivated. Chemicals can be leached out by water, they might be altered and inactivated by cold temperatures, they might just break down with time, or in some species they are inactivated by a chemical in smoke. This is the system found in many plants from areas where fire is a regular component of the ecology and where the parent plant is killed by the fire.

The final category of dormancy involves the morphological barrier, normally a small, immature embryo. This is the case in many orchid species where not only is the embryo tiny, but also there is no food in the seed and for the embryo to develop it must be infected by a fungus. I realize it may sound very strange that a seed must be infected by a fungus in order to survive, but frankly orchids are odd in almost every way. These three broad categories of dormancy are not mutually exclusive and so the germination of some seeds will be inhibited by more than one category, making breaking the dormancy even more interesting.

continued from page 131

How do you handle the seeds before you get home?
So you have found the plants and you are ready to plan the trip. You need collecting equipment. This is quite simple. Paper envelopes and bags and cloth bags are used for the first stages because there is a risk that the seeds will rot off in plastic bags or sealed pots. You must have labels to attach to your envelopes or to put in the bag with the seeds or fruits. If you are going to be in a region for a long period of time, then you might place sheets under plants to catch falling seeds, or you could place stockings over the maturing fruit. To collect seeds that are beyond reach from the ground, a tree climber might be required. Ben Jones, curator at the Harcourt Arboretum in Oxfordshire was collecting seeds in South America on one occasion by shaking a tree so that the cones fell on a sheet spread out below the canopy. Things were going well until a local cow walked through the vegetation and mistook the cones for her breakfast.

What information do you collect with the plants?
You will need to decide what information you want to record about each plant, and you will need a form with boxes to ensure that you collect the same information about every plant. This may have to be in a paper form if you are working in remote areas where there is not the facility to charge up electrical equipment every night. You cannot have too much data, but it is essential that all the data is closely and permanently connected to the seeds. This is normally achieved with a unique collection number being given to every packet of seeds. The type of information that you need to record includes where you are, perhaps GPS coordinates, the type of habitat, other plants, the soil type, the altitude and aspect of the land, evidence of human activity, and how common the plants are. The collection and handling of data in seed banking is critically important and is a hidden but expensive part the process. Photographs of where the plant was found are useful but there is no substitute for a herbarium specimen. This provides a permanent

record and enables researchers in the future to check your identification skills.

Next is the difficult question.

How many seeds do you collect?
Never more than 5 percent of all the seed is an overriding principle for some organizations while others will take up to 20 percent. For big conservation projects twenty thousand seeds is seen as a minimum. Some collection protocols recommend sampling from a minimum of fifty individual plants and ten to twenty seeds from each so long as this is not more than 10 percent of the seeds. Whatever the upper limit, collection should be random. This is not as easy as it sounds because one's natural propensity is to collect from the largest plants, but you want seeds from the full range of the populations because this year's big plants may not do so well next year.

What do you do before the seeds are prepared for storage, assuming that they can be stored?
Seed collection can be seriously compromised if the seeds are not cared for properly from the moment that they go in the bag. When you are on a collecting trip, the work carries on long into the evening because every bag has to be opened and checked for signs of rotting and to check that you have not inadvertently collected a bug who is merrily munching his way through what are now your seeds and not his. You also want to start the process of cleaning the seeds away from the debris of the plant and the remains of the fruit. This should not be rushed, but if you have been able to collect at the right time and the seeds and fruits are both dry, then the seeds should fall out of the capsules easily.

Having got them home safely, how should you handle the seeds?
At this point you can find that the envelopes have small holes in them at the bottom that are bigger than the seeds; this is very irritating! The

more debris that you can clean off before sending the plants home, the lower will be the shipping costs. If you are collecting herbarium specimens, these too have to be checked every evening and the papers changed. The quicker that the seeds can be sent to the seed bank, the better, and in many countries there are now seed banks set up with help from the Millennium Seed Bank Project.

Are there quarantine procedures?
One of the beauties of seeds is that very few pests and diseases are transported with them. The majority of contaminants that do travel are on the surface and so can be washed off with a mild sterilant. If any pests or diseases remain, then they will hopefully be killed off by the freezing that awaits most of the seeds in the seed bank. However, any plants raised from newly collected seeds must be grown in isolation for long enough to be sure that contaminants did not get through.

How are the seeds dried and chilled?
When the seeds and herbarium specimens arrive at the seed bank, they must be inspected for any signs of disease and pests. The latter are easily killed by a few days in a freezer at -20°c (-4°f). The data has to be checked and put on the database along with any photographs. The seeds can now been cleaned further if it is required. Seed cleaning does not have to involve highly technical equipment. Sieves of different sizes are commonly used. A more sophisticated piece of kit is a zigzag aspirator which blows the debris away from the seeds and blows the seeds away from bigger pieces of the fruit.

What to do before the seeds are prepared for storage, assuming that they can be stored?
The clean seeds are then checked for signs of life. X-rays might be taken if you have an X-ray machine. You could try the tetrazolium test described elsewhere in this chapter. In the absence of both of these, you

could cut open the seed to check for an embryo and food supply, which you should only do for a small proportion of the seeds. The seeds are then counted, normally using a combination of physical counting and then extrapolating the quantity by weighing the seeds.

Drying the seeds prior to freezing is simple. The packets are placed in a drying room where the air is at 15 percent relative humidity at 15°C (59°F) or thereabouts. After about a month the seeds will also be at 15 percent moisture content. The seeds are now placed in airtight storage jars or packets at -20°C (-4°F) and that is the end of the first part of the process.

How do you know that you can germinate the seeds?
This is the point at which the gardeners at the seed bank come into their own. Experience and good record keeping often reveals that seeds from the same species, genus, and even family will share germination requirements.

How do you check that the seeds are still alive, and what do you do if they are not?
The seeds in the store must be checked after a month to be sure that they have not been killed by the drying and freezing. At this stage a great deal has been learned about the dormancy and germination requirements of different species. If the percentage of germination is good enough, then the frequency of testing can be reduced. The seeds are now ready to be used when required.

Seeds would not have evolved if they had not given their plants an advantage over the other plants around at that time. Furthermore it is hard to see how this evolutionary innovation could have become used by so many plants if animals have started eating the seeds straight away.

continued on page 142

Artifical Seed Banks: Pros and Cons

Several benefits can be derived from using artificial seed banks as part of a species recovery program. Conversely seed banks also have their critics.

The conservation benefits

Let us consider ten categories of advantages to be derived from using seed banks over other strategies.

First, when compared to growing plants, the seeds are completely removed from the threats they face in their habitat—whether a disease, another plant, mismanagement of fire, or simply the destruction of the habitat. This was the case with *Banksia solandri*. So far just under a thousand seeds have been collected, which itself gives an indication of the extreme threat that this species faces. These have been split between the bank in Australia and the Millennium Seed Bank in the United Kingdom—you should not put all your seeds in one bank. The seeds are not only protected from the threats that we have identified, they are also safe from threats that we have not spotted yet. This was the rationale behind collecting and storing the entire UK flora even though many of the plants do not appear to be in any danger at the moment.

Second, seeds take up much less space than living plants, and space can often be very expensive or needed for something else. Related to their compactness, seed banks can be portable and can be rehoused or merged.

Third, seeds of many species can be stored safely in seed banks for decades if not centuries.

Fourth, the daily maintenance of a seed bank is relatively simple. Checking the temperature of the freezer is not an onerous task, but it is also vitally important for the seeds in the store to be checked regularly to ensure that they are still alive and are capable of germination. This can be more complex.

Dormancy may have to be broken before the seeds will germinate, which leads to the fifth advantage: our understanding of dormancy and how to break it has been greatly enhanced by the research carried out at seed banks around the world.

However, if the seeds are dead, then the bank will have to be restocked from wild plants, and this might be difficult if the species is very rare already. An alternative is to collect seeds from plants raised from seeds from the seed bank, which brings us to the knotty issue of genetic diversity. As mentioned earlier, Charles Darwin (and many other natural historians) realized that no plants go on self-fertilizing for ever: "Nature abhors repeated inbreeding." This is because the genetic diversity of the population falls, leading to inbreeding depression—that is, inbreeding over a long period of time, which is also referred to colloquially as a reduction in the gene pool. If you collect seeds from a small number of plants, raised from seeds in the seed bank, then you run the risk of those seeds containing embryos whose collective genetic diversity is sub-optimal. If the plant is critically endangered like *Banksia solandri*, then you are probably going to be grateful for any viable seeds, but different batches or seeds with different provenances (or origins) must be kept apart.

With the correct collection methods, in a seed bank you can conserve much more genetic diversity of a species in a much smaller area or volume than if you are growing mature plants, especially if those plants are trees, which is the sixth advantage. At the Threatened Flora Seed Centre (TFSC) in Western Australia, they aim at collecting at least 75 to 80 percent of the genetic diversity of the species, from as many locations as possible, across the full range of the species. Collection methods, which we will consider separately, are important.

The seventh advantage is also related to genetic diversity: when compared to removing live plants, the removal of seeds, if done properly, will have no impact on the survival of the wild populations. It has been shown that the removal of 5 percent of the seeds from a population of plants will not reduce the chance of that population surviving.

The eighth benefit to be derived from the development of seed banks, namely collaboration and support, is exemplified in the joint programme to save *Banksia brownii* involving the Millennium Seed Bank Project in the United Kingdom and the TFSC in Australia. Not only are duplicate collections established, but this is often a way for developed countries to assist less economically developed countries.

The ninth reason for using seed banks is a practical one: the seeds of many different species are available at the same place at any time of the year. This is particularly important where a number of different species are being used in a habitat restoration programme. This new and expanding use for seed banks may require very large weights of seeds—tons rather than ounces and grams.

Finally, the tenth reason: seed banks are a good addition to the various means of plant conservation because they are attractive to funding bodies including individuals who want to give money to projects on a human scale (one species at a time) and to projects that they perceive as being safe. The word "bank" suggests that element of safety, and although this perception may have altered in recent years, we all still have our money in The Bank. Seed banks can be used very successfully as a focus for education programmes and for raising awareness of the plight of many plant species and their habitats.

A critique

You may by now be so convinced of the wonderfulness of seed banks that you may be wondering why anyone would need to embark on any other form of plant conservation. Well, it has to be said that seed banks have their detractors and their limitations.

First, not all species react well to being dried and frozen. A good example of this is oak trees. Acorns do not survive in orthodox seed banks, and for this reason they are refereed to as recalcitrant seeds. The word "recalcitrant" does sound like a scolding from a primary school teacher, but up to 30 percent of plant species produce recalcitrant seeds, and for these other strategies have to be found. Some of them can be stored for a number of years just above freezing. This temperature slows metabolisms thus preserving the food supply. For others it might be possible to use cryogenic storage where the seed or just the embryo is stored at -196°c (-320.8°F). This type of storage has also been used by Margaret Ramsay at Kew to conserve mosses very successfully. Since mosses do not produce seeds, obviously seed banks are totally inappropriate for them.

Another criticism of seed banks is that other parts of the ecosystem that the plant requires are not conserved. This is undeniably true for some species. For example, the fungus required for the germination and growth of an orchid seed is not necessarily included in the seed bank, nor are the pollinators which are often specific to one species of orchid. However, it must be remembered that these are the exceptions. Most plants do not have a specific pollinator and even those who use only one pollinator *in situ* will often use another *ex situ*, as we know from watching pollinators in our gardens. Likewise most plants do not require a specific animal to disperse their seeds, and most do not use animals at all. Most plants have an association with a fungus around their roots, but these are very generalist relationships and there is little specialization here with several fungi providing mycorrhizal services to most plants.

Others claim that by putting seeds in a freezer, you are also freezing evolution and that by removing the plants from evolutionary pressure, you are reducing to zero their ability to evolve and adapt to a changing climate. This has not been proved, but an experiment has been started that over the next fifty years or more will measure and compare the genetic diversity of seed collections in the freezer with the diversity found in the population from which the seeds were harvested. Whether fifty years is long enough for evolutionary changes to be selected remains to be seen, but it is a nice simple way of answering the critics of seed banks with a simple scientific experiment. My guess is that you will actually have more genetic diversity in the seed store because it will be safe from random events causing a genetic bottleneck.

Another criticism of seed banks is that they give out an ambiguous educational message. The argument goes that if you tell people that seeds from every species of plant in the United Kingdom is safe in the Millennium Seed Bank, then they will see no reason to preserve intact habitats. In reality this does not happen because there are many powerful reasons for preserving complete communities *in situ*. These are mostly related to the ecosystem services that intact habitats provide. No one ever said that seed banks are an end in themselves. They are the start of many conservation programmes and the insurance policy in case of failure.

continued from page 137
And yet as happens the seeds have been exploited by animals, much to the annoyance and inconvenience of the plants. As ever the long-suffering plants have found a wide variety of work-around solutions to survive the greedy animals. It is not only ants and birds and others who depend upon seeds for their lunch; without seeds there would be no *Homo sapiens*. It is worth mentioning here that now, at the beginning of the twenty-first century, the resilience of seeds is giving seed plants an advantage that they could never have foreseen—namely the tolerance of being dried and frozen and being preserved in a deep freezer.

In the year following the Royal Botanic Gardens, Kew, meeting on conservation genetics in 1976, the author of a book on animal behaviour suggested that we are all just vessels for our genes, which selfishly exploit the bodies they are in. Richard Dawkins, in *The Selfish Gene*, explained nicely why the concept of nonhuman animals behaving for the good of the species was nonsense. He suggested that altruism could be explained by kinship—and that plants do not behave in such a way as animals because, for one thing, they are rooted to a spot. However, their genes are very important, and *Homo sapiens* has selfishly and very (perhaps *too*) successfully exploited the genes of one particular group of plants—plants grown as crops. More than 25 percent of the world's surface is now under some form of cropland production. These regions of the world and the plants growing thereon are understandably essential to our survival. And what we need are plant conservation programmes not only to protect the genes of crop plants for future breeding (and future food supply), but we also must protect croplands and the biological resources extracted from those production lands as well.

In 2010, I heard Peter Raven, the former director of the Missouri Botanical Garden, speak in Dublin at the Fourth Global Botanic Gardens Congress, which had been organized by Botanic Gardens Conservation International (BGCI). He recalled that at a meeting in 1975 at Kew, the decision was made that genetic conservation was vital—and that it was not just enough to preserve *one* example of everything; it was also necessary, in addition to the establishment of seed banks, to establish large conservation lands and plantations.

Thirty-five years after that meeting, 10 percent of all plant species are in the Millennium Seed Bank. The MSBP had become the linchpin of plant conservation. Peter Raven turned on those people who moaned about seed banks being just a collection of seed packets. He pointed out that we are in a much stronger position now than we were then all those years ago. Why? Because, quite simply, without a seed bank's collections, you have no bank of seeds to *start* your conservation!

2020 STRATEGY

TARGET 9 Conserve 70 percent of the genetic diversity of crop plants, their wild relatives, and economically valuable plants while preserving indigenous and local knowledge and practice

PART THREE

And Justice for All: Diversity Without Adversity

In much of conservation a compromise is required between the needs of today's population and the needs of future generations. It has been known for a long time that many plants are happier outside their current range—a happiness that can be manifested as rampant growth and reproduction that smothers all around them, and that can eliminate other plant species, lower the water table, change the fire regime, and cause the loss of animal species.

The threat posed by invasive species can be controlled, with the cooperation of lay and professional gardeners and the implementation of well-designed management programmes. We also need to preserve the fertility of our production lands. We will need to feed nine billion people by 2050—but the planet can only realistically support 1.5 billion people and a massive population reduction is not going to happen quickly. Individuals and institutions need to find ways to promote living within Earth's biological means.

4 Moving Away from Home: Mobile Plants, Natural or Unnatural?

There are several different ways of classifying the threats to plants. Scientist and author Jared Diamond has suggested the evil quartet of habitat destruction, overkill, introduced species, and secondary extinctions; biologist and author E. O. Wilson is credited with HIPPO: Habitat destruction, Invasive species, Pollution, (human) Population growth, and Overexploitation. But the International Union for Conservation of Nature (IUCN), as ever, has produced the gold-standard classification for threats: a list with nine headings, each of which is subdivided into three, four, or five areas. The heading for invasive and other problematic species and genes is subdivided into invasive non-native species, problematic native species, and introduced genetic material.

It is often stated that the study of biological invasions began properly in 1958 with the publication of what became a classic work, *The Ecology of Invasions by Animals and Plants*. Its author, the famed ecologist-biologist Charles Elton, wrote it no less than a hundred yards from where I am now sitting. At the time of his writing, the Bureau of Animal Population of the Department of Zoological Field Studies of the university was housed in the Oxford Botanic Garden. (And although the bureau moved out decades ago, we still occasionally receive their mail!) While there can be no doubt that Elton's work brought the study of non-native species into the biology syllabus, others before him had already noticed the effects of plants taken beyond their natural boundaries. Among these were Linnaeus and Alexander Humboldt—yet, once again, Charles Darwin gets the credit. In *Origin of Species*, Darwin frequently commented on plants that had been taken out of their natural ranges. In one of his most profound and important passages, he wrote:

> No country can be named in which all the native inhabitants are now so perfectly adapted to each other and to the physical conditions under

which they live, that none of them could anyhow be improved; for in all countries, the natives have been so far conquered by naturalized productions, that they have allowed foreigners to take firm possession of the land. And as foreigners have modified with advantage, so as to have better resisted such intruders.

Darwin realized that evolution neither produces the fittest organisms nor perfection, but evolution does make allowances for every species to be *better*. There has to be, however, some advantage to making such changes, meaning that, if there is no pressure, or advantage for the improvement, then it may not happen.

So what does happen when a plant or animal arrives in new territory and the need to survive there does not present challenges? Everything is easy, no pressure. To begin with, to use Darwin's word, these "foreigners" already have survival abilities ahead of the natives. They did get there; and they did get established. To the natives, catching up with this adept, high-performance newbie in town would be like trying to compete with an Olympic 100-metre champion turning up at their primary school sports event. The local kids ("native" population) would do nothing but just stand stock-still and gawk, getting overrun quite quickly.

Does this meant that Darwin's theory of how species evolve—the advantage of favoured, adaptable individuals being selected for—gets disproved? In other words, putting aside the humiliated "natives," does the fact that some plants from Country A perform better in Country B, better than its own native, local species, disprove his theory? Not at all. Rather, we all know that different parts of the world contain different plants; what is not obvious to us is that each of these plant species has different strengths and weaknesses. And what is important here is that these strengths and weaknesses are related to the past and not to the future.

Evolution has no foresight and can only improve on what worked yesterday and sometimes the best plant for Country B *did* evolve in Country A! Darwin *never* described evolutions as being about the survival of the fittest. Evolution, and biology in general, are all about survival of the slightly less mediocre. Plants and animals only have to be better than their neighbors. As he says later:

> As natural selection acts by competition, it adapts the inhabitants of each country only in relation to the degree of perfection of their associates; so that we need feel no surprise at the inhabitants of any one country . . . being beaten and supplanted by the naturalised productions from another land.

At this point it would be good if we could agree on a definition for what a native species is. As this is my book, I am going to present my definition. Other people will likely disagree with me. Their primary claim may be that not all non-native plants are the same. What they mean by this is that some non-native species will have been present for so long, and have become integrated so harmlessly into native plant communities, that they will have attained the status of honorary native. But *harmless*, as you will learn, will be the operative word here as we try to come to some agreeable ground for reducing the risks that "other plants" (non-natives) pose for natives and, in the larger picture, extinctions and plant biodiversity. Perhaps George Orwell would have said that all plants are native, but some plants are more native than others.

My approach to establishing parameters for defining "native" is to, perhaps in the process, cultivate some agreement and to draw a distinction between native and non-native. The definition goes by way of making a distinction in a plant's mobility: the movement of a plant for "natural" reasons as already described (nonhuman-induced mobility, such as migrations that occur with migrating animals or climate change conditions) distinguished from the movement of a plant for "unnatural" reasons (human-induced movement, such as for commercial exploitation of beauty or to create botanical gardens). Since, in Europe, the year 1500 has caught on with ecologists and is already widely used for the purpose, I will consider it as suitable as any other

> **Native** A plant species that arrived in its present country without the aid of humans, or was brought into that location as a result of human activity before 1500. These plants are known as archaeophytes or, more commonly, as natives.
>
> **Non-native** Plants that were transported beyond their "natural" home range after 1500 are known as neophytes; and it is from the ranks of these species that we find the villains of worldwide ecological peace of mind—the invasive, non-native species.

arbitrary date and as good a definition as consensus. And since 1500 is so conveniently close to America's historic date of 1492, I will include North America as well.

So it is becoming clearer now that it seems illogical and wrong to condemn non-native species simply because they cause change. Plant migration in itself is not a threat to biodiversity. Nature is made up of a fascinating matrix of interactions that scientists are still trying to unravel. Biology has been changing for ever. Sometimes the change happens very slowly and over very long periods of time; sometimes it happens quickly and is noticeable in our own backyards. But geographical origin—nativeness—is not the be all and end all to the dilemma for plant conservation and risks to extinction.

For example, a plant moved to the United Kingdom is unlikely to become a problem if it cannot survive below freezing point. The same would be true for many parts of the United States but not all, because a plant that is never going to be a problem in New England could well be a problem in Florida. So in this particular case, the detrimental nature of the plant is not circumscribed by the country of origin but by the growing conditions of a different region in that country; it is invasive there but doesn't fit the parameter of "foreign" and detrimental to the place.

continued on page 154

A Very Short (Very Early) Evolutionary Plant History of Conquerors and Invaders

About 470 million years ago a plant "discovered" that it was able to survive for at least part of the year out of water, and thus began what has been called "The Invasion of the Land." This description makes a pivotal episode in the history of our planet sound like a Hollywood B-movie. It should more accurately be known as the invasion of the air and dry land. Life in the water is easy compared with trying to survive in the air or on dry land. Water is very helpful to life. When you get out of water, desiccation is a serious problem; and once you are on land, support provided previously by the buoyancy of water is an even a bigger issue. But once Earth's first plants acquired the ability to survive out of the water for the whole of their life cycle, biodiversity and competition for survival started.

This "invasion" all those million of years ago—plants moving from water to proliferate on land—was not the result of human activity, nor were there threats from other species. Darwin wrote that "the struggle [for survival] almost invariably will be most severe between the individuals of the same species." And once on land, a plant species would have found no soil (as we know it), only bare rock. The new dry-land habitats would have had more variations, or challenges to survival, than there had been in the sea or fresh water. There might have been lichenized fungi already on the rocks, which, it is not impossible to imagine, were helpful to the new kids, providing a bit of dead organic matter for the early land plants, with precious few roots, to grab onto; or, there was a bit more heterogeneity in the habitat, such as a rough surface, which might have been beneficial for a spore to lodge into and then germinate when water came available. This "invader" would then have spread out across the land, migrated, adapted, and diversified. So the stage was set and the players amassed in a mutual competition and struggle for survival.

But then things changed: the continents on which the plants were growing moved (for neither the first nor the last time). For example, 362 million years ago Gondwana and Laurasia started to collide, and by 248 million years ago there was land from pole to pole. And when these continental movements separated, plant communities were moved along with their newly conquered habitats. These "new" environments, each split-up community, would lead to a species' reproductive isolation, and then slowly to new adaptations. The islands of Madagascar and New Zealand, with their unique floras (and faunas), are exemplary of how, after millions of years of separation from their one-time cohorts on the same land, their island floras diversified into what can be seen today. These island floras are very different from Africa and Australia respectively and, of course, very different from each other. As Darwin wrote, "Barriers of any kind . . . are related in a close and important manner to the differences between the productions of various regions." Darwin was among the first natural historians to realize the value of studying the biology of islands: "Cases could be given of introduced plants which have become common throughout whole islands in a period of less than ten years. In St. Helena there is reason to believe that the naturalised plants and animals have nearly or quite exterminated many native productions." However, the continental alterations were not all about separation. Drifting continents can drift together as well as drift apart. When land masses meet, or meet up again (as is the history of continental drift), the species, which have had different evolutionary histories, come together (maybe even again). Imagine the meetings of India with present Tibet, perhaps 34 million years ago, or more recently North America and South America during the Pliocene geological period 2.5 to 5.3 million years ago, when separations formed the Isthmus of Panama. Plants and animals with quite different characters and traits on each of the continental habitats found themselves trying to survive, competing for the same space.

Yet when two land masses merge, not all the plants and animals meet their doom. They may have found that there were new opportunities.

How plants cope with new conditions and competitors is complex; no one knows for certain because plants have hidden talents. Ecologists referred to this hidden talent as pre-adaptation. This is an adaptation that the plant acquired in the past but which was not evolutionarily lost, such as when a plant survives a frost in a new habitat but it has never seen a frost before in its originating, native land.

So, for such an immobile, rooted organism, plants are readily moved and the history of their mobility is deep, their having arrived on dry land 470 million years ago and since then migrating around the world. Sometimes the migration was slow, as when the plants were passengers on drifting land masses; or surprisingly fast, as when they hitched onto a journey across oceans atop migrating animals or rafts of driftwood. Such migrations have historically led to the colonization of the vast majority of Earth's land. Plants that arrived, and then survived, in a region or country found their way there by biogeographical processes—and they are, despite their invasions, considered the native species.

Yet there is still another paradox of plant mobility beyond the distinctions native/non-native and invader/naturalized species: migrations both promote species diversity (which is Good) and reduce species diversity (which is Bad).

Now it is believed that as many as four out of every five plant species make no attempt to distribute their seeds more than a few inches. It is not unreasonable for a plant to drop its seeds at its feet, or rather at its roots, where they are randomly distributed around the parent plant, because if the parent plants grows well there, then so should the offspring. But there may appear to be a bias to one side or another; and thus the direction of the seed dispersal, and consequent plant mobility, can be driven by changes in climate: the seeds may be dispersed, but only those that find themselves spread toward the correct, favourable climatic conditions (sometimes referred to as the climate envelope for a species) will survive. That is, if the temperature of the locale is falling year after year, the seeds that fall on the equatorial side of the parent plant, or further down the mountain if they are alpine plants, will germinate, and only those individuals will survive for another generation.

And this process of seed dispersal is exactly what is thought to have influenced plant mobility during the cyclical ice ages during the past three million years. Plants appear to have been pushed so far south ahead of the advancing glaciers as to be found on promontories and islands of the Mediterranean region; some are even believed to have found their way to the Macaronesian Islands in the Atlantic. This led to two processes that have resulted in great species diversity and richness in those parts of the world: hybridizations, forming new species from two that previously would not have met but are now sharing the same promontory; and varieties, same species that were isolated from each other, on separate islands, were unable to interbreed and thereby repeatedly recombine their unique gene pool; and their separate populations experienced slightly different selective pressures in their respective locales, which took them down different evolutionary pathways. The result would be the emergence of new varieties and, later, new species entirely. So seeds and spores do travel, and arrive—proving that Darwin, once again, was correct in writing that "During the vast geographical and climatical changes which will have supervened since ancient times, almost any amount of migration is possible."

continued from page 149
Native or non-native, we can see that there is another, perhaps less "natural" mechanism influencing the dispersal of plants—and that is us, *Homo sapiens*.

Leaving Home for "Unnatural" Reasons

Depending on your stance on the naturalness or unnaturalness of the species *Homo sapiens*, or her or his influence on all things Earth, arguing this is neither natural nor unnatural is better left to be sorted out elsewhere—rather with a philosopher than a horticulturalist. So, moving on, the next thing that comes to mind is the big question: why does *H. sapiens* move plants anyway?

There are many reasons why people have, and still do, take plants beyond their natural range. Plants are, for one, intentionally imported—for gardeners to grow in their back-, side-, and front-yard gardens or in their institutional demonstration botanic gardens (think of the New York Botanical Garden, England's Oxford Botanic Garden, Oregon's Lan Su Chinese Garden, and such). The garden is the major conduit for introduced invasive species into a locale or country. Meanwhile, given all these human pleasure domes for distraction and entertainment, only a minority, as quantified in the Tens Rule, of the introduced plants into the garden become invasive and damaging to a habitat there and beyond.

There are, among the many reasons for why people move plants around the world, other circumstances beyond the garden. As with introductions into gardens, these can be intentional, decisions with both beneficial and unintentional unbeneficial outcomes, as well as unintentional, inadvertent outcomes from lack or knowledge about or awareness of the malevolence of a particular species.

The Tens Rule

What is the likelihood that a plant will not only escape from the garden where it was first grown but also go on to do significant damage in its new, adopted home? There is a simple rule of thumb (that does not work all the time but is nonetheless helpful). It goes like this:

- If you took seeds from 1,000 species of plants not naturally growing in the UK or USA and sowed them in your garden, then plants of 100 of the species would set seed and that seed would germinate and, if not weeded out by a diligent gardener, would result in flowering plants that set viable seeds.
- Of the 100 species that did set seed that germinated and resulted in flowering plants that set viable seeds, 10 species would disperse themselves, not only around the garden but out of the garden gate and into the countryside.
- Of those 10 species one of them would not become a benign part of the plant community but would go on to change the countryside and not in a good way.

So, very roughly, the likelihood of a non-native plant species becoming a problem is 1 in 1,000, or 0.1 percent. If you think that these are low odds and not a problem, then remember that, by example, there are more than 70,000 plants listed in UK nursery catalogues and that equated to 70 invasive plants. Just think, if the lottery gave odds of 1,000 to 1, how many more people would buy a ticket! You must also remember that the damage done by invasive non-native species is out of all proportion to the number of species involved because the damage is lasting if not permanent.

Non-Native's Adopted Home: Predator or Not

American visitors to the Oxford Botanic Garden are always surprised to see us growing purple loosestrife (*Lythrum salicaria*) in one of our exhibits, the Bog Garden. Well, the simple answer to polite questions about our sanity is that this is a British native species as well as being a great garden plant and it is not the problem in the United Kingdom that it became when it was taken to the United States and to New Zealand.

So why does it not pose a problem in the United Kingdom? We simply do not know. Darwin stated that predicting which species will survive in a new country is a very tricky business because "The degree of adaptation of species to the natural conditions under which they live is often overrated. We may infer this from our frequent inability to predict whether or not an imported plant will endure our climate" and that "we know not exactly what the checks are in even one single instance." While it's still tricky business, today one of the most commonly stated reasons is that in its adopted home, the invader experiences **predator release**.

Predator release is the simple idea that a plant in its native range will probably have a lot to put up with: animals will try to eat it and fungi will try to infect it; other plants will compete with it for local resources. Take that plant away from all the predators—the herbivores, the fungi, and other plants that have jostled with it for generations—and move it to a new home, the plant will probably be very grateful.

Once in its adopted home, if there are no pathogens to infect it and no herbivores to consume it, then it is instantly at a selective advantage over its new neighbours. Of course that is a big **if**, and in many cases there will be an herbivore or a disease to which the newcomer has no defence, and this will stop the invasion before it, the outsider, can do any damage. This is one of the reasons why the Tens Rule works as it does.

Moving beyond the pleasure principle of gardens and city botanicals, some non-natives have been put to well-meaning use to stabilize soils. Like gardening, this is not an evil thing to attempt. Soil is the most precious part of our gardens and the most precious part of any ecological system. The bottom line in all conservation activity is to protect the soil because once that has gone you are back 470 million years before the plants got out of the water. One of the most pernicious of this group that has been used to this purpose is the ice plant (*Carpobrotus edulis*) from South Africa. The problem is very serious in the European Mediterranean region, in California, in Australia, and more recently in Cornwall, England, where ice plant can be seen quite literally escaping over garden walls and spreading along the coast. It produces large areas of nothing but itself; and if you ever need convincing of the ability of an invasive species to reduce biological diversity, go and have a look at an outbreak of this one.

A similarly dreadful sight is produced by the kudzu vine. This is thought to have been introduced into America from Japan in 1876 at the Centennial Exposition in Philadelphia. Since then it has swamped large areas of vegetation in the southeastern USA. This species has been used elsewhere for erosion control, and even as fodder for goats being grazed on sub-optimal agricultural land. This is a very unholy alliance, as many people see goats as one of the biggest threats to biological diversity. If you need proof of the destructive powers of goats, even kudzu will give up after a few years of the kids' intensive grazing. And finally perhaps the most bizarre reason for the often-reported introduction of kudzu into the islands of Fiji and Vanuatu by the US military during World War Two: as camouflage for equipment. The war ended but the invasion by kudzu did not.

Moving further afield, some introductions are unintentional and inadvertent and unavoidable—that is, until the awareness of the damage alerts us to the cost of these invasions, ecologically and economically. The problem is that we may have a hard time doing something about it.

In 1984, the green alga *Caulerpa taxifolia*, native to the Indian Ocean, was accidentally dumped into the Mediterranean when someone was cleaning out an aquarium tank and let a piece go down the plug hole and from the drain into the sea. Unfortunately it was hardier than assumed; someone had not read *Origin of Species*. Eradication from the Mediterranean Sea is a nonstarter. Fortunately, luck has played a role in this instance: a small population of *Caulerpa* was spotted by vigilant divers in California in 2000 and it was dealt with thoroughly and apparently successfully using bleach and a piece of tarpaulin.

Farmers and foresters have also played their part; and given the girth of Earth under cultivation by them, the area is far greater than that of our gardens. Among the problems arising from forestry are *Eucalyptus globulus*. A native of Australia, this plant grows vigorously in Spain, Portugal, and California. It spreads beyond the plantations and into woodlands, outcompeting the local species. However, by the sort of contradiction that is so common in biology, a native species suffering in Portugal is *Pinus pinaster* (maritime or cluster pine), which is itself in the list of the top one hundred most damaging invasive species as a result of the huge areas of it in South Africa. There is a further twist in this biological retribution because the Californian Monterey pine (*Pinus radiata*) has become a serious pest in Australia where it is grown as a timber tree. While farming and silviculture cover an immense area, there are fewer different species that can potentially escape. It is the huge number of species being grown in our gardens that make these gardens the number one habitat threatening biodiversity. This is an uncomfortable fact, but it does not have to be so.

What's the Damage? The Cost of Leaving Home

The first and most obvious damage is the reduction in biological diversity as a result of swamping and outcompeting native plants for light. This can not only kill the original vegetation but also prevent the growth of any seedings. The knock-on effect of the reduction in biological diversity can be an increase in the instability of the plant community and thus an increase in the possibility of a complete breakdown of the ecosystem services provided by the vegetation. Furthermore, an alteration in the plants in a community will have an effect on the species of animals in the area. The plant invasion might not result in a monospecific stand of the non-native, but the balance of the natives might be changed and some of the less common species will be swamped and killed. Conversely some minor members of the community might become more common at the expense of other native species. Examples of the cost of invasions include changing soil conditions for all the existing plants, alterations in a beneficial fire regime, changes in the water table in a region, and increases in the need for public spending from these ecological events.

When *Myrica faya* (faya-tree or fire-tree) was brought from Tenerife to Hawaii, it felt so much at home that it spread, pushing out *Metrosideros polymorpha* among others. In addition to elbowing out some native vegetation, *Myrica faya* fixes nitrogen, releasing much of this into the soil and thereby altering the ecosystem further. In addition the fruits of *Myrica* are eaten by and therefore support the non-native birds that have colonized Hawaii. Biology is all about interactions, and the effects of non-native invasive species are no exception.

It is sometimes difficult for gardeners to see fire as anything but bad (or a way to dispose of diseased material) and yet in many parts of the world, fire regimes are a regular part of the ecology. Fire can vary from place to place; its intensity depends on how much flammable material has built up since the last fire but also on the calorific value of the plant material being burned. The more material there is, then the slower the fire moves across the land, giving it more time to burn right up into the canopy of the trees which otherwise would be heated but not incinerated. The plants have evolved to survive the normal fire but can suffer badly if they get caught up in the wrong sort of fire. This is the situation in South Africa where the Port Jackson willow (*Acacia saligna*) from Western Australia forms thickets that burn too hot for the natives.

If the disruption of the fire regime was not enough, the Port Jackson willow also has a severe impact on the water table. Its roots can grow deeper than the native vegetation and it can "steal" water from greater depths. This not only reduces the amount of water available to the other plants and the animals, it also seriously reduces the volume of fresh water available to the human population. In South Africa it has been discovered that it is cheaper to control the acacia than it is to build water treatment or water storage facilities, but still money has to be found to invest in control measures. And the economic cost of non-natives is increasingly coming to the fore in politics as public spending is cut. In 2011, the parliament in Scotland awarded £15 million to the Forestry Commission to rid 66,000 hectares of *Rhododendron ponticum*. In England the control of Japanese knotweed (*Fallopia japonica*) costs £189 million each year. The removal of this plant from the 2012 Olympic Park site cost £70 million. The recent introduction of the herbivore *Aphalara itadori* might help to reduce the cost.

2020 STRATEGY

TARGET 10 Prevent biological invasions and manage important areas of plant diversity that are invaded

---

So, then, how do we approach conservation, justice for all—achieve diversity without adversity—when to begin with, it has been so difficult to just untangle the native/non-native–natural/unnatural matrix? What may be the best possible approach amid what seems so impossibly vast? Change directions entirely; reconsider, perhaps a new,

The Seven Stages of an Invasion

No two invasions are the same because no two invaders are the same. Some introduced non-native species, the stereotyped invader, may never make it to becoming true invaders. And by breaking this stereotype and making specific distinctions, we are better equipped to spot potential invaders (with similar characteristics) and to identify the characteristics and vulnerabilities in those habitats where the invasions take hold.

1. The species will have to be introduced into the new country or region by people.
2. Once it has been introduced, the plant has to be able to tolerate the conditions: soil must be the right pH, water availability must be adequate, if there is fire it must be tolerated, minimum and maximum temperatures must be known.
3. Once the plant is established, the plant will reproduce, which may involve a very specific pollinator or an animal, but if the plant is wind pollinated, then it will be fine in its new home.
4. Now that the plant is producing viable seeds, it will have to be capable of germinating and this might require an animal, or a period of cold, or a fire to break the dormancy.
5. The next stage is the dispersal of the seeds, which could require an animal.
6. If all the above criteria have been met, the conditions are welcoming to the newcomer but not necessarily open to it: physical space is needed to accommodate the new growth.
7. The final stage is the battle between the natives and the non-native. If the latter wins then it will cause major, perhaps irreversible, changes to the habitat and qualifies for the title of invasive species and joins the list of problem plants. It will also then be on the target list and attempts to control it will begin.

not "illogical" approach. Stop trying to define and instead look closely elsewhere: to the problem—damage to our ecosystem—and subsequently, solutions. The problems were the things that stopped everyone in their tracks in the first place. Start there and work back: from *damages*, created by certain adverse plants that manifest as invaders, to *strategies*, created in response to the need to find a solutions to the problem (and coincidentally, just what inspired this book).

In order to do this successfully, first we need to understand the specific conditions that lead to the damage, that allow any new plant species to become an invader and adversely change its environment and habitat.

At this point, having recognized that damage has resulted from an invasion and knowing the conditions that need to exist for an invasion to occur, actions can be taken by the conservation activists aware of the destructive ramifications of rampant, invasive growth (for example, driving out established species as well as the animals dependent on those plants) and the disappointed backyard gardeners, who within one or two seasons will begin to see the demise of their garden idyll.

As you may have already experienced in your own backyard, if you inherit a beautiful garden and do not look after it, within one or two seasons it will look horrid. There will be certain plants that appear stronger that will have swamped the weaker-seeming plants. New plants that you do not want will have arrived either as seeds or by growing under the fence from next door, or perhaps you introduced, unawares, the pretty thing flaunted at a local nursery. And restoring the backyard to its former glory will take much more than the one or two seasons taken to undo it.

In the light of all this gloomy information, can any movement of plants be justified? There would be an outcry from gardeners if the importation of non-native species were to be banned completely and yet countries such as New Zealand and Australia, where the negative effects of non-native species are most visible, seem to be going in this direction and the United States seems to be close behind. Should we ban all non-native species to protect native species from the 1-in-1,000 Tens Rule that will cause very serious, irreversible, problems? This is a solution, but can science find a better solution? Can we look at the stages in an invasion and find the weak links where we can halt it? Can we examine the species that do cause problems and find common features that make them into non-native, invasive species that can grow outside their natural range where they cause major changes to the ecology of their new home and it cannot be controlled easily? And finally what if the climate changes? Darwin said that "Change of climate must have had a powerful influence on migration," and presumably it will in the future.

Still, the damages that have resulted from invasive plants indicate that there are problems we face on Earth that impinge on a matrix of species and their habitats, and we need to address them. In the words of the GSPC 2020 vision—"Without plants, there is no life. The functioning of the planet, and our survival, depends on plants"—and this includes the matrix of interactions among species. So we also need to keep in mind that the conservation strategies to protect threatened species are conservation strategies whose benefits reach beyond the plant kingdom. This is especially important, perhaps to some of paramount importance, when it comes to threats to our livelihoods and food security, to our day-to-day survival and our longer-ranging survival as a species.

> This Strategy recognized the vital importance of maintaining global plant diversity in providing essential resources for human well-being; food, shelter, medicines, fresh air and water and a healthy environment, as well as cultural and spiritual well-being.
> —Plant Diversity Challenge, The Joint Nature Conservation Committee

5 Meeting the Needs of Today and All Our Tomorrows

Most animal species survive by finding food in their habitat and consuming it. The more food there is, the larger the population grows, but as food decreases so does the population size of that species and its chance for survival. One exception is ants, which actively promote their own continued existence: they milk aphids for honeydew—a sugary waste liquid they produce—and can also cultivate their own fungal gardens to nibble on by protecting the fungus from other predators and by providing a material for the fungus to grow on. Apart from these clever little bugs, it is really only humans who promote their own survival as a species by increasing the so-called carrying capacity of their habitat—the capacity of an area to continue to supply needed resources—by using more land, and more of that land as production land. And we are very, very good at this. There is not a species on Earth that would, if they could, not envy our ability to turn the balance sheet of nature in our own favour.

Only the most arrogant, shortsighted, and spiritually bereft of our species would say that, at any cost to other species, we need only worry about our own. We are the species capable of looking at the things we do, and how our decisions and actions can create conditions that are both not in our own favour but also not in other species' favour either. If anything, the destructiveness of such witting and unwitting actions would be apparent. What we now well know and understand about our ecosystem is that the interactive ecological services therein work in a kind of call-and-response effort to keep things in balance, which can promote the survival of our species as well other organisms.

It is this very interdependence of ecosystem services that is of direct relevance to the management of what is produced on our production lands. For example, wild plants that are relatives of our cultivated crop plants will contain genes essential for ensuring that we will have future crops to cultivate; pollinators working and living among our current crops will also live in and around surrounding hedges, woods, and meadows, and the pollinators' predators and other crop pests will also live on these boundaries. Any decisions that we make that deny the survivability to one or more pieces of the puzzle of this network of production can jeopardize part or all of that production, in the short as well as in the long run.

Regard for of all of these species, our necessary biodiversity, and understanding the science of their interactions are the necessary components of any food security policy and strategy that will be able to successfully feed the ten billion people predicted to populate Earth by 2050. It is a model that needs to include production land management strategies that grow our food and produce commodities and the safeguards to ensure supportive habitats and crops for the future. A compromise between the need for calories today and genes for tomorrow must be designed.

Production Lands and Management

Production lands are any area from which biological resources are regularly extracted, ranging from intensive arable fields to vineyards and from pastures to woodlands. Just how much of Earth's surface area falls under this heading is debatable. A commonly quoted figure is 25 percent, and half of this might be under some form of direct management as arable or pastureland. In the United Kingdom, 77 percent of production land is classified as agricultural; another 10 percent is for forestry, leaving just 13 percent for the 52.5 million people who live in its towns and cities. This does not leave much room for Lord Alfred Tennyson's wild, rampant "nature, red in tooth and claw."

Cropland: Fraction of cropland (arable land & permanent culture)

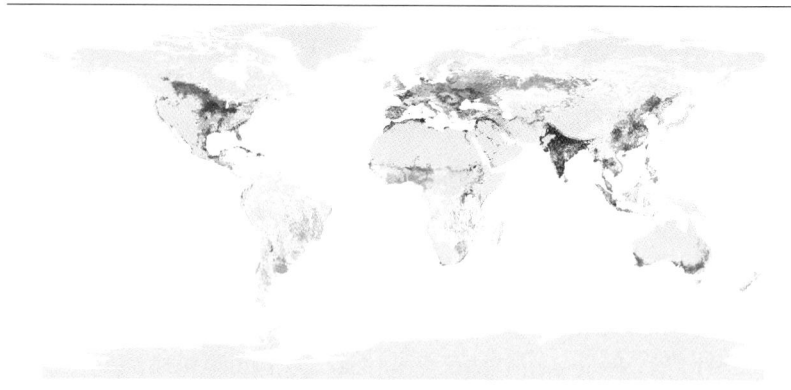

Grazing land: Fraction of area used for grazing

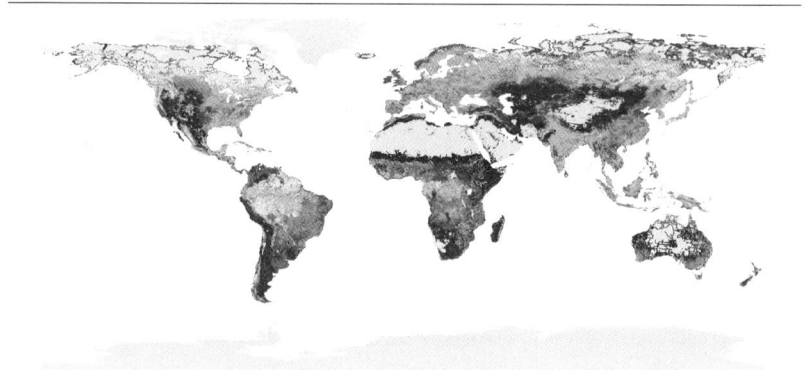

Forestry: Fraction of forestry land use

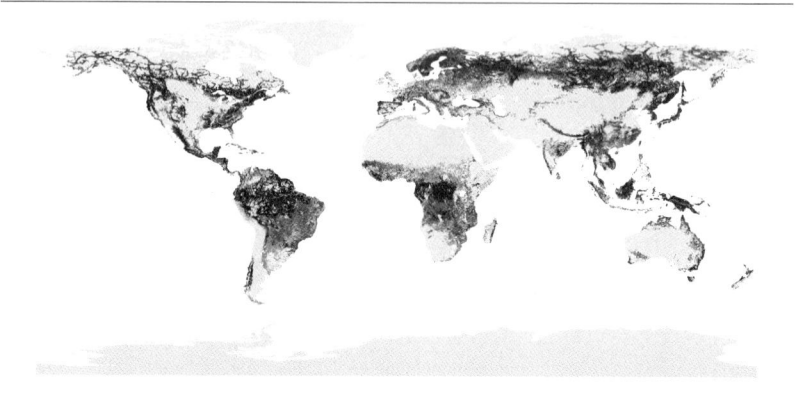

Infrastructure: Fraction of infrastructure & settlement areas

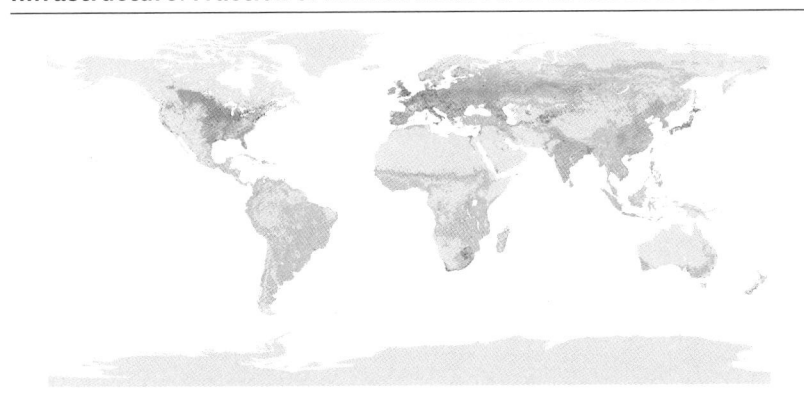

Wilderness & unproductive areas: Fraction of areas without land use

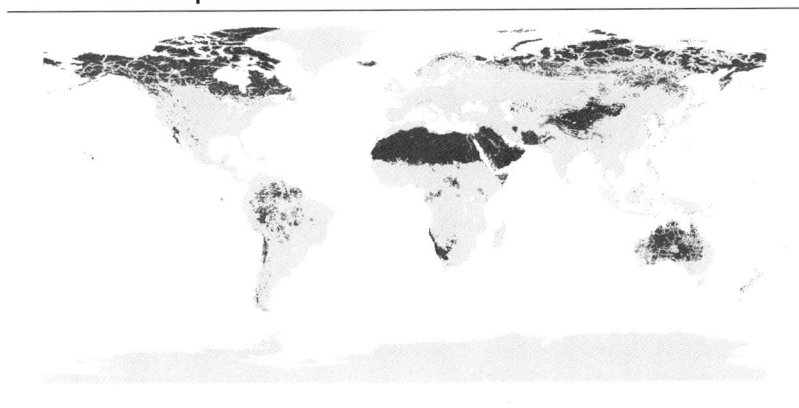

Areas of production and wilderness

Researchers used land-use data for the year 2000 to show five classes of land use: cropland, grazing, forestry, urban and infrastructure areas, and areas without land use.

Percent per grid cell

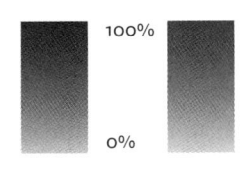

100%

0%

K. H. Erb, V. Gaube, F. Krausmann, C. Plutzar, A. Bondeau, and H. Haberl. 2007. A comprehensive global 5 min resolution land-use dataset for the year 2000 consistent with national census data. *Journal of Land Use Science* 2(3): 191–224. Courtesy of Taylor & Francis Ltd.

> **2020 STRATEGY**
> TARGET 6 Manage at least 75 percent of production and croplands for sustainability and biodiversity

As one travels through the United Kingdom by train, as I am currently doing, it is very common to see a strip of land around the edge of farmers' fields that does not contain a monoculture of wheat, barley, oilseed rape, legumes, or sugar beet. This is its headland; and this production land usage, which leaves a six-metre-wide strip for wildlife, can qualify the farmers for payments from the UK government and/or the European Union, payments that were designed to encourage wise production-land management to promote biodiversity. So if there is a hedge of native woody species in the middle, then for every 800 metres of field boundaries, you have one hectare (2.4 acres) of nature reserve. In imperial terms, this means that for every 375 yards of field boundaries, you have an acre of nature reserve—areas of critical importance for the conservation of not only plants but also birds, mammals, butterflies, moths, and many other smaller beasties. In China such incentives have also been created, whereby the government gives, in UK pounds, £1,340 million to farmers and nomadic people in its western areas for the conservation of the grasslands that are such an important supplier of ecosystem services such as fresh water to the rest of China.

Sometimes, as another example of such beneficial management practices, production and conservation happen together to support biological diversity. This is practiced in the mixed orchards found in the Algarve, Portugal. Here, four different crops—figs, olives, almonds, and carobs—are grown in a matrix in which each species of tree takes slightly different things from the habitat both above ground and below, as they grow to different depths and the plants need different resources at different times of year. The farmers in the Algarve also have on their orchard lands herds of cattle, goats, and, in the past, pigs, which were particularly satisfied feeding underneath the carobs. Now add to that a particular orchid flora that is very rich and grows beneath these trees and you have a picture of a model of production land management: organisms that, in the process of sharing the same production land, will balance the need to grow food and other commodities with the need to sustain a habitat as well as protect native plants.

Another very good example of land sharing can be found on organic farms in the United Kingdom. These farms are both economically viable as producers of prime beef and are designated as Sites of Special Scientific Interest, as defined by the Countryside Conservation Act of 1981. In Lincolnshire, there is one farm with a pond that is home to the nationally rare bog bean, *Menyanthes trifoliata.* This is a beautiful plant that we grow in our ponds at Oxford Botanic Garden and at the Harcourt Arboretum. When we put a photograph of its flowers on the cover of our newsletter, the image provoked more phone calls than for any other issue to date, proving that it is easier to protect beautiful plants than dull plants. As with many aspects of conservation biology, there is not one answer nor a one-size-fits-all approach. The scientific data shows that, generally speaking and depending on the species, land sparing, such as a nature reserve, is less harmful to the wildlife and less damaging to crop yields, than land sharing, such as headlands.

Genes and Seeds: Plants and Food for the Future

The land production systems described so far—both those that take useful measures to ensure biodiversity as well as those that have yet to do so—present a problem for many people. There is some very serious doubt that the current population level can be fed by even the best methods we have. At one time it was suggested that sustainable organic farming would provide enough food for 1.5 billion people, and that this could be achieved virtually overnight (unless God has another nasty diluvian surprise in a bucket behind his back).

Norman Borlaug's inspired Green Revolution of the 1960s is credited

Hay, for Example: Putting It All Together for a Better Future

Compromise might be seen by some as weakness, but there is no reason why conservation and agriculture need to be mutually exclusive. Commercial products can be grown or raised in such a way that nature can survive alongside them. I have already mentioned an organic farm in Lincolnshire, England, but other examples of conservation-friendly agriculture are beginning to emerge.

Hay meadow ecosystems are rich in plant species, and rich in the pollinating invertebrate species (such as bees, butterflies, and moths that the species need, not the grasses, which are all wind pollinated). The hedges will provide further food, not only for invertebrates but also for birds and mammals. The invertebrates, in turn, become food for larger animals. And the larger animals will be feeding and grazing off of the hay. Such is what we know about the rich hay meadow ecosystem; and with this knowledge and understanding, there is an opportunity to support the meadow ecosystem biodiversity. Land sharing is one management and land-use method.

At one time farms that grazed for sheep and cattle also produced the hay for forage. Such grazed hayfields were a common feature of the countryside in the early part of my childhood; but sadly, during my lifetime, agricultural subsidies and incentives have encouraged specialization—alongside the tyranny of large supermarket chain monopolies that has forced down the payments paid to farmers—and hence UK farmers got out of livestock and, consequently, mixed farming and out of land sharing as well. So during my lifetime hay meadows have almost been erased from the UK: only 2 percent of the 1958 hay meadows remain.

Now, what's interesting is that hay meadows require very low inputs, but if only 2 percent remain, is it too late? Can we recreate a sustainable production system for this crop?

The answer is yes, and faster than you might think.

At the University of Oxford Harcourt Arboretum, six miles south of the city of Oxford, a thirty-acre hay meadow has been recreated in just four years. And it is not just in the affluent West that this type of work is happening. In Sri Lanka a wonderful project has recreated a tropical woodland in just thirty years—a process that would normally take at least 150 years. This is habitat restoration on steroids, but what is particularly encouraging about this project is that it has been achieved by a mixture of local professionals and amateurs without any government funding—and, to boot, their long-term planning for reserves supports biodiversity by protecting it through managing resource extraction, which in turn ensures the future of this Sri Lankan woodland.

with saving more than a billion people from starvation, earning him the Nobel Peace Prize in 1970. Green Revolution agriculture was based on high-yielding, disease-resistant dwarf varieties of wheat, which demonstrated what we could achieve if the right genes were put into crop plants. However, since the 1970s, farmers in developed nations and increasingly in the developing nations have been encouraged to specialize. Increasingly they rely on a small number of high-input, genetically pure cultivated varieties (sometimes referred to as cultivars). And we are seeing now across our fields just this sort of erosion to genetic diversity—which is important everywhere, and seeing it in agriculture is no exception.

GENE BANKING AND SAFE DEPOSITS: ENSURING CROPS FOR TODAY AND TOMORROW

Food security is becoming a popular academic subject, bringing together agriculturists, plant scientists, zoologists, soil scientists, and economists with research conducted and experiments designed to address long-range planning for our food supplies and the threats that will reduce them. Limitations on land acquisition, land use, fertilizers, and water supplies; pollution and war, and other known and yet unknown threats, are just some of the politicized concerns that influence the food we grow and consume.

Notable is the long-term security of food supplies, clearly linked to global insecurity during wartime. One example from 1994, the Rwandan Civil War, demonstrates how a local food economy can be destroyed—and how important the local landraces, if protected, would be for reconstruction. We can see in this example just how valuable and irreplaceable landraces are and how swiftly they can be lost. Before the Rwandan war, more than five hundred different varieties of beans were grown in the country. During the war, landraces disappeared and crops were destroyed, preventing Rwandans from saving more seeds and adding to their seed banks. Furthermore, the existing seed stores were consumed by the population to stay alive. After the war, modern "improved" varieties were brought in, but not being specifically bred for the conditions in Rwanda, they yielded 30 percent below what their landraces had been known to produce.

It is understandable, then, that in recent years geneticists have become increasingly keen to preserve the seeds of crops as well as the wild species to which the cultivated crops are related, because from the wild plants, new genes might be obtained. Russian botanist-geneticist Nicolai Vavilov is sometimes credited with setting up a way to do this; he is thought to have been the first to establish an international seed bank, in St. Petersburg in 1926. Luckily, he did this before he fell from political favour and was condemned to die in a labor camp. The story of this seed bank is as tragic as Vavilov's. During the siege of Leningrad, from September 1941 to January 1944, the staff in that seed bank starved to death rather than eat the seeds.

There are older collections of cultivars than the one begun in 1926 in St. Petersburg. At the Rothamsted Research Station in England there are jars of seeds of cereal cultivars harvested in the nineteenth century, but these are a historical record rather than a conscious attempt at conservation genetics. With the explosion in our understanding of genetics following the discovery of the structure of DNA by Watson and Crick in 1953, the concept of gene banks as a synonym for seed banks was finally

Landraces

In some parts of the world farmers do not grow genetically uniform cultivated varieties; instead they have cultivated landraces. Landraces are much more genetically diverse than cultivated varieties and they are normally lower yielding, but they are considered to be more tolerant of particularly challenging local conditions. Additionally, the seeds are kept from year to year. These landraces, then, provide a reliable crop yield. It is surely lower than what could be obtained from higher-yielding varieties, but more important is that it is not unreliable. In parts of southeast Africa, for example, you find villages where different families cultivate slightly different landraces. Year to year, landrace yields may vary—some higher in one year but not in the next—yet across the village, year-to-year yield is stabilized enough to maintain the local diversity and sustain their cropland production. The same thing happens in the central valleys of the Oaxaca in Mexico; landraces there are constantly being exchanged, crossed, and improved.

Such processes have been happening for millennia, and it is believed that many of these plants contain genes that will be used to confer resistance to drought, pests, and diseases. In northeast Africa, in Morocco, for example, farmers grow a simple rotation of legumes, then cereals with a common combination of fava beans alternating with barley. The vast majority (97 percent) of these bean plants are of varieties that were selected and bred for growing there because they tolerated the pests encountered in Morocco.

The Food and Agriculture Organization (FAO) of the United Nations has had a checkered history and still has many critics. However, one of its current programmes is to preserve landraces. It is believed that this programme has encouraged 1.5 billion farmers to save their seeds from year to year and improve the genes in the plants through selection and/or breeding. Such an improvement process can be low-tech, but it requires great skill. The work is often carried out by women who collect seeds from "good" or "better" plants in the fields. These plants may be chosen because they are disease free or high yielding or any other desirable combination of characters. The seeds from the selections will then be mixed together and sown to encourage cross breeding. If this sounds a bit primitive, consider that I was once told by a leading UK geneticist that modern plant breeding in the UK has the same three components: *select* the best, *cross* the best, *hope* for the best.

up and running. There are now about 1,500 seed banks for crop varieties and their wild relatives. It could be said that while the heroic workers in the St. Petersburg seed bank were starving to death, a movement began on the other side of the world that was to result in a global network for the conservation of the crop genes.

It might be surprising to learn that only about 150 crops are grown in significant quantities around the world. They do, however, come in an almost uncountable number of varieties. In 1943 the Rockefeller Foundation and the Mexican government founded what was to become the International Maize and Wheat Improvement Centre (known by the unfathomable acronym of CIMMYT). Then, in 1963, the Rockefeller Foundation and the Ford Foundation came together to establish the International Rice Research Institute (known by the more fathomable acronym of IRRI). Between them, these two organizations had three major crops covered—wheat, maize, and rice. The output and impact were immense, turning countries such as India from centres of malnutrition and hunger in the 1960s to net exporters of cereals within two decades.

The benefits of research in India have not ceased. For example, in the 1980s there was great deal of interest in no-tillage systems of crop growing, where you did not disturb the soil between crops. We were taught this at horticultural college, where it was known as the "no-dig technique" and we most unfairly put its popularity down to the sloth of the lecturer. It turned out that we were being very unkind. It is now believed that no-tillage systems have brought economic benefits totaling $165 million to the Indo-Gangetic Plains in Northern India in the two decades to 2010. One of the major advantages of no-tillage systems is how they help to reduce the loss of topsoil. Surface erosion is one of the most worrisome changes in our farmers' fields along with rises in salinity caused by over-irrigation.

IRRI and CIMMYT (the champions of rice, wheat, and maize, in case you are drowning in the sea of acronyms) showed the way forward; and at the beginning of the 1970s the Rockefeller Foundation proposed a coordinated global network of research institutes that covered not only the three major crops but also other aspects of farming. This idea gained the support of the World Bank, the Food and Agriculture Organization of the United Nations, and the United Nations Development Programme—and in 1971, CGIAR was born. CGIAR stood for the snappily entitled Consultative Group on International Agricultural Research. (If only it had been the Consultative International Group on Agricultural Research.) The remit of their research widened into other crops including cassava, chickpeas, sorghum, potatoes, and millet. Of these only potatoes are a familiar sight in the United Kingdom, but already sorghum is seen regularly in Oxfordshire due to its ability to grow well with less water in the soil.

Now CGIAR has fifteen active institutes all around the world that carry out cutting-edge research into all aspects of the production of food and other natural commodities such as forestry, livestock, and fishing. They also investigate improving the nutrient content of food, food policy, and food security, and most importantly the management of the world's water supplies. Very appropriately, the latter activity is run out of the International Water Management Institute in Sri Lanka. This is appropriate because the Sri Lankans have been managing their water supplies in ingenious ways for centuries. One of the oldest gardens in the world is at the Sigiriya Rock, and in it is a water garden, in honor, I guess, of the god of water.

If you are skeptical about the impact of these large international partnerships consider this. A report was published in 2003 by CABI (now the Centre for Agricultural Biosciences International but formerly the Commonwealth Agricultural Bureau) that examined the impact of international agricultural research. The report's authors, Robert Evenson and Doug Gollin, found that in 1998 (compared with the situation in 1965) improved varieties of ten crops were being grown on 65 percent of the land being used to grow those crops—namely wheat, rice, maize, sorghum, millet, barley, lentils, beans, cassava, and potatoes. Across the ten crops, on average 60 percent of these improved varieties had their origin from CGIAR cultivars, and if you looked at just lentils, beans, and cassava, 90 percent had their origins in CGIAR institutions.

GENE BANKING AND LOCAL KNOWLEDGE

The CGIAR scheme of crop improvement relies on free global exchange of seeds with partner institutions and others. This is fine when everyone trusts everyone else, but the genes in plants can have a huge commercial value and some countries are wary of giving over their genetic inheritance. This is why the Millennium Seed Bank Project principle of enabling countries to establish their own seed banks is a great idea. At the centre of the trust is the 2004 International Treaty on Plant Genetic Resources for Food and Agriculture (ITPGRFA).

Most countries have contracted into the treaty, some have chosen to just sign it but not be bound by it, and others have ignored it presumably because they do not want access to other countries' genetic resources and/or they do not want to share theirs with anyone else. It has to be remembered that the majority have contracted in. (The ITPGRFA website gives the most up-to-date information on membership.) Another outcome of this treaty was the twelve-page Standard Material Transfer Agreement that sets out clearly the responsibilities of the donor and recipients and any subsequent payments for commercial exploitation. Up to this point all exchanges of genetic material had to be negotiated afresh

continued on page 180

Case in Point: The International Potato Centre—Creating a Model Gene Bank

Given that the annual world production yield for potato crops is enormous—more than 325 million tons each year, with China's production being the largest, growing nearly 25 percent of this number—some agricultural analysts believe that China is going to play a major role in the feeding of an extra 2,000 million people in the next forty years, especially in the developing countries. In order to keep food production in line with added consumption, China's estimation is that half of the extra calories will come from potatoes in the next two decades.

There are at least four thousand named cultivars of potato, and the gene bank in the International Potato Centre (CIP) in Lima, Peru, contains more than seven thousand plants from different localities. Some of these are seed collections for the 141 of the 187 wild species that are relatives of potatoes in the genus *Solanum*. It is believed that the CIP holds more than 80 percent of the global genetic diversity of potatoes. So far samples have been supplied to institutions in more than one hundred countries.

The CIP also looks after sweet potatoes that share nothing with potatoes except their name and the fact that they are flowering plants with tubers. Sweet potatoes (*Ipomoea batatas*) are less widely cultivated than ordinary potatoes, but they are very important. They have a reputation for being an emergency food. For example, after typhoons wiped out rice fields in Japan, when China experienced famine in the 1960s, and when the cassava crop in Uganda was decimated by viruses in the 1990s, sweet potatoes were grown to fill the gap. In Sub-Saharan Africa the area being used to grow sweet potatoes is growing faster than any other crop. It is a very forgiving crop, growing over a wide variety of conditions and often in poor conditions where other plants will not grow. The final reason for growing sweet potatoes in developing countries is that just five ounces of fresh sweet potatoes contain sufficient vitamin A for a toddler—and without vitamin A, under-fives will go blind.

Given the nature of the crops cherished in the International Potato Centre (CIP), which uses a full range of conservation techniques, it is a useful model for how to create a seed bank.

First, there are the field-grown gene banks of living plants at Huancayo, 3,200 metres up in the Andes. These collections have to be propagated each year and so are more labor intensive than a packet of seeds in a freezer.

Second, small potato and sweet potato plants are grown in test-tubes using a nutrient jelly instead of soil. If these are kept in low light conditions at 6° to 8°c, they survive for two years and take up less space than a field gene-bank. This is known as *in vitro* conservation, and the CIP collection is the largest in the world.

Third, there is orthodox freezing of dried seeds at -20°c. This is used for seeds of the wild relatives of both types of potato and has been shown to work for at least forty years.

Fourth, there is cryopreservation of growing shoot tips at -196°c using liquid nitrogen. This works well for potatoes but has yet to be perfected for sweet potatoes.

Fifth, CIP has a DNA bank. This is a unique reference collection of the pure genetic instructions of 2,400 named varieties stored at -70°c.

Sixth, there is a herbarium of more than 25,000 pressed specimens of potatoes, sweet potatoes, and other Andean root and tuber crops. These voucher specimens provide a priceless historical record of these plants.

The seventh strategy is the potato park, a very different way of doing things and part of the innovative Ruta Condor Project running down the Andes. The vision of this scheme is to establish a chain of conservation sites from Merida, Venezuela, in the north, down to Jujuy, Argentina, in the south, following in part the Qhapaq ñan, or Main Andean Road, that was central to the Inca Empire and the economic power of that empire. Since 2000 more than 4,600 samples of 1,200 disease-free verified varieties of potatoes have been repatriated to local communities living high up in the Andes at forty-one different locations. The Picaq Potato Park in Paucartambo, Cusco, Peru, is one of the sites, situated in the Sacred Valley of Peru.

The park covers 12,000 hectares (or 28,800 acres or 120 square kilometres or 46 square miles) and the altitude varies from 3,150 to 5,000 metres. In the Potato Park more than six hundred varieties of potatoes are grown, but this is about more than the conservation of the genes of potatoes. It is part of a much bigger project to reestablish the local Quechua communities who have been struggling for many years to assert their land rights in the region. An alliance between the CIP and the Quechua-Aymara Association for Sustainable Communities (ANDES in Spanish) drove this project. The Qhapaq ñan is a major tourist route and visitors can enjoy the varied tastes of these potatoes as they travel along the Andes; ecotourism can help to provide sustainable livelihoods.

Near to the Picaq Potato Park is the San José de Aymara communal seed bank in Huancevilica, which won the BBC Global Challenge Award for its part in the Tikapapa Projects, which commercialized these native potato varieties. Also in South America, at the Inheritors of the Earth near Pasto in southern Colombia, a workforce with an average age below twenty is taking their future into their own hands by cultivating their landraces of potatoes in a botanic garden.

continued from page 176
and the legal community was able to help with this, but not always on a pro bono basis; even lawyers have to eat. The creation of a standard transfer agreement saved a great deal of time, money, and suspicion.

Then, in 2010, access to genetic resources and the fair and equitable sharing of benefits arising from their utilization received a boost—with the Nagoya Protocol, agreed upon at the meeting of the parties to the Convention on Biological Diversity held in Nagoya, Japan. The protocol took the process of the 2004 itpgrfa agreement of access and benefit sharing to the next stage. It facilitated fair play while at the same time allowing for new varieties to be created, enabling us to feed a population of ten billion people by 2050. While we are now confident that we can conserve the genes upon which our future depends, fair and equitable sharing of benefits is a complex issue. It must be remembered that this is not just about genetic resources; it also includes local knowledge, and as was pointed out by Sir Francis Bacon in 1597 (and by many, many people since), knowledge is power. Socrates went one step further by stating that there is only one good, knowledge, and one evil, ignorance—suggesting that knowledge, the one good, is invaluable. Take the case of the hoodia plant and its use.

One problem facing many of us is being overweight. If one could suppress one's appetite, that would help to remove one of the reasons why one eats too much. *Hoodia* is a succulent plant growing in southern Africa. The indigenous San peoples have used this plant as a hunger and thirst suppressant for donkeys for years. If it works for donkeys, then it seems like just the thing that fat people like me have been looking for. In 1996 the South African–based Council for Scientific and Industrial Research (csir) patented the active ingredients of *Hoodia* for potential commercialization of the plants' molecules as a dieting aid. csir then entered into agreements with members of the pharmaceutical industry to develop hoodia-inspired products and to bring them to the shops.

Unfortunately the csir forgot to consult with the San peoples whose valuable knowledge was being exploited. Nongovernmental organizations took up the right of the San peoples to demand to benefit from this commercial exploitation of their knowledge. Following a press campaign the right thing was done, and a benefit-sharing agreement was reached. Benefits do not have to be hard cash. In this case some monetary compensation was agreed to that included milestone payments during the development phase and then royalties from sales following successful commercialization. Nonmonetary benefits agreed on included development and delivery of education for the San peoples and the implementation of programmes and projects to further safeguard their heritage and knowledge.

> **2020 STRATEGY**
>
> TARGET 9 Conserve and protect genetic diversity of crop plants, their wild relatives, and economically valuable plants while preserving indigenous and local knowledge and practice

Food Security Conservation: Safeguarding and Funding Our Genetic Resources

Bioversity International (BI, formerly known as the International Plant Genetic Resources Institute, IPGRI) is a partnering organization whose conservation work revolves around the agricultural industry, targeting "hunger, malnutrition, poverty, and environmental degradation." The intersections of their investigations address agricultural biodiversity to achieve these aims. One of their stated research priorities is "to promote the conservation, exchange and sustainable use of plant genetic resources." But gene banks are not just for Christmas, but for ever.

One of the biggest problems in conservation, as you might imagine, is finding ongoing funding. BI happens to be an important conduit for

continued on page 184

A Global Flora Protected: Svalbard Genes

No staff are permanently based at the remote site for the Svalbard Global Seed Vault; security is by remote cameras and by the most unusual security staff—polar bears who outnumber residents on the arctic archipelago. And the back story is that the Norwegian government, persuaded to supply $9 million to build the facility, complied. The vault was opened in 2008, having taken just eight months to build, with added help from the Global Crop Diversity Trust, which agreed to provide the $300,000 annual running costs.

These funding figures seem ludicrously good values, to my mind, because there are already 700,000 samples in storage. The first consignment of seeds was placed in the vault at the opening ceremony and it symbolically contained rice seeds from 123 different countries. In the same year 3,000 kg of seeds from CIMMYT were deposited. This is something for which we should all be grateful because it important for the long-term security of our food. Zoologist Charles Godfray of Oxford University put this very clearly and forcibly when he wrote the real decisions in conservation are dominated by politics and economics and "governments will have the luxury of acting on biodiversity only if their populations enjoy food security; protecting biodiversity and ensuring food security are part of a single agenda."

Another beauty of the Svalbard vault is that there are no ownership issues. The Norwegian government owns the building, but the seeds remain the property of the donor country. In addition to the polar bears, any thieves would have to get past four sets of locked doors. Depositors only have access to the part of the vault that houses their seeds, which are cached in locked boxes. However, there still remain issues surrounding the exchange of genetic material. A central principle of the Convention on Biological Diversity is that countries can expect fair distribution of the benefits derived from the exploitation of their biological and genetic inheritance. This was one of the reasons that many poor countries ratified the convention, hoping that their natural genetic resources would be safeguarded. It is also one reason why the USA chose not to ratify the convention—because it feared that it might harm the US economy by preventing access to the genetic resources of other countries. This is probably why the USA has only signed, but not contracted into, the 2004 International Treaty on Plant Genetic Resources for Food and Agriculture (ITPGRFA). This does not mean conversely that anyone can help themselves to the genetic resources in the USA. What is in the US stays in the US, and quite rightly so perhaps because genes are money.

continued from page 181

money; some of their funding comes through the Global Crop Diversity Trust (GCDT), whose own mission is to fund the conservation and correct management of the genetic diversity of crops where funding is not possible from local governments. The GCDT gets its money from many sources, including the Bill and Melinda Gates Foundation—the source of funding for what can be seen as GCDT's landmark project: the Svalbard Global Seed Vault.

If we think of the major threats that a seed bank might face, besides that already mentioned—wars, which have in our centuries of life (the twentieth and twenty-first span) been nearly continuous round the world—we can also add natural disasters and economic recessions both regional and, freshly documented, global.

One solution to such problems is for there to be a central storage facility where landraces can be stored securely and repatriated if or when required. This is sometimes referred to as black box conservation, from the survival capabilities of an aircraft flight deck records. Thanks to the efforts of the GCDT, the Svalbard Global Seed Vault has as its sole purpose the preservation of genetic diversity of crops against all possible disasters.

The 2004 International Treaty on Plant Genetic Resources for Food and Agriculture (ITPGRFA), along with the Convention on Biological Diversity, signed and ratified in 1992 by the majority of the world's nations, set the scene for the Svalbard Global Seed Vault. The Consultative Group on International Agricultural Research (CGIAR) appealed for a central repository for backup samples from all gene banks around the world. A triumvirate was formed between the government of Norway, the Nordic Genetic Resource Centre, and the GCDT. Plans were drawn up to build a vault deep in the permafrost-ridden land at Svalbard. This was not only chosen because of the cold. It's true that the region is geologically stable, enjoys low relative humidity, has very low background radiation that might cause damage to the seeds, is 130 metres above current sea level, and for much of the year the -18°C (-4°F) temperature is maintained by drawing cold air into the vault. Even if the summer refrigeration fails, the vault will remain frozen. But the extraordinary aspect, of the most far-reaching import, is the international agreement that Svalbard will not be fought over.

The conservation of plant genetic resources happens beyond the global safeguard project of the Svalbard collection, within a country proper as well, with some of the fifteen national institutes that are members of CGIAR holding other major gene resources for their respective countries and for others. This is an essential part of a global strategy, the essential work of the GSPC, whose programmes and ideas cutting across sixteen global aims—the targets for 2020—along with a complex of frameworks encourage cooperation and working together at the local, national, regional, and global levels.

Cooperation is fundamentally centred on us, whether at the simpler level of the individual—you, me, our communities; or at the more complex level of a socioeconomic entity, which can be political (such as countries), cultural (such as nations of people), or geographical (such as land regions).

What can unite all of these entities, and us, and perhaps must, is a truth that is universally acknowledged: life on Earth is not sustainable if it consumes the resources faster than they are replaced.

6 Pay As You Go: Sustainable Resource Use

Sustainability is one of the most abused words in the politician's phrase book. It is usually followed by the word *development*, changing the meaning completely. Development is about expansion, but biology is not: biology cannot expand because there is just one world that will support life. The Class M planets, other than Earth, so popular and central to *Star Trek*, do not exist as far as we know. So if everyone on the one planet we know of as habitable, Earth, consumed the planet's biological products as quickly as, say, the Europeans, we would need three planets to support seven billion people. If everyone consumed the biological products as quickly as, say, the Americans, we would need twelve planets to support seven billion people. These are very uncomfortable calculations.

The economics of biology are far simpler than the modern banking system: credit cards cannot be issued for biological resources because biology only lives in the present. The plants upon which we depend do not know that the sun will come up tomorrow. Our use of fossil fuels is living on savings, but those savings are being consumed without being replaced. Also, those savings do not accumulate any interest. In biology, plants make useful stuff fueled by the process of photosynthesis; the plants make useful stuff and we consume the stuff. If we consume that stuff faster than plants can make it, then we shall run out and will have to wait until the plants have made some more. Anyone who grows their own potatoes will know this. If you plant your seed potatoes in the spring, harvest them at the end of August, and then proceed to consume all of your potatoes before the next planting's crop is ready to harvest, then it's no chips for you. But what about the bigger picture—what about everyone else?

Sustainability and Food Production

The population of the world continues to increase. There are websites that give constant ticker-tape updates of birth and deaths, and hence net growth in population for today and the current year. It's strangely mesmeric to watch with joy and hope the births, and with grief and loss for deaths, as the number clicker like the one used on petrol pumps goes up and up while we fill our car tanks. In fact, in the time that it has taken me to type *this* sentence, world population has increased by seventy-five people.

There are many estimates for how our population will grow, with one common feature: at some point in the twenty-first century, the numbers will stop going up and will start to decline. The United Nations Development Programme is working on an estimate—roughly, that world population will peak at 9.3 billion in 2050. Another estimate, by a group of Austrian scientists at the International Institute for Applied Systems Analysis, suggests a peak of nine billion by 2070; and they go on to say that by 2100 one-third of people will be over sixty. The "problem" with this is that the contribution of the over-sixty population to the economy has in the past been more consumption than production in terms of both food and economic wealth. There are a number of ways to get around this problem of too few workers trying to support too many retired people. One is simply to abolish the expectation of retirement.

The fact that both calculations find that the population will level and then fall is a good thing. No one seems to want to say where the population will bottom out, but some researchers are suggesting that 1,500 million people is a good figure for how many humans can be supported by the planet indefinitely—that means, sustainably. There are limits on the survivability of any biological population; factors include such things as food, space, predation, and disease. For the production of food for humans and their survivability, the limitations can be specified: land, fertilizer, water, pests and diseases (both pre-harvest and post-harvest), yield, and waste.

LAND

It is generally agreed that there is not much land on Earth that is suitable for intensive arable agriculture that has not already been cleared, ploughed, and incorporated into intensive agriculture. Many areas of marginal land might be suitable for new and emerging crops such as sweet potatoes, but we cannot assume that these can be farmed for ever. In fact, we cannot assume that all the land currently farmed will be available for ever. For example, at present 0.5 percent of farmland in Western Australia's wheat belt is becoming too salty to support crops. At this rate all that land will be unavailable by 2200.

FERTILIZER

A feature of modern agriculture is its dependence upon large quantities of fertilizer and in particular inorganic fertilizers. Let's look at the two most important of these in terms of the quantity used: nitrogen and phosphorus. Ammonia is produced by the reaction of nitrogen and hydrogen gas in what is known as the Haber process (or Haber-Bosch process) and then changed into nitrates and ammonium nitrate which can be applied to the soil. A problem with this way of supporting the nutrient requirements of plants is that the process needs the methane in natural gas as a starting point, and this is not present in unlimited quantities.

The significance of the invention of the Haber process cannot be overestimated. It is believed that between a third and half of the yield of food crops is the direct result of the application of nitrogenous fertilizer produced through the Haber process. Furthermore, half of the nitrogen in human proteins began its journey into our bodies in the Haber process. "For dust thou art, and unto dust shalt thou return" never seemed more true!

Phosphorous can be obtained in a number of ways. Many of us have applied superphosphate fertilizer to our soil. The development of this is attributed to several people, but the story begins in Oxford. In 1801

William Buckland came up to Oxford University to study theology at Corpus Christi College. Buckland was a polymath and attended the chemistry lectures of Professor John Kidd. This fueled further his interest in mineralogy and fossils. In 1829 he described coprolites, which are almost the ultimate fossil fuel because they are fossil animal dung—fossilized faeces. Another student studying under Professor Kidd a few years later was Charles Daubeny who succeeded Kidd in 1822 as professor of chemistry at the ridiculously young age of twenty-seven and became professor of botany in 1834 at the age of thirty-nine.

John Bennet Lawes developed his interest in plant nutrition while studying under Daubeny. Theirs was a meeting of kindred spirits as they began experiments on plant nutrition in the Botanic Garden on the banks of the River Cherwell. They soon ran out of space here and so moved to experimental plots at the end of the Iffley Road where Daubeny Road commemorates their work. When he left Oxford in 1832, Lawes was able to continue his work at home because in 1822 he had inherited Rothamsted Manor in Hertfordshire from his father. This is now the home of the Rothamsted Research Station. Here in a field at Rothamsted, the Park Grass Experiment, the soil has been studied continuously for more than 150 years and is still revealing unknown properties of biological communities and of soil and their behaviour after decades of continuous cultivation and fertilizer applications. Rothamsted is also home to one of the oldest seed banks in the world.

In 1842 three men discovered independently that pouring sulfuric acid onto either bones (Justus von Liebig) or phosphate rock (John Bennet Lawes) or coprolites (Rev. John Stephens Henslow, Professor of Botany at Cambridge University, England) resulted in the formation of monocalcium phosphate or superphosphate as it is better known. Whoever gets the prize for being first, Lawes started to manufacture superphosphate at a factory in Deptford, UK, and the Fison Company began manufacturing in Ipswich, UK, where there is still a road called Coprolite Street.

Unfortunately the Lawes process has a side effect, because by using rock phosphate you are inadvertently introducing fluorine into your soil. This has the same effect as bromine over a long period: soil sterilization, which reduces the number of useful fungi in the soil (the mycorrhizal fungi). This explains one of the attractions for organic farming—the use of organic, animal-derived fertilizers. I have already said that organic farming probably cannot provide, overnight, enough food to feed the world's population, but when the population falls, maybe it will.

At present rock phosphate supplies world farming with the majority of its artificial phosphate fertilizer. Our known supplies may run out within fifty to a hundred years. If this is correct, then the supply should see our grandchildren past the peak in human population. However, in the meantime those countries blessed with large deposits of phosphate rock will become as important as the oil-producing countries. Nearly one third of the world's known reserves of phosphate rock is in Morocco. Other countries currently with exportable reserves are Western Sahara, South Africa, Jordan, and Syria. How much undiscovered phosphate rock exists is unknown (obviously). Some countries, such as China, have begun to use export taxes to try to preserve their own supply for their home market.

WATER

The next limiting factor on crop production is fresh water. As I sit writing this, England has just enjoyed the wettest April in recent history and many homes in northern England are flooded in late June, so suggesting that there might not be enough water might seem strange. And yet this follows one of the driest years of record in England (2011). It is a generally accepted fact that there is not enough fresh water to irrigate more than 50 percent of agriculture, and that is stretching it very fine. In 2009 it was reported that groundwater was becoming depleted at a rate of up to 40 mm each year on the Indo-Gangetic Plains in Northern India. Quite simply the groundwater was running out.

Water is too scarce to be used to produce biofuels; it is also too precious to use regularly on growing ornamental plants. It is always going to be possible to find ornamental plants to grow in our gardens that will survive without irrigation. At home we do not water our ornamental borders because of how we plant them and because of the species that we choose. If a plant needs irrigating, we give it away. Planting is a critical moment, and this is how we do it. Dig a hole (always a good start). This must be the right depth so that the crown of the plant is at the soil surface. Put the plant in the hole and backfill halfway. This soil should be firmed with your foot to the same firmness as the soil around the hole. Now fill the top half of the hole with water and continue filling until the water does not drain away and you have a puddle. At this point leave this plant and dig the next hole. When the water has all drained away finish filling the hole and firm the soil very lightly with your fingers. This technique encourages the plant to root well below the surface where the soil is more likely to remain moist all the year round. If the roots are restricted to the surface, then it will wilt when there are a few weeks without water. The no-watering rule is not applied to the vegetable plot, but we do use rainwater, which we harvest from almost every roof and gutter. Home-grown food is a treat and reduces the need to import food from overseas.

FUEL

Now there is a lot of concern at present about another commodity that is running out: oil and other fossil fuels. All of the energy held in fossil fuels was originally captured by photosynthesis. Each year we are currently releasing the energy that it took ancient organisms three million years to capture. It is easy to see why it will run out. There is also concern about the volume of carbon dioxide that is being released when the fossil fuels are burned. If we think of burning fossil fuels as essentially photosynthesis in reverse, it is logical to think about recapturing the carbon dioxide in a plant that we can then use as fuel to boil the next kettle or drive the next mile.

A number of plants will grow very quickly, often on poor soils and with low inputs, that are either already being used or are being considered for fuels for power stations or as the starting point in the manufacture of biodiesel or bioethanol. Some of these are familiar to some of us as good garden plants or crops while some are unfamiliar: miscanthus (an ornamental grass, *Miscanthus*), switchgrass (*Panicum virgatum*), giant reed grass (*Arundo donax*), sweet sorghum, reed canary grass (*Phalaris arundinacea*), willows (*Salix* species), poplars (*Populus* species), sugarcane, jatropha (*Jatropha curcas*), soybean, maize, oilseed rape, and palm oil. It sounds like a great idea. In Brazil there are already nine million vehicles powered by ethanol manufactured from sugarcane. Although energy has to go into processing the sugarcane into ethanol, it is believed to have fewer greenhouse gas emissions than burning fossil fuels in engines.

In the United States, maize is being developed further as a source of bioethanol and soybean as a source of biodiesel. It has to be said that the benefits to natural resources and to the environment derived from producing vehicle fuel from plants are less clear. There is one major drawback to both of these, which is the volume of water needed to produce energy. Petroleum extraction currently requires 25 litres of water for every megawatt hour of energy. Corn ethanol needs 6 million litres of water for every megawatt hour and soybean biodiesel requires 20 million litres. Putting aside all the technical and infrastructure problems, these water requirements seem to be the death knell for many people's hopes.

An old idea that is receiving a great deal of attention is cellulosic ethanol made from lignocellulose in plants. There is lots of lignocellulose out there. Lignocellulose is what makes trees stay upright and it is immensely strong. You can see this by looking at many of the improbable angles at which huge branches grow. It takes a great deal of energy to make lignocellulose, and so it contains a great deal of energy that can be released and used by us. Over 60 percent of non-fossil-based carbon on

Water Requirements for Energy Production
(LITRES PER MEGAWATT HOUR)

Petroleum extraction	10–40
Oil refining	80–150
Oil shale surface retort	170–681
Natural gas combined cycle power plant, closed loop cooling	230–30,300
Coal integrated gasification combined-cycle	~900
Nuclear power plant, closed loop cooling	~950
Geothermal power plant, closed loop tower	1900–4200
Enhanced oil recovery	~7600
Natural gas combined cycle, open loop cooling	28,400–75,700
Nuclear power plant, open loop cooling	94,600–227,100
Corn ethanol irrigation	2,270,000–8,670,000
Soybean biodiesel irrigation	13,900,000–27,900,000

Earth is in the form of lignin or cellulose, which is very easy to believe if you drive down the West Coast of America. There is a great deal of cellulose in the byproducts of agriculture. However, the technology is in its infancy. The same can be said for the idea of using algae to produce fuel.

PESTS AND DISEASES

The limits on food production from pests and disease attacks are being tackled through breeding programmes. This is why the wild relatives of our crop plants are so important. For example, resistance to rice yellow stunt virus was discovered in a plant growing in Turkey. Many home gardeners believe that you must have the pesticide spray to hand when growing food at home. The chemicals that we used when I was a schoolboy helping my father on the vegetable plot would make your hair curl, or fall out in my case. Today we use nothing at home and still we can grow many of our vegetables. Most food waste is of vegetable and fruit that go off post-harvest. This is not an issue if you grow your own.

YIELD

Increasing yield is also being tackled by conventional breeding and new techniques grouped together under the infamous term *genetic modification*. For example, if we could persuade a plant to have hairier roots, would it not grow bigger because it is better able to take more resources out of the soil? One way of potentially achieving this is to duplicate the genes coding for root hairs. Whether this is any different from crossing two species that would never have met without the intervention of humans is debatable, and it will be debated until we are so hungry that we shall not worry about any potential fallout.

WASTE

The final limit on the food supply to the world's population is the wasting of food, and here there is the potential of a very quick gain because the difficult part has been done in that the food has been grown. Waste or post-harvest loss is different in different parts of the world and in different social groups. The UN Food and Agriculture Organization has reported that a third of all food, more than 1,000 million tons, is not eaten. If this calculation is correct then we can already produce sufficient food for the peak population of 9,500 million people. The richest countries waste more food than the whole Sub-Saharan part of African produces in a year—that is 222 million tons. (Sub-Saharan Africa is Africa without Egypt, Libya, Algeria, Tunisia, Morocco, and Western Sahara.)

In industrialized countries the wastage is mostly the result of throwing away food after it has reached shops or homes. On average, everyone in Europe and North America throws away 100 kilograms (or 220 lbs) of perfectly good food every year, or 10 ounces per day. This equates to about 10 percent of the daily food of each person. In contrast, people

The Science of Feeding the World and GM

Science is a method of working that starts with a question followed by an experiment designed to answer that question fairly. It is easy to make assumptions but more difficult sometimes to back these up with hard evidence. As Norman Borlaug said, "The first essential component of social justice is adequate food for everyone." By asking some big questions and applying scientific methodologies, he pursued scientific work resulting in an increase in the world's food production and a reduction in human suffering from starvation. He also said that "Civilization as it is known today could not have evolved, nor can it survive, without an adequate food supply." If this is true, then civilization as we know it is, through and through, dependent on science.

We are now facing the problem of feeding a world population that is approaching ten billion people. And how we breed the varieties of the future depends on the crop, and the characteristics of that crop, that we want to improve. For example, if we want a modern variety of rice that will tolerate flooding, then this can be achieved thought traditional breeding techniques, because some old-fashioned varieties are already tolerant of flooding. However, if we want to breed a banana that is resistant to root nematodes, then traditional techniques are useless because bananas are sterile—they do not reproduce sexually. In this case the technique nicknamed genetic modification, which bypasses the need for pollen and ovaries, has to be used. Genetic modification, or GM, is a misleading term in that all plant breeding results in genetic modification. GM differs from pollen-on-stigma breeding in that genes can be taken from completely unrelated species and inserted into the crop plant. Bananas are very important in some parts of the world. In Uganda, the per capita annual consumption of bananas is 200 kg. Protecting the banana crop is therefore very important.

GM techniques are controversial in some parts of the world, most notably Europe, where hunger is not very common. Trials of a wheat variety at Rothamsted Research Station are currently being threatened with destruction by people who do not like the idea of a wheat variety that contains an artificial gene, created in the laboratory, that enables the plant to produce an aphid pheromone E-beta-farnasene. The aphids produce this when they are threatened; and so aphids, flying up to the GM wheat, are frightened away. This could not only reduce the proportion of the wheat crop lost to aphids, but it could also reduce the quantity of synthetic pesticides that need to be sprayed onto the crop. There are claims that this crop might not be safe for human consumption and that the genes for the production of the aphid pheromone could spread to native grasses, which could then resist aphids, leading to a decline of wild-aphid populations which could have an impact on their predators such as birds and ladybirds. These claims could be tested using the scientific method. Many of the opponents of GM prefer direct action to debate and open science, and so presumably they do not want to know the truth in case it is not what they believe.

GM is often criticized as being yet another way that multinational corporations can exert control over poor people by breeding varieties of which the seeds cannot be saved and so seeds that have to be purchased each year. A simple way around this is for the GM varieties to be bred by public funding or from philanthropic donations. For example, all the varieties produced by grants from the Bill and Melinda Gates Foundation have to be varieties that can be saved from year to year. GM crops will not solve all the problems. They will not address the problem of soil erosion, and the availability of water for irrigation.

in Sub-Saharan Africa and most of Asia throw away 1 percent of their food. In developing countries the problem is losses during production, or processing of distribution. The solution for this includes better plants through breeding and better infrastructure for distribution and storage.

Sustainability and Health Care

In the 1960s the National Cancer Institute in the US made the life-changing discovery that the bark of the Pacific yew (*Taxus brevifolia*) contains a molecule that is very effective in the treatment of ovarian cancer in mice. Further studies showed that the molecule, named taxol, was very useful in the treatment of ovarian cancer in women. The problem was that paclitaxel (as taxol was renamed for trademark protection) could not be synthesized and the only source was the bark. Further, in order to extract enough pure taxol to carry out clinical trials, tens of thousands of kilograms of bark were required. The removal of the bark did the tree no good whatsoever—it killed the trees.

Now, if it is you or your wife, mother, sister, or daughter who is suffering from a cancer that can be treated with paclitaxel, there is no dilemma because the life of a loved relative is more important than a few trees in a woodland in the Pacific Northwest of North America. Taking a longer view, however, the methodology that was employed was never going to be a sustainable way of producing the drug anyway. Additionally, extraction of the bark from trees in the woods severely disturbed the forest overall. At this point, a movement developed to save the woods. Eventually a team, in France, found a way to synthesize paclitaxel from a molecule in the leaves of the English yew (*Taxus baccata*). The beauty of this discovery was that there was already a supply of yew leaves every August when English gardeners went out and trimmed their yew hedges. Rather than putting the leaves on the compost, on the fire, or in the bin, yew leaves could be sent to France, where they were used in the synthesis of not only paclitaxel but of the synthetic molecule docetaxel (trade name Taxotere), widely used in the treatment of breast cancer.

> **2020 STRATEGY**
> **TARGET 11** Protect wild flora from overcollection
> **TARGET 12** Source wild-harvested, plant-based products sustainably; don't manufacture products from wild plants faster than the plants can regrow

China grows a small tree (*Eucommia ulmoides*) that is very important to the practice of traditional Chinese medicine, and now it is on the Red List as "near threatened," a result of overcollection. The reason for this overcollection is built on a superstition that is based on a small amount of truth. The superstition is that medicinal plants are not efficacious if they are cultivated in a farmer's field and that only plants harvested from the plant's habitat will work in herbal medicine. This is clearly untrue as the millions of acres of poppies for the production of opiates proves. However, this is why the wild populations of some plants have been overcollected to the point of extinction. It must be remembered that this is not quite the same as killing off big animals for the extraction of dubious potency aids, for example, because plant-based medicines are very often effective, whereas animal extracts used for virility are bunkum. Traditional Chinese medicine has been unfairly tainted by the idiots who hunt these creatures. But, as I said, there is a grain of truth in this superstition and it is this: we extract molecules from plants because they happen to have properties that make them useful medicines, but some of these plants only make these molecules when they are stressed in their habitat and not when grown in the stress-free luxury of a farmer's field.

Why the plant makes the molecules in the first place is not always clear. The most commonly cited reason is self-defence, based on the well-known fact that most drugs when taken to excess are not good for you. In some cases our discovery of a new medicinal molecule comes after someone uses the molecule as a poison. This was true of the arrow poison, strophanithine, derived from *Strophanthus*, which has subsequently been used to treat heart disease. What the defence is against may vary. If it is against a herbivore, then it would be good to have the poison there all the time. This might explain the presence of digoxin (and digitoxin) in foxgloves, which is currently keeping my old mother alive. However, if the attack is by a slower organism like, say, a fungus, then maybe the plant has time to manufacture its chemical weapons before too much damage is done. In this case, the active ingredient may not be present in the plant until it is invaded by the fungus. The molecules are known as secondary compounds because they are not part of the day-to-day or primary metabolism. They can be elusive and more commonly exploited in herbal medicine where identification of the active ingredient is less important than saving life.

Secondary compounds have unusual properties, and they are regularly used in medicine. If the medicinal plant only produces them in response to a stress then they might not always be present in cultivated plants. There is a programme in China that aims to discover what the stresses are that stimulate the production of the useful secondary compounds, but these are the exceptions. Most medicinal plants are very happy to be cultivated and produce the molecule that we want, and this is the principle behind an exciting project in the West African country of Ghana.

Case in Point: Ghana—Herbal Medicine and Happy Plants
Ghana has a population of 20 million people living in a country the size of the UK. Eighty percent of the population live in the rural areas, and like 80 percent of the world's population, they depend on herbal medicine for their primary health care. All of the plants used in this herbal medicine are harvested from their habitats. None are cultivated, and many other plants are also collected for industry. It is known that the populations of medicinal plants are declining at the same time that the number of medical practitioners is increasing, and there are now more than 2 million people collecting medicinal plants. The medics are finding that they have to walk further and further to find their plants, and when they do find the plants, they overcollect or use inappropriate collecting methods that are leading to the decline of the medicinal plants and their associated biological diversity.

In the southeast corner of Ghana is the small town of Aburi where a botanic garden started life as a British research station to test the possibility of a wide variety of crops including cocoa, rubber, cotton, and many spices such as vanilla, pepper, cardamom, and nutmeg. The Aburi Medicinal Plant Garden, as the garden is called, was made possible by money donated by the Hong Kong and Shanghai Bank Corporation with the botanical expertise being provided by the World Conservation Monitoring Centre (WCMC) in Cambridge UK and Botanic Gardens Conservation International. The mission of the project is to promote the sustainable use and conservation of the medicinal plants of Ghana, and a guiding principle is that the local community are the best guarantors of the sustainable use of the plants so they must be involved in the design of the scheme.

Fifty acres of degraded forest have been transformed into a model medicinal plant garden. Before this was planted, an ethnobotanical survey was carried out to identify and list the important species and to assess their conservation status. Field trips were organized to collect plants and seeds and data about how they are used. Training sessions were then organized for trainers who then went out to train the practitioners.

The benefits of the project have been tangible from the start. The medical practitioners have been taught how to harvest plants in a sustainable way. Protocols have been established for how to conserve the most important species. The project has increased the capacity of the local people to propagate and cultivate their own plants; and 2.5 million seedlings have been raised and planted in schools, churchyards, and villages. This project has shown that this type of effort can sensitize people to the need to support and sustain a conservation programme. It has made the simple point that when these plants are harvested for their medicinal properties, the future of the plants might be threatened. Most importantly it has given the local people the skills necessary to conserve their plants.

Sustainability, Nurseries, and Forestry

The ability to grow plants is something that gardeners take for granted and yet not every country has a tradition of horticulture. In the Philippines, for example, until the end of the twentieth century, up to 75 percent of exported ornamental plants were harvested from the wild, many of them taken from protected areas. Orchids and members of the arum family were particularly targeted as there is an insatiable demand from collectors in Europe and North America for these plants. There were insufficient nurseries in the Philippines to grow enough plants for the collectors until now. Following the introduction of an accreditation scheme, new nurseries are being established and the trade has been legalized. This is a great example of targets 11 and 13 being satisfied.

On a larger scale, among the most controversial areas in which humans have had an impact on the world's biology is in the destruction of woodlands. Timber can be used for a wide variety of commodities.

We have already considered the pharmaceutical exploitation of paclitaxel in the bark of the Pacific yew. This case and forestry are two sides of the same dynamic: commercial use of limited biological resources.

If you fly into the Seattle-Tacoma International Airport it is difficult not to be impressed (that may not be the right word) by how some of the hillsides around the city have been very neatly and systematically clear-cut of timber; and as you drive down the Ocean Road through the magnificent forests, it is hard to avoid the number of timber trucks taking the trees away. However, if you pay attention you will see many information boards explaining when the woods you are looking at were felled for the first or second time and how what is being felled is a small amount of the annual growth.

With careful shopping you can find timber harvested by sensible foresters. There are many schemes around the world that certificate whether the timber has been harvested from a woodland that is being sustainably managed. The Forest Stewardship Council (FSC) scheme has been in existence for nearly twenty years. It is an international non-governmental organization that recognizes that, while it is not sustainable to cut down an area of woodland the size of the United Kingdom every two years, it is equally unreasonable to deny indigenous peoples the opportunity to make a living from the responsible exploitation of their biological resources.

A simple (non-woody) example of this idea that is working well is found in Western Australia, where florists can apply for a permit to harvest featherflowers (*Verticordia* species) in the national parks. The number of blooms collected is tightly controlled, a way for parks to bring in money and support business. It also means that there is a reason for the local people to support the management of the park. If it works for featherflowers in Western Australia, then why not for timber products? At least 60 million people are totally dependent on forests for all of their needs, and a further 1,600 million people are supported by forest products.

Certification for Sustainably Managed Forests

The Forest Stewardship Council (FSC) certification system has two components. First there is the assessment of the forest and then there is the chain of custody system in which a product can be traced from the moment the tree is felled to the point when the product is purchased, perhaps on the other side of the world, a scheme that now operates in fifty countries. When a woodland has been awarded its certificate, then all of the potential products from that woodland are covered whether they are timber or otherwise, although this does not mean that growing cocaine would become legal and FSC certificated.

The assessment of the forest has ten principles. These cover so many different aspects of woodlands that they serve as a reminder of how many issues come together when one is trying to conserve the world's biology. (The list here is not necessarily in the order of importance.)

1. The management of the woodland must follow the law of the country where it is situated. This includes any international treaties or agreements to which that country is a signatory such as the Convention on Biological Diversity.
2. The long-term ownership of the land must be clearly and legally established.
3. It is recognized that indigenous people have a right to determine how their resources are managed. If this were to include the clear felling of the woodland, then it might not qualify!
4. The FSC insist that the operations in the woods must maintain or better improve the standard of living of the local community.
5. The management of the woodland must look at the widest range of product possible. This helps to make the management more resilient to fluctuations in product values.
6. The management of the woodland must not impact in a negative way on the biological diversity of the area and nor

can it affect the ecosystem services provided by the woodland. These will include water and soil quality. The management plan must recognize the potential fragility of the ecosystem and the role of the woodlands in the landscape.

7. There must be a clearly written, comprehensive management plan. This plan will state what will be extracted, how it will be extracted, and what the impact of the extraction will be. The plan will reflect the size of the operation and the complexity or simplicity of the woodlands being assessed. The plan also has to be updated regularly.

8. The principle of monitoring and assessment of the forest: obviously the monitoring is closely connected to the chain of custody scheme. However, it is vital that the volume of timber or other products extracted from the forest is closely recorded. The monitoring also includes checking that the community is benefiting from the trade as planned and that the profit is not being collected by middlemen.

9. Areas of high conservation value, often in biodiversity hotspots, cannot be damaged by the extraction and if possible should be enhanced in some way. This enhancement could involve the removal of non-native invasive species or active regeneration. Where a forest of high conservation value is being assessed, the precautionary principle is automatically applied, so the answer is no until there is a good reason to say yes.

10. The FSC schemes will consider plantations especially if they are involved from the start. However, the plantation must fulfill all the same criteria as natural forests and woodlands. Plantations can score extra points if they can be shown to take pressure off, and hence enhance the conservation and/or restoration of, natural woodlands.

If the woodland negotiates the assessment process successfully, then the FSC logo can be attached to those products extracted from the woods and to the finished article. This could be anything from a table to a bag of charcoal to a ream of paper. When we built a new staff facility at the Oxford Botanic Garden, it was written into the tender documents that all the timber should be FSC certificated. This was not just because of the environmental benefits derived from the proper management of forests, nor just because the UK has signed and ratified the Convention on Biological Diversity that commits countries to using the world's biology at a sustainable rate. A significant appeal of the FSC scheme is that there is a much better chance that the people felling the trees will have the sort of training and personal protective equipment that UK forestry workers enjoy. There is also a greater chance that the processing factories will enjoy the sort of health and safety standards that we have in this country.

Even without an FSC certificate, though, we can manage woodlands in line with similar principles. In the English bluebell wood at the Harcourt Arboretum, the veteran trees deep in the wood are allowed to die standing up because they become home to different invertebrates from those who will live on the tree once it has fallen over. While the tree is still standing it can also be home to bats and birds. However, on the fringes of the woodland there are oak trees that we can cut to provide us with green oak for our new barn. In fact, when this barn is constructed it will be a focal point for our education programmes at Oxford Botanic Garden, particularly those related to the sustainable use of woodland products in the UK. While we may not have the magnificent woodlands of the US Pacific Northwest, we do have some ancient woods and coppices of hazel (*Corylus avellana*), birch (*Betula pendula*), and sweet chestnut (*Castanea sativa*). Our coppice at the Harcourt Arboretum is already providing us with all the staking material that we need for the borders at the Botanic Garden. All of the brash, bits and pieces of

What *You* Can Do for Biodiversity: Drink Wine, Conserve Plants—Cheers!

You do not have to live in a woodland to use woodland products in your everyday life. Every time that you pull a cork out of a bottle of wine, you can drink the wine in the secure knowledge that by buying that cork (which obviously comes with a bottle of wine that must be drunk or it goes off), you are contributing to the conservation of biological diversity. Cork is harvested from the outside of the main trunk of the cork oak (*Quercus suber*). The outer bark is skillfully removed from the trunk every nine years. You might be wondering why this does not kill the tree because if you take the bark of almost every other tree species the tree dies. The cork oak survives this because it has two layers of bark and the outer one can be removed without damaging the vascular tissue (the plant's plumbing), which is protected by the inner bark. Why does the tree do something as extravagant as making two layers of bark? To protect it from fire which is a regular component of the natural ecosystem in this part of the world. It is an extraordinary sight (as happened in 2003) to see the cork oak woodlands on fire and then to come back in seven months' time to see the oak trees sprouting new shoots.

The oaks live on sloping land that is not suitable for the cultivation of many other crops. The maritime pine (*Pinus pinaster*) can be grown here for the production of turpentine and increasingly eucalyptus for timber. The wild strawberry trees (*Arbutus unedo*) are preserved here and protected because the fruit is used to make a powerful liqueur called medronho. Underneath the oaks, on the poor soil is a diverse mixture of shrubs (dominated by several species of *Cistus* and members of the legume family) with a range of bulbs and climbers. The understory is rich because of a range of factors of which the fire is one and the bark removal is another. These two disturbances help to prevent this community getting settled for very long. It is a strange quirk of the dynamics of natural communities of plants that while high levels of disturbance (such as annual fires or flooding) or low disturbance (as in a temperate conifer woodland) result in lower levels of diversity, intermediate levels of disturbance, such as a fire every eight to twenty years in the cork oak woodland, promote diversity.

If you don't drink wine or any other beverage that comes in a bottle with a cork, then buying linoleum floor covering is a good substitute. Linoleum floor covering may look like plastic but it is actually made from almost 100 percent renewable sources: linseed oil (*Linum usitatissimum*), rosin (from *Pinus* spp.), cork (*Quercus suber*), very fine sawdust (known technically as wood floor made from hardwoods), calcium carbonate (from rocks), and some natural fibres in the form of hessian (burlap) made from jute (*Conchorus* spp.) or sisal (*Agave sisalana*) as the backing. Whatever use the cork is put to, the production systems in Spain and Portugal make this crop one of the best for the other organisms in this ecosystem.

leftover wood, from the coppice and from other work in the arboretum is now used in the charcoal kiln. Charcoal-making is an art and a skill; it involves sleeping next to the kiln and checking the temperature endlessly (all with the hope that our charcoal will be used in our barbecues come summer). When the kiln first arrived it looked like a shiny sputnik; now it is burnt and rusty and looks the part. What this shows is that even as quintessential a feature of the countryside as a spring woodland in flower can have a commercial value, but that the exploitation of that commercial value does not have to destroy the woodland. In fact, it may even pay for its maintenance and therefore its survival.

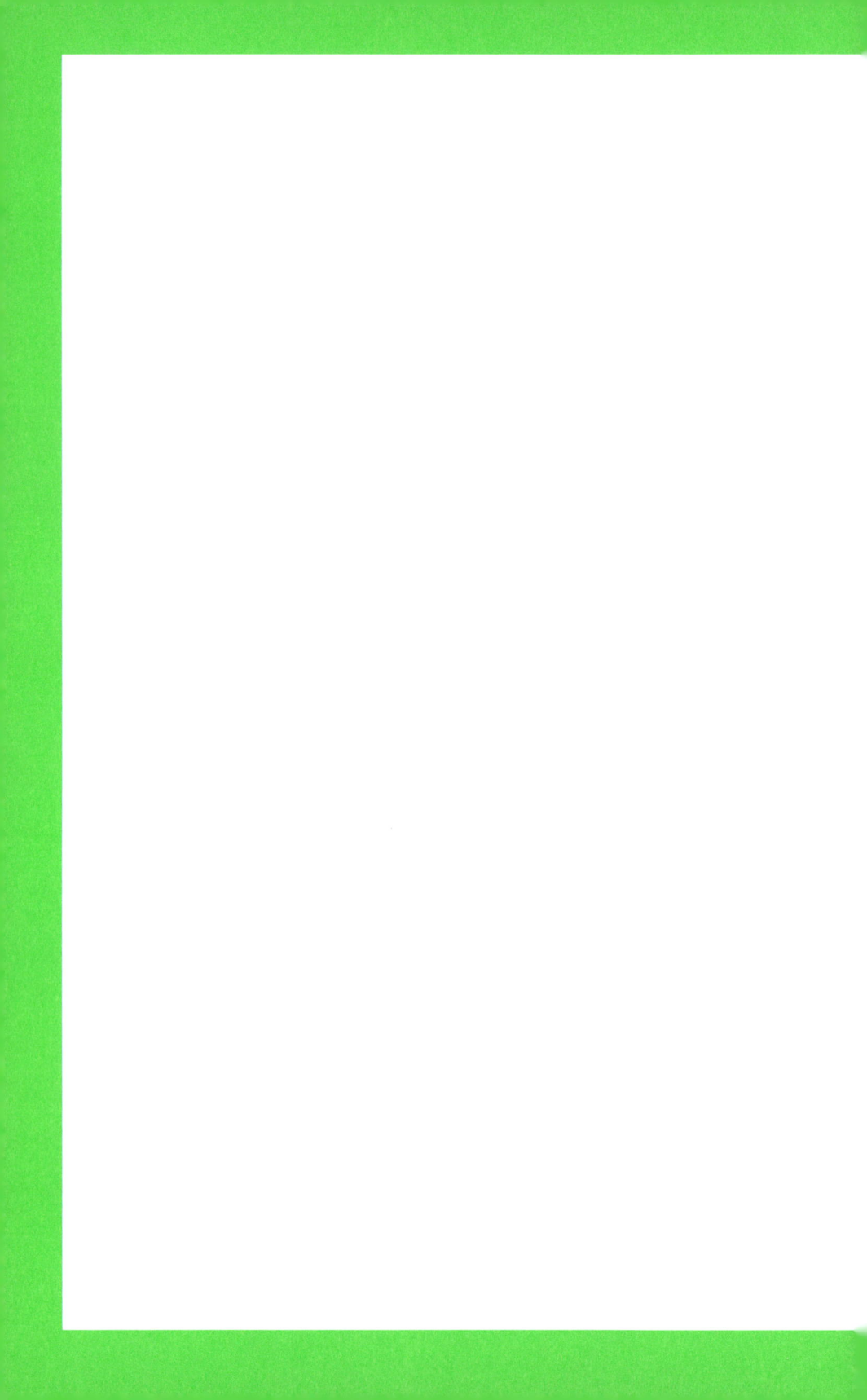

PART FOUR

What Can You Do? Partnership and Practice in Plant Conservation

No man, nor woman, is an island and we all can, and we all should, behave in a way to reduce our personal impact on the world's finite biologically produced resources. We do not have to become hair-shirted Puritans. We just have to be sensible and not selfish. However, in addition to a few modifications in our day-to-day lives, we can go further and give our time to the cause.

7 Gardeners Getting Involved

It could be said that plant conservation is all about the activities and thinking of living, playing, working people—it is about what we do and how well we can persuade and be persuaded that Earth's capacity to provide and sustain our human well-being is linked to the well-being of Earth's plants. The urgency of this knowledge, and the necessary mission intrinsic to it, is expressed by the Global Strategy for Plant Conservation's 2020 vision: "Without plants, there is no life. The functioning of the planet, and our survival, depends on plants."

And the strategy that has been outlined is, from the get-go, designed to make this work as an engagement at several operational levels, "national, regional, and global—to understand, conserve and use sustainably the world's immense wealth of plant diversity whilst promoting awareness and building the necessary capacities for its implementation." Taking this one step beyond, and yet closer to each of us, we can consider research by geneticist David Chamovitz, whose interest in a plant's use of light for its growth led him to identify "plant-specific" genes that are also in our human DNA. Perhaps understanding our commonalities can highlight our interrelated existence—and our interrelated, interdependent survival. The organisms that help to support our human existence on Earth are in a sense our relatives. So maybe the proverb "You scratch my back, I'll scratch yours" is not so much anthropomorphized as it may seem.

I want to address just one question in this final chapter: what can we do? What on earth can we do in kind for the plant organisms that we depend on, and which in turn depend on our right thinking for their survival? Getting involved in plant conservation requires a wide variety of skills and knowledge: field botanists with the ability to identify plants and create checklists of existing and threatened species, managers for nature reserves, custodians for seed-bank collections, scientists who can design research projects and execute programmes to work toward and achieve successful conservation outcomes, and professional and lay teachers. There are many career-sized contributions that can be made, and many routes into these careers; and there are many ways in which trained and highly motivated volunteers can be involved in conservation goals and programmes—all of which we can examine here by way of the 2020 conservation mission to promote plant conservation work at home and abroad.

> **2020 STRATEGY**
> **TARGETS 13** Maintain and conserve indigenous and local knowledge associated with plant resources
> **TARGETS 14** Communicate the importance of plant diversity
> **TARGETS 15** Train enough people
> **TARGETS 16** Establish or strengthen institutions and plant conservation networks to achieve the targets

International Cooperation: Global Seed Collections

In addition to the Svalbard Global Seed Vault there are some major plant gene banks around the world which house a selection of important gene reserves that are more specifically valuable to the regions in which they reside. It is interesting to note that the current major areas of crop production are a long way from where the crops originated. The map on page 212 shows where we should look for useful new genes.

MEXICO: INTERNATIONAL MAIZE AND WHEAT IMPROVEMENT CENTRE (CIMMYT)

Probably the largest is in Mexico at the CIMMYT headquarters there. The collection of maize cultivars and landraces numbers more than 27,000, plus samples of the wild relatives of maize including not only

Food origins and production

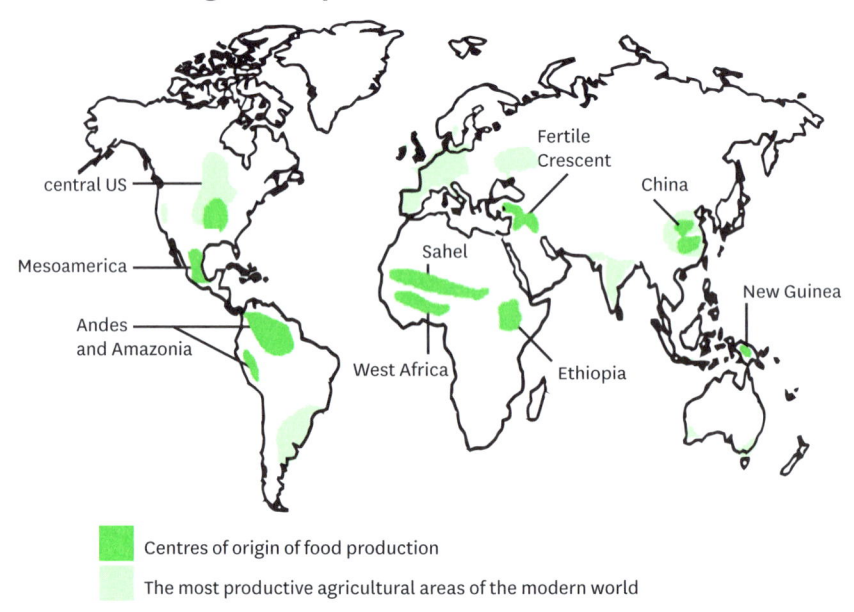

- central US
- Mesoamerica
- Andes and Amazonia
- Fertile Crescent
- Sahel
- West Africa
- Ethiopia
- China
- New Guinea

■ Centres of origin of food production
□ The most productive agricultural areas of the modern world

the teosinte from which it has been bred but also *Tripsacum*. Maize is the most important crop in not only Latin America where it first arose, but also in Sub-Saharan Africa. However, the maize collection pales in comparison to their wheat collection of more than 150,000 collections. These have been sent from more than one hundred countries because wheat grows over a huge range of different conditions, such is the diversity of the plants that we call wheat. The crosses performed at CIMMYT are then supplied for trials around the world and the results are returned for analysis.

PHILIPPINES: INTERNATIONAL RICE RESEARCH INSTITUTE (IRRI)
Their seed bank has more than 113,000 types of rice, plus collections from twenty-four wild species of rice including the two most widely domesticated, Asian rice (*Oryza sativa*) and African rice (*Oryza glaberrima*). There are in fact two seed banks at IRRI: the active collection

kept at 2–4°C (36–39°F) from which withdrawals are regularly made and the long-term base collection, where the seeds are kept at -20°C (-4°F). Oxford Botanic Garden has had small quantities of seeds from IRRI to grow in our tropical house. In this way we can show local school children where their breakfast cereals come from.

COLOMBIA: INTERNATIONAL CENTRE FOR TROPICAL AGRICULTURE (CIAT)

Here there are three gene banks. In the first they keep the most diverse collection of beans in world, with more than 36,000 collections of wild species and cultivated varieties of more than forty-four of the sixty species of *Phaseolus* that have been gathered in 109 countries. Nearly 2,000 of the collections are from wild populations that may have genes for resistance to pests, diseases, and environmental stresses such as flood and drought. This collection represents the diversity of forms found in the beans from shrubs to climbers. The climbing beans are particularly important in mixed production systems with maize. By the end of 2011 423,303 samples had been distributed from this collection to institutions in 107 countries.

The second collection at CIAT is of cassava (*Manihot esculenta*). This is one of the oldest domesticated crops, believed to have been first grown in Brazil ten thousand years ago at the same time that wheat was being domesticated in Eurasia. Despite being domesticated in South America, cassava is now most widely grown in Africa with Nigeria the largest grower. It is the third most important starch-producing crop in the tropics with a calorific yield per acre greater than that of any of the big three crops, and yet it is almost unknown in temperate regions. It should be said that proper cooking is required to remove the toxic substances in cassava. Proper cooking here means soaking, heating, or fermenting.

A problem with cassava is that if the tubers are damaged, the plant tries to heal the damage and in the process makes the tuber useless as food. This has be solved by introducing genes from the Texas species

Manihot walkerae (Walker's manihot, no relation). The *Manihot* gene bank differs from those described above because it is not just a seed bank but also a tuber bank. The tubers grow at the base of a shrubby tree. The CIAT cassava collection has 883 different forms of the one-third of the ninety-nine species of *Manihot*. It also has nearly six thousand cultivated varieties (or clones) of *Manihot esculenta* from twenty-eight countries. It is a sign of the success of the CGIAR network that sixty-nine countries have received plants from CIAT. To date more that 33,000 samples have been distributed. One of the problems with vegetatively propagated crops is that a disease is more likely to be transmitted from generation to generation. All the materials supplied by CIAT for breeding are certified free from three viruses (cassava common mosaic virus, cassava virus X, and frog skin disease). This has been achieved through the same aseptic tissue culture techniques used in some commercial horticulture nurseries.

The third gene bank collection at CIAT is of a group of plants defined by their function on farms—the forage crops. These are simply any plant that animals will munch. The group includes a wide variety of growth forms from annuals through herbaceous perennials to shrubs and even trees. There are more than 23,000 accessions in this bank from more than 700 species in more that 120 genera from more than 72 countries. These are mostly grasses and legumes (the Poaceae and Fabaceae respectively). More than half of the collection was collected in sixteen years from 1977 in seventy-five expeditions to forty-one countries. In an age of national conflict and international brewhaha (and brouhaha), the international collaboration on the area of agricultural research is inspirational and gives one hope for the future of *Homo sapiens*. In the three decades to 2011 more than 87,000 samples were supplied to institutions in more than 100 countries. One interesting difference between forage crops and crops for direct human consumption is that forage crops are being bred that are resistant to flooding as well as drought. This will enable grazing on wetter regions that are currently no-go areas for livestock farmers.

NIGERIA: INTERNATIONAL INSTITUTE FOR TROPICAL AGRICULTURE (IITA)

In this African country, IITA is looking after the global gene bank for cowpeas (*Vigna unguiculata*). This is a legume and so is good for inter-cropping on poor soils. It is also very good for stabilizing fragile soils and reducing erosion and loss of topsoil. This is a crop for the future and to date the IITA gene bank has 15,122 accessions from 88 countries. This compares interestingly with the pea gene bank at the John Innes Centre at Norwich, UK, which holds 3,450 accessions of garden peas (*Pisum sativum*). These are mixture of wild plants, landraces, and cultivars.

IITA has recently embarked on a new gene bank for yams with the initial target of three thousand accessions. This project is important because yams are part of the staple diet of 60 million people. It became even more urgent following a fire at a large collection of yam varieties in Togo, West Africa. Like cassava, yam is a vegetable crop that has to be stored in fields but in the future cryopreservation at -196°c will be used. Obviously this type of high-tech storage is beyond the economic resources of most of the countries where yams grow. So far there are 3,200 yam accessions with 847 from Benin. The Ivory Coast plans to send another 5,500 varieties.

UNITED STATES: US DEPARTMENT OF AGRICULTURE

In 1980 the USDA established the National Plant Germplasm System (NPGS). Germplasm is just another word for a bank of material from which plants can be propagated. The NPGS was established specifically for the conservation of clonally propagated fruit and nut crops, and for conserving some of the wild relatives. Fruits and nuts cover a vast number of crops ranging from pecans to pineapples and from cranberries to cocoa. It should also be pointed out, before pen is put to paper by botanists reading this chapter, that nuts are a type of fruit.

There are eight centres in all. The institutes at Brownwood in Texas, Corvallis in Oregon, Davis in California, and Geneva in New York State are responsible for the temperate fruits and nuts. The institutes at Hilo on Hawaii, Miami in Florida, Mayaguez in Puerto Rico, and Riverside in California look after tropical and semi-tropical fruits and nuts. More than three decades later these are now all internationally recognized as centres of expertise in the crops that they protect.

Together the eight NPGS institutes hold more than 30,000 different clones from 1,600 different fruits. As so often happens with ideas like the NPGS, their work and scope widens beyond the original vision of supplying genes for crop improvement. The centres have become places for conserving rare species and landraces, understanding plant genetics, storing historical data, and educating politicians and the public alike.

UNITED KINGDOM: NATIONAL FRUIT COLLECTION AT BROGDALE IN KENT

This facility holds probably the best collection of apple trees anywhere in the world. I have already mentioned the pea collection at Norwich, but there are also world-class collections of onions, carrots, and brassicas at Warwick. The Scottish Crop Research Institute at Invergowrie holds the Commonwealth Potato Collection of 1,500 accessions from three different species of *Solanum*.

Regional Networks and Local Know-How: Restoration Ecology

A problem facing conservation scientists is diversity itself in that every species is different in its requirements, so there are a multitude of reasons why a species may decline, and thus a multitude of conservation solutions. Take, for example, three threatened North American species: *Cirsium pitcheri* (Pitcher's thistle), *Asclepias meadii* (Mead's milkweed) and *Platanthera leucophaea* (eastern prairie fringed orchid). These species present three very different problems, and thus solutions. The thistle grows for three to five years, flowers, and dies; the milkweed is a long-lived perennial that is shy to produce seeds; and the orchid is a short-lived perennial plant with a half-life of just three years and requires continuous reseeding for the population to be maintained. The cost of saving *Platanthera leucophaea* has been estimated at $5,315,000. The table on pages 218–219 displays, for three very different plants, their very different conservation problems and conservation solutions.

Borneo is the only island in the world to consist of three countries: Brunei, Indonesia, and Malaysia. (This will of course change when Scotland and Wales are given independence from England.)

Borneo is a botanical treasure trove. Sadly it has suffered in recent years from two different activities. First, there is illegal logging for timber where just the biggest and most valuable trees are felled and quickly removed. Second, there is the clearance of all vegetation (and animals) in preparation for the planting of oil palm trees. Since 2000 there has been a very significant reduction of 70 percent in the volume of illegal logging.

However, it would be better for the native plants and animals if more effort could be put into preventing the clearance for palm oil because biodiversity can recover after logging much better than after clearance for palm oil. For example, after just two rounds of logging 70 percent of the bird species returned to the regrown woodlands as opposed to just 30 percent living in the plantations.

In the middle of Borneo is a nature reserve the size of the United Kingdom known as the Heart of Borneo area. The $1 billion funding for the reserve came from the Norwegian government as compensation for not extracting materials. This is an act of pure of altruistic charity on the part of the citizens of Norway, extraordinary generosity based on sound scientific research. The research has shown that while some

Three Different Recovery Scenarios for Three Threatened US Species

SPECIES	***Cirsium pitcheri*** **(Pitcher's thistle)**
HABITAT	Endemic to Lake Michigan foredunes
LIFE HISTORY	Flowers after 3–5 years and dies
BREEDING SYSTEM	Self-compatible, pollinated by many insects
GENETICS	Low diversity
RESTORATION STRATEGY	Add new plants to populations
RESEARCH NEEDS	Assess different populations for germination success

habitats recover from disturbance such as illegal logging, most forms of forest degradation have an overwhelmingly detrimental effect on tropical biodiversity. This means that when it comes to maintaining tropical biodiversity there is no substitute for primary, undisturbed, virgin forest. However, we do not yet live in Utopia and so there are already many altered habitats that require long-term management following ecological restoration.

Restoration ecology is a growing discipline. When it is well done, then restoration consistently enhances biodiversity and ecosystem services, even if it is unlikely to lead to a full recovery of the biodiversity and ecosystem services found in undisturbed systems. In all restorations there is going to be a balance to be struck between the complexity of the restored system and economic reality.

If one orchid species is going to cost more than $5 million, think how much an entire landscape is going to cost. There is little doubt, however, that *preventing* damage is more cost effective than trying to

Asclepias meadii (Mead's milkweed)	*Platanthera leucophaea* (eastern prairie fringed orchid)
Dry Midwest prairies and glades	Established prairies, sedge meadows and fens
Long-lived perennial but poor seedling establishment	Short-lived perennial, half-life of three years, requiring a fungus in roots
Self-incompatible; requires genetically different individuals for successful pollination	Must be pollinated by hawk-moths; small populations tend to be inbred
High diversity between populations but little diversity within populations	Moderate genetic diversity between populations
Increase genetic diversity within populations and implement fire management	Hand pollination in the absence of the hawk-moths and hand sowing
Assess effects of outbreeding on genetic diversity	Assess success of hand pollination. Culture the symbiotic fungus

repair the damage. This is where plant conservation and species recovery come into play, with seed banks one means to this end. And there is a spectacular example of just how beneficial seed collecting can be in the UK, where *Bromus interruptus* has been brought back from being extinct. Oftentimes, it takes only one person to make a difference.

To give a thorough and instructive account of how a species recovery programme works in reality, I am going to describe in detail one project that as of this writing is in various stages, both completed and ongoing. One recurrent feature in this and similar conservation projects—and clearly galvanizing this project—is simply how few people need to be involved and how quickly a few people, in this case five women, can save a species from extinction. This project began over twenty years ago here in Oxford at the Botanic Garden.

continued on page 222

Case in Point: *Bromus interruptus*, Species Interrupted *and* Recovered

Bromus interruptus is a tall, annual-biennial grass that was first recorded in 1849 at Odsey in Cambridgeshire, UK. It is believed to have been a new species that arose as a mutant form of the soft brome (*Bromus hordeaceus*), making it one of very few species endemic to the UK. It spread quickly through its habitat of arable fields, particularly of legume crops such as clover and sainfoin (*Onobrychis viciifolia*), reaching a peak in the 1920s. It then went into a decline, perhaps as a result of the rise of the internal combustion engine and the decline in horse-drawn carriages and thus a reduction in the need for horse fodder such as sainfoin. The intensification of agriculture also may have played a part in its decline. It does not help that the seeds appear to be short-lived in the seed bank. The species was last seen in the wild at Pampisford, also in Cambridgeshire, in 1972, and by the end of the twentieth century this species was generally thought to be extinct in the wild.

Fortunately seeds had been collected by Philip Smith, a grass botanist from Edinburgh University, in 1963. He kept the plants going at his home, and in 1979 distributed seeds to friends and colleagues at the Botanic Society of the British Isles. Plants were also raised and cultivated at the Royal Botanic Gardens in Edinburgh and Kew. Seeds were added to the Millennium Seed Bank because the first target of the MSBP was to have all 1,500 UK native plant species safely stored in the freezer by 31 December 1999.

By the time that there were 62,000 seeds in the MSB, there was sufficient material to carry out an assessment of the genetic diversity of the population. There were concerns that because all the plants had resulted from the plants collected by Philip Smith, there would be too little diversity to reestablish a viable population. However, genetic analysis carried out at RBG Kew revealed that everything was fine and that a reintroduction into the Cambridgeshire countryside should be undertaken.

This was important, not only because of its endemic status, but because it had only declined as a result of changes in agricultural techniques and through no fault of its own.

So in February 2003 a piece of land on the margin of an arable field at Whittlesford south of Cambridge was ploughed, harrowed, and sown with seeds from the MSB. Germination was good and by late August there were many flowering and, more importantly, fruiting plants. The seeds from these plants were allowed to fall into the soil, and by Christmas 2003 seedlings were visible. These survived the winter and by July 2004 the second generation was well established. Importantly for the farmer who kindly supplied the land, there was no evidence of this species invading the rest of the field. It did seem that some cultivation of the field margin would be necessary to reduce competition from other plant species and to give the seeds some clean soil in which to germinate.

Following the success of the second generation at Whittlesford, it was decided to sow at a second site, this time in Oxfordshire on a former arable field next to the National Nature Reserve at Aston Rowant. This field was attractive to the projects because it was on an organic farm where the practices more closely resembled those in the nineteenth century. The field was ploughed (12 August 2004), harrowed two weeks later, sown by hand the next day, and then raked in. Germination and subsequent flowering were so successful that new seeds could be added to the seed bank in 2005, and the species is still present at Aston Rowant. Philip Smith died in 2004 at the age of just sixty-three, but he did live long enough to see the species recovery programme enter its final stage.

This story is being repeated all over the world using different species. We have seen the US example of three threatened North American species, *Cirsium pitcheri* (Pitcher's thistle), *Asclepias meadii* (Mead's milkweed), and *Platanthera leucophaea* (eastern prairie fringed orchid). These plants are all different and so are the programmes for their survival, but the programs illustrate three important points. First, these successful species recovery projects only happen because individuals choose to get involved and many of them work in gardens or are gardeners. The UK project has involved Tim Upson from Cambridge University Botanic Garden; Ian Turner from Paignton Zoo and Botanic Garden who bulked up the seed supplies; Ron Porley and other English Nature Staff at Aston Rowant; Robert Holme and Ashley Arbon, the farmers in Oxfordshire and Cambridgeshire; Michael Fay and colleagues at the Millennium Seed Bank; and finally Richard Wilford and Stewart Henchie (inventor of the bicycle pump pollinator for cycads) from the RBG Kew. Second, the projects show that plants that have become extinct in the wild can be reestablished. Third, they show clearly that seed banks lie right at the hub of species recovery programmes and plant conservation.

continued from page 219

The Oxford Botanic Garden is home to a wonderful collection of euphorbias. This was developed in the late 1970s and early 1980s to support the teaching work of David Mabberley, author of the classic *Mabberley's Plant-book*. David used the many diverse species of euphorbia to demonstrate how species in a genus can become diverse vegetatively while retaining the same flower structure. Within the genus *Euphorbia* there are two thousand species, and while some of these are small annual herbs that we think of as garden weeds, some are succulent trees that look for all the world like cacti until they flower. In 1979 the National Council for the Conservation of Plants and Gardens (NCCPG) was founded in the UK. This less-than-snappy title has now been changed to Plant Heritage. While the name has changed, the aims have not; at its heart is the National Plant Collections Scheme wherein gardens or rather gardeners apply to have their collection of a particular genus or other group of plants designated as a national collection.

So, for example, at Painshill Park in Surrey, England, you can see the John Bartram Heritage Collection of woody plants that were sent to this country in Bartram's five guinea boxes in the eighteenth century. Oxford applied for national collection status for its euphorbias, which was granted in 1985.

One responsibility of a national collection holder is to pay particular attention to those species that are either rare in cultivation or threatened in their natural habitat. One such euphorbia is *Euphorbia stygiana*, which grows on the Azores in the middle of the Atlantic Ocean and nowhere else, and is therefore endemic to the Azores. All species that are endemic to ocean islands are automatically vulnerable to extinction because of a number of factors—in particular, the risks posed by non-native species and the problems that can result from small population numbers and inbreeding depression. Island populations are particularly vulnerable to non-native species because, as Darwin observed, "Isolation probably acts efficiently in checking the migration of better adapted organisms after any physical change such as climate or elevation of the land." This means that the species on islands are not constantly being forced to improve by incomers. The constant immigration of competitors that occurs on the mainland does not happen on oceanic islands because of their isolation. In a way they have a quieter life. The Azores rose out of the ocean just over eight million years ago and all the organisms there have evolved in glorious isolation, and yet within a decade a non-native invasive species could spoil things badly.

The Portuguese know this of course, and there are programmes on the Azores, led by Luis Silva at the University of the Azores, to ensure that this species does not die out there. However, as insurance policies are a good idea in all of life, so in the 1990s an *ex situ* species recovery programme was initiated.

The first thing that we wanted to know was whether we could grow this plant outside its origins, here in Oxford. Even if its future was not guaranteed in the wild, it was not sustainable for us to grow this plant under glass where we would have to burn fossil fuels to keep the plants alive. The climate of the Azores is best described as mild temperate with average air temperature between 11°c and 26°c (52°f–79°f) and the possibility of rain on any day of the year with average precipitation of over 42 inches per year. The climate in Oxford is very different from that of the Azores with minimum temperatures well below freezing and around 24 inches of rain each year. But never forget what Darwin wrote in *Origin of Species*: "The degree of adaptation of species to the climates under which they live is often overrated. We may infer this from our frequent inability to predict whether or not an imported plant will endure our climate." This could not be more true for *Euphorbia stygiana*, which has survived temperatures as low as -15°c (5°f) and many weeks without any rainfall. So hurdle number one was cleared and we knew that *Euphorbia stygiana* can grow very well in Oxford. It was also apparent that it makes a handsome garden plant. While this should not influence our decision whether to grow a plant, it is undeniably true that attractive plants are more likely to be grown by gardeners than dull and boring, botanically interesting species. ("Botanically interesting" is perhaps the most damning thing that you can say about a plant.)

So we were growing a small number of plants raised from the seeds we were sent. These plants were reluctant to flower, so that no seeds were set in the first few years. This was disappointing because the first target for this project was to get this species growing in two hundred gardens in Britain and Ireland. Repeated attempts to propagate this from cuttings failed despite cuttings from other euphorbias being easy to strike. Clare Kelly, the Oxford garden's propagator, who could root a broom handle, persevered and eventually discovered a technique whereby if she dipped the bottom of the cuttings in charcoal to stop the bleeding sap and then dipped them in hormone rooting gel, the cuttings would root. These cuttings were then put into coarse horticultural sand and into the heated propagating frame. The sand was warmed to 20°c while the top of the cuttings was regularly misted. After six weeks the roots had formed; and after growing them on for a few months, we had plants that we could give away.

We did not want to be the only garden growing these precious plants because if we killed ours, or they died for other reasons, all the work to date would have been wasted. Before plants were sent out, particularly to gardens on the west coast or Ireland where the conditions are closer to those found on the Azores than the conditions in Oxford, we did consider whether this species might become invasive. While there are no well-known examples of oceanic island endemics becoming invasive elsewhere and no well-known examples of threatened species becoming invasive, the assessment had to be carried out. Two things convinced me that *Euphorbia stygiana* was a low risk. Firstly, although the plants in the Botanic Garden were now flowering and setting seeds, there were no observed self-sown seedlings. This later became a problem as we considered earlier in our discussion of the risks of *ex situ* propagation. Secondly, the plants could easily be killed by cutting them off just below ground level. However, I have repeatedly refused requests to send seeds of this species to New Zealand because not only would this be against New Zealand law, it would also be unwise given the proven vulnerability of New Zealand to invasions.

The next target was to make the species available through the nursery trade and Marina Christopher of Phoenix Perennial Plants was the first to offer the plant. It is now listed by more than a dozen nurseries in the UK, and it has appeared at the London Chelsea Flower Show—the highest accolade for any plant. So we had achieved the basic insurance for the future of the species in cultivation *ex situ*, but there was much left to do. The next stage was to improve the success of our propagation of this species from seed. The ripe fruits containing mature seeds were harvested in July-August and stored in open paper bags on the potting shed shelves until January. By this time the seedpods had dried and opened and the relatively large seeds (3–4 mm long and 2–3 mm wide) were easily separated from the remains of the fruit. The seeds were sown in the propagation greenhouse and more than 90 percent of them would germinate. However, we would subsequently lose up to 75 percent of the seedlings to a mixture of disease (mildew) and herbivores (slugs).

The next person to get involved in the project was Susan MacBurney, a Oxford biology undergraduate from Somerville College. For her second-year project, Susan looked at drawing up a seed propagation protocol for *Euphorbia stygiana*. Susan used two types of seed compost; a loam- (or soil-) based and a peat-based compost. Seeds were sown individually in two-inch pots. This was partly to make counting the failures more easy and partly because euphorbias resent root disturbance and have brittle fibrous roots. As expected the seedlings sown into peat-based compost grew quicker.

When the seedlings were big enough to pot on, half of those raised in peat-based seed compost went into a peat-based potting compost. The other half went into a loam-based potting compost. Similarly, half of the seedlings raised in loam-based seed compost were potted on into a peat-based potting compost. The other half went into a loam-based potting compost. Again those seedlings in peat-based composts grew away faster but after two years the differences became negligible. Susan was able to control the downy mildew by keeping the seedlings well ventilated, and controlled the thrips by using a predatory mite. Slugs were controlled by vigilance. At the end of Susan's project we had a blueprint for the seed propagation of *Euphorbia stygiana* that enabled us to get eighty-five flowering plants from every one hundred seeds sown.

The next thing we wanted to know was how to store the seeds. Could we leave them in a paper envelope in the seed drawers in the potting shed or should we dry and freeze them? Research carried out at the Millennium Seed Bank Project in Sussex, England, has shown that euphorbias do have orthodox seeds. Observations and experiments carried out in Oxford by Julia Jeans, another biology undergraduate, showed clearly that storage at room temperature was not a good idea because after two years nearly all the seeds were dead. We also found that if you do not control the mice in the seed store, they would eat the seeds.

Julia also followed up another observation made by the garden staff. They had noticed that despite the viability of at least 90 percent of the seeds produced by the plants, there was no flush of seedlings underneath the parent plants. The fact that such a high proportion of the seeds are viable means that there is no problem with the pollination of this Azorian species in England. This was not unexpected because euphorbias do not have specialized flowers. There are no adaptations to restrict pollination to just small number of pollinators. Put bluntly, euphorbias are completely relaxed about who moves their pollen around. Flies, wasps, bees, ants, and even snails and birds have been recorded visiting the flowers. It also became apparent that *Euphorbia stygiana* is self-compatible, and a plant can produce viable seeds using its own pollen. Self-compatibility is a useful trait because it is the only way a lone plant can guarantee its propagation.

Julia demonstrated that the fresh seeds were in fact dormant and would not germinate until the following spring, six or seven months later. Dormancy means that viable seeds will not germinate even if the soil conditions are correct. This was not expected. Why would seeds from a plant growing on the Azores not germinate straight off the plant? The mild and moist conditions of the Azores would appear to be perfectly good enough for young seedlings. This innate dormancy is a classic adaptation found in plants from a Mediterranean-type environment that want to avoid germinating at the beginning of a long, hot, dry, summer. Did this mean that the seeds that colonized the Azores originated from Iberia or the Canary Islands where dry summers can be found? This was to be expected because as Darwin tells us "The most striking and important fact for us in regard to the inhabitants of islands, is their affinity to those of the nearest mainland, without being actually the same species."

We seemed to be very nearly at our goal of establishing, within the Botanic Garden, a self-propagating population of *Euphorbia stygiana*, but there was still the final problem to be overcome. Susan's work had given us many plants that we could plant out in a corner of the garden, but why were there no self-sown seedlings under the parent plants? Up stepped the fifth woman in this story, Helen Humphreys, another biology undergraduate. Helen started her project by testing whether the soil under the parents contained something, perhaps secreted by the parent plants' roots. This is known as allelopathy and is often put forward as an explanation for the failure of seedlings to grow, but I do not believe that it is as widespread as claimed. It is a good example of the anthropomorphizing of plants. To some parents the idea of their children staying close to them for their entire lives is not attractive. This cannot be true for most plants because most plants drop their seed under the canopy of their leaves.

Whatever the truth may be about allelopathy, it is not an explanation here. Helen sowed two hundred seeds underneath the parent plants and sowed two hundred seeds in a greenhouse using the soil from under the same plants. The seeds sown under glass germinated exactly as expected; more than 90 percent came up as seedlings. On the other hand, none of the seeds sown outside grew into seedlings. Other species of *Euphorbia* came up as weeds under *Euphorbia stygiana*, but not one of them was *E. stygiana*. Something appeared to be preventing germination outside, and when Helen inspected the soil under the parent plants carefully she discovered the remains of seeds. She found empty seeds that had been bitten in half and the centre scooped out.

There had been reports from others gardeners growing *Euphorbia stygiana* that they had seen mice climbing up their plants and eating the seeds fresh out of the fruits. Were Oxford mice doing the same thing? Another perpetrator of this crime might have been ants taking the seeds away. This is normal behaviour for ants and is generally encouraged by euphorbias. They produce, on the outside of the seed, a relatively small lump of fat called an elaiosome which is taken back to the ants' nest with the seed still attached. The elaiosome is removed and eaten and the seed discarded, but it is in effect sown by the ants. Helen sat and watched to see who was stealing and eating the seeds. It was not ants. Nor was it mice. It was birds. Occasionally European robins (*Erithacus rubecula*) would take the seeds, but the most common thieves were wrens (*Troglodytes troglodytes*). The irony of this is that although wrens can be seen taking seeds and other human gifts from feeders, they are predominantly insectivores. We seemed to have acquired some vegetarian wrens.

Helen thought that might not be the whole answer because the many other species of *Euphorbia* in the collection seemed to be able to seed around and some of these produced seeds similar to those of *Euphorbia stygiana* and some were bigger. Leaving no experimental stone unturned, Helen carried out a consumer survey of the wrens. She gave them trays of seeds containing a mixture of ten different species and then she put out ten trays containing seeds from just one of the species. When presented with the mixture of ten species, the wrens would pick out just the seeds of *Euphorbia stygiana*. When given ten different trays, they would preferentially feed from the tray of *Euphorbia stygiana*. It appears that when given a choice, nine out of ten wrens prefer *Euphorbia stygiana* to any other euphorbia and as Sod's law would have it, the wrens prefer the threatened species.

All is not lost. A few self-sown seedlings have emerged next to rocks on the Rock Garden in the Botanic Garden. It seems that if the seeds can slip into the soil out of the reach of the birds' beaks, then they are safe. A mulch of coarse stone, like an alpine scree, will be enough to enable this species to survive *ex situ*.

HABITAT RESTORATION

There are many reasons why a habitat may have been altered and so there are many different types of habitat restoration projects. Habitats may be changed for agriculture and other economic purposes, or by invasive non-native species, or by unsustainable extraction. As a result

continued on page 234

Conservation Ideology or Conservation Economics— Or Both?

Reasons for habitat destruction are varied, including being driven by economics. Many conservation practitioners have tried to ignore this, preferring to remain unsullied by the filthy lucre. This naivety resulted in the failure of projects because short-term economics normally trumps the prospect of longer-term benefits. If, however, there can be short-term economic benefit from a restoration project, then that will make the local people more supportive of the work.

China

In southern China, where clearance of the woodlands has been blamed for the extreme weather events of 2008, forests are being replaced by eucalyptus, rubber, and oil palm plantations. The drive to grow rubber is very powerful: between 1988 and 2003, there was a ten-fold increase in income for rubber farmers; between 1976 and 2003, rubber expanded ten-fold and the tropical montane forest shrank by 80 percent. And the establishment of the rubber plantations has forced villages to be moved—the plantations now cover 300,000 hectares (720,000 acres) and are draining water from village wells because surface water run-off has tripled and soil erosion has increased by forty-five times. Despite this expansion, it is estimated that by 2020 there still will be a 10 percent underproduction of rubber unless more is planted. An alternative production system is being trialed by scientists to ensure a long-term income and establish provisions for ecosystem services.

The major species for this production system is *Cunninghamia lanceolata* (Chinese fir), but there are in all twenty hardwood timber species.

These species are a mixture of pioneer through mid- to terminal succession trees, each with different ecological roles, from soil formation to providing food for birds. The soil under this vegetation is richer and better at holding water than plantations, and it is more resilient to pests and diseases. The selective logging of the trees is more expensive than clear felling plantations, but there is a premium price for these certified sustainable hardwoods. The result of these projects is a healthy forest ecosystem that is a reasonable facsimile of natural vegetation in China. The underproduction of rubber can be satisfied by plantations elsewhere in Asia.

Restoration ecology is not a precise science. The 28 million hectares of plantations created in China between 2001 and 2007 can provide ecosystem services and have a role in fauna conservation if they are part of a carefully designed mosaic of landscapes. In some cases doing nothing and leaving nature to its own devices has been more successful than aggressive restoration programmes. Biology is never black and white.

South Africa
The problem here has been caused by invasive species and in particular *Acacia saligna* (Port Jackson willow). This and other non-native species currently take 7 percent of South Africa's rainfall, and this will rise to 20 percent if left unchecked. Working for Water is an organization with more than three hundred projects costing more than $100 million each year, employing more than 29,000 people. In the past fifteen years, these projects have cleared one million hectares (2.4 million acres) of non-native plant species. Part of the weaponry has been seventy-five imported insect species that have been used to control

forty-five invasive species. Sadly, these million hectares are just 10 percent of the invaded area, which currently consumes 3.3 billion cubic metres of water each year. However, the cost of clearing the invasive species is less that building water supply systems such as dams and reservoirs. Once the non-native species are cleared, then the restoration can proceed. There have been successes already. For example, the Ceres stream damselfly and the Cape bluet dragonfly have been taken off the extinct species list following invasive clearance and pond restoration.

Indonesia

Following the establishment of democracy in Indonesia, nongovernmental organizations have been able to start restoring 98,000 hectares of heavily logged forest. The goal is to create sustainable livelihoods for local communities, so planting five million trees has started. These trees have been raised by Indonesian gardeners in the community tree nursery, and already a Sumatran tiger has been seen with cubs in the young woodland. This and the other projects in Indonesia, such as the Harapan Forest project in lower Sumatra, have shown that success depends on a number of factors. The habitats should be as large as possible. The restored habitat will need continued maintenance. Areas should be connected rather than isolated from each other. The local community must be involved, and sustainable, commercial extraction must be permitted.

Australia

In the southwest corner of Australia in the state of Western Australia, the inspirational work of Kingsley Dixon (professor at the University of Western Australia and one of the greatest living biologists) and his colleagues are aiming to restore tens of thousands of hectares of former farmland in a corridor of a thousand kilometres along the southern edge of the state. The project is known as the Gondwana Link. In the Pilbara region, twenty thousand hectares (fifty thousand acres) of former mine is to be restored, but it requires at least 120 tons of seeds which will cost about $90 million. Even if the money is available, that quantity of seeds probably is not, and there must be a scaling up of seed banks for the production and supply of restoration quantities of seeds. This will require agricultural-scale horticulture. We also have a lot to discover about improving the success of seedling establishment because it is calculated that currently only 4 percent of broadcast seeds result in flowering plants.

Ecosystem services are another aspect of restoration biology that must be factored into habitat conservation projects, especially the restoration of pollinator services, which are necessary to sustain the reproductive potential of the community and the genetic resilience of the ecosystem. Specialized pollinators are often the first casualties of degraded ecosystems, but the loss of generalists has a more fundamental and pervasive impact. It has been calculated that 60 percent of the global landscape that has been disturbed by humans is in the twenty-five biodiversity hotspots defined by Myers and colleagues in 2000. Worse still, 70 percent of the land in these twenty-five sites has been cleared or fragmented. Fragmentation is a particular problem for pollinators (both generalist and specialist) with low dispersal potential.

Reestablishment of pollinators in restored habitats is not always easy. Obviously wind-pollinated plants are going to be fine, but the scientists in Western Australia have discovered that generalist pollinators are easier to reintroduce than specialists and pollinators that can move around well are easier to establish than those which cannot roam around freely. This means that specialist pollinators with limited mobility will have to be assisted in their migration.

The proximity of undisturbed habitat helps restoration projects because these areas act as a reservoir for pollinators. If no undisturbed habitats are near enough, then corridors are required, and in order to get the pollinators to travel down the corridor you need three types of plant species: frameworks species that provide a major amount of nectar and pollen, bridging species that provide resources in otherwise quiet times, and magnet species that have attractive flowers that catch the eyes of the pollinators for the drab flowers that might otherwise be missed. Agricultural headlines are important here in the landscape mosaic. Any consideration of the science of restoration ecology has to mention the impact of climate change. For example, if the predictions of a reduced growing season in Mediterranean-type regions comes true, plants and pollinators will be affected negatively: there will be less precipitation and shifts in seasons, reduced plant vigor and delayed plant maturation, less nectar production, and an asynchrony of pollinator and flowering. However, climate change predictions are still controversial. Vital details of global changes in temperature are eluding the weathermen and women.

continued from page 229
of these changes the balance between the different species can change. Losses and gains of species in a stable community is a normal process. However, we know more about the effects of species gains (that is, invasions) than we do about species loss, because the loss of a species may go unnoticed for much longer than the arrival of an invasive species.

In some restoration projects the ecologists are looking at the *function* of a plant in a community rather than the *name* of the plant. This means that they might use a non-native species in habitat restorations rather than rigidly sticking to the list of species present in the past. This is rather like the herbaceous border (again). Sometimes we are looking for an effect rather than a specific species or cultivar. If you want a big yellow daisy at the back of the border you are going to be spoilt for choice and it won't matter which one you use. However, if ecological restorations are not going to be species specific then we need *ex situ* conservation of species in seed banks or in botanic gardens and arboreta or preferably in both.

The idea that instead of restoring a habitat to its so-called natural state you create a new community might send shivers down the spines of the fundamentalist ecologists but is it really logical that restoration targets are based on what was there before at some arbitrary point in history? In 1783 Goethe wrote, "Nature is ever shaping new forms: what is, has never yet been; what has been, comes not again." By the same token John Sales, chief gardens advisor to the National Trust of England, often stated that "A garden is a process not a product." And likewise, as stated by Christopher Lloyd of Great Dixter renown (his garden in Kent, England), "You can never visit the same garden twice."

"Natural states" for a habitat are generally assumed to be what was there before European colonization and the onset of land clearance, agriculture, grazing, and the control of wildfires. However, this view needs to be revised for three reasons. First, pre-European *Homo sapiens* exerted significant influence on habitats; second, nonhuman-facilitated climate change makes restoration to a historic standard anachronistic; and finally the changes wrought by humans have ecological legacies that are impossible or very hard to reverse or override. In the same way as you do not have to live with someone else's garden when you move into a new home, you do not have to restore a habitat to what was there at some arbitrary point in the past—but the restored habitat must work. A further complication for restoration programmes is that for many parts of Europe, Asia, and Africa, undisturbed landscapes are too remote in time to provide restoration targets. This is not true for the USA, but what is the natural state for North America? Is it before the Europeans showed up or is it before the humans came over from Asia via Alaska or is it some other arbitrary date in the past?

We have sufficient data from fossils and pollen deposits and other paleoecological records from the past twenty thousand years to draw a three-braid conclusion from this data. Firstly, ecological and environmental changes are the norm and the world has always been in a state of constant flux. Few of the major terrestrial ecosystems have existed *in situ* for more than twelve thousand years and most are much younger. Everywhere has experienced a series of ecosystems, so there is no inherent natural ecosystem or landscape configuration for any region—that is, there is no ecological default setting. Second, many ecological combinations come and go as the environment changes so the late-glacial communities have no analogue at present. Third, for any given place there are many possible alternative natural states, just like there is no one type of garden for your own backyard.

Some new school restoration ecologists think that we should break free from the shackles of the concept of objective natural states; instead we should be driven by three principles. We should aim to restore the functions and services of the ecosystem. We must accept that novel ecosystems are inevitable with new combinations of species, which may not have existed anywhere before. And we should go into the restoration project assuming that it is a dynamic process and that further changes are inevitable. Habitat restoration, like gardening, is a process not a product.

Restoration ecology is a newish departure for botanic gardens but it is a logical evolution of their activities. Public gardens and their gardeners are pre-adapted to this activity. The gardens contain gardeners who can grow plants and are particularly familiar with raising wild species as opposed to cultivated varieties. Botanic gardens are visited by 200 million visitors each year and so are clearly well placed for invigorating public awareness and providing educational programmes and resources. Additionally, many botanic gardens have links to academic institutions, where teaching, research, and practice are integrally combined for what is hoped to be cutting-edge and up-to-date knowledge. To illustrate this I want to describe in detail a project that we have been involved with at the University of Oxford Harcourt Arboretum in Oxfordshire. I am telling this story not for self-congratulation but to illustrate how local and regional communities can address issues in their area when sufficient numbers of people want a solution to be found.

OXFORDSHIRE, ENGLAND
This story begins in 1712 when Sir Simon Harcourt purchased several square miles of land just to the south of Oxford at the village of Nuneham Courtenay. At the end of the eighteenth century, the Harcourts built a "villa" overlooking the River Thames with a view of St. Helen's Church Abingdon in the distance and even the dreaming spires of Oxford on a clear day when you can see for ever. The estate was a mixture of pleasure grounds, woodland, and deer park for grazing animals and thus it remained until 1947 when Nuneham Park was sold. The various components were dealt with differently and some of the park land was rented out to tenant farmers who either ploughed it up and grew cereals or left it as pasture and grazed sheep.

In 1963 fifty-five acres were purchased for the University of Oxford Botanic Garden because part of Nuneham Park had been planted up in the nineteenth century by William Vernon Harcourt between 1835 and 1865 with a mixture of native oak and lime woodland and exotic trees in a landscape designed by William Sawrey Gilpin. By the middle of the twentieth century these plantings had matured and were a valuable addition to the Botanic Garden collection. Twelve acres of the arboretum were a remnant of the original parkland. This is known as Windmill

Hill meadow because it is on the (north) side of Windmill Hill. (There is not now, nor has there ever been, a windmill on Windmill Hill.) From 1963 onwards this meadow was cut once a year in early August. The hay was turned and then baled and taken away. This minimal maintenance regime produced a mixed sward that eventually contained a growing population of common spotted orchids (*Dactylorhiza fuchsii*). The meadow also contained a large population of pignut (*Conopodium majus*), a distinctive member of the carrot family that is a classic indicator of ancient undisturbed pasture. It is called pignut because of the small tubers that are loved by pigs.

For how long the meadow had gone unploughed we do not know. Traditional hay meadows were common in this part of England before the Black Death in the middle of the fourteenth century. Following the reduction in the population there was abandoning of the land followed by enclosure of land. Many UK farmers practiced mixed farming with hay meadows to feed their cattle and sheep. The hay meadows became a recognized community of native species, the component species of which varied with soil type and other factors. However, in the 1970s and 1980s farmers were encouraged to stop mixed farming and to concentrate on being 100 percent arable or 100 percent livestock. The result of this specialization was that in the past fifty years the area of hay meadow in England has been reduced by 98 percent. In this part of Oxfordshire the meadow would have belonged to the MG5 community as defined by the British National Vegetation Classification. MG stands for mesotrophic grassland, mesotrophic meaning a soil with moderate inherent fertility. MG5 contains a basic community of grasses and other perennial herbs, shown in the accompanying list.

Plant Species Always Found in British Mesotrophic Grasslands (MG5)

Agrostis capillaris	common bent (a grass)
Anthoxanthum odoratum	sweet-vernal grass

Centaurea nigra	black knapweed
Cynosurus cristatus	crested dog's tail (a grass)
Dactylis glomerata	cock's foot (a grass)
Festuca rubra	red fescue (a grass)
Holcus lanatus	Yorkshire fog (a grass)
Lotus corniculatus	bird's foot trefoil
Plantago lanceolata	ribwort plantain
Trifolium pratense	red clover
Trifolium repens	white clover

So from 1963 to 1998 the twelve-acre meadow was slowly and effortlessly changed into an MG5 community. At the bottom of the hill there was a small dew pond that filled with water through the winter but then dried up through the summer. In 1971 this pond was enlarged and lined with rubber to create a permanent naturally fed pond in which the nationally rare bog-bean (*Menyanthes trifoliata*) has flourished. Around the edge, on the roots of the willow trees grows the bizarre parasitic toothwort (*Lathraea squamaria*).

Then in 1998 the field adjacent to the meadow, known as Pylon Meadow because of a huge electricity pylon in its centre, came available because the tenant farmer went out of business. For many years he had grazed sheep on the field and not improved the sward at all with the result that the sheep had not grown very well. We applied to the landowner to take over the rent offering to pay a commercial farm rent for the land. The owner was not convinced initially because he was more inclined to rent it to one of the existing tenant farmers since the minimum area for a viable farm increases each year. We wanted to have control of the land because any farmer wishing to make a living from the land would apply fertilizer, lime, and pesticides and this would inevitably drift and seep into our 35-year-old species-rich meadow.

We invited the landowner and his agents to walk the land with us one sunny afternoon so that we could pitch our bid and answer their questions. These men of money came out to the countryside and you could see that they were returning to the days of their childhood when they used to walk across meadows on their way to the village school. They were beginning to forget the bottom line and to remember that some things have a value that is measured in different units from those found on a balance sheet. The appearance of two hares twenty yards from us clinched the deal. Those battery-operated hares were a very sound investment and Pylon Meadow was ours: we now had thirty-seven acres of meadow. The fact that the previous tenant had chosen not to apply any fertilizers meant that the soil was already poor.

From 1998 the management of Pylon Meadow mirrored that of Windmill Hill with a cut for hay in early August. However, the aftermath, the remains of the sward that escapes the baling machine, was dragged with a chain harrow from one side of the meadow to the other thereby mixing up the seeds of the plants in the two different populations. Two alternative strategies were now considered. Either we could allow the plants to grow unhindered until the end of July when the hay would be cut and removed. Following the removal of the hay then sheep and or cattle could be introduced to graze the aftermath and generally scuff up the soil surface to provide a space for annuals. This is a good strategy if you want to encourage lady's smock (*Cardamine pratensis*) and it is essential if you want to grow yellow rattle (*Rhinanthus minor*). Alternatively we could cut or graze until the end of May and then allow the plants to grow, flower, and set seed until the end of September when you either cut the hay crop and then graze or just cut in October–November leaving piles of grass for the grass snakes.

We went for the hay and graze option because it was close to previous regimes and we had been offered some animals on loan (and I really do not like snakes). The cutting date is important with 25 July being the rule of thumb because this gives a high nutrient hay which is good for the farmer taking the hay. If you leave the cut much later you run the risk of a monoculture of knapweed. It does have the disadvantage that there may still be some pollinators about. To help them you can cut a strip around the edge of the meadow to 150 mm (6 inches) in May to stimulate a second flush of flowers that will provide nectar after the main part of the meadow is cut on 25 July.

From 2002 the meadow received support from the UK government's Countryside Stewardship scheme After the hay was cut in 2002, eighteen Aberdeen Angus cattle were introduced on to the field to add their disturbance and manure. It should be said that estate railings had to be erected to make sure that the cattle did not escape, but there was capital grant for this. Undergraduate projects carried out before and after the introduction of the cattle shows clearly that the diversity in the meadow has increased. Countryside Stewardship is connected with not only the agricultural use of the land but also public access and the history of the landscape. The grant enabled us to lay an all-weather path through the middle of the meadow so that all visitors could enjoy the meadow without damaging the plants. It also gave us access into the middle of the meadow for teaching purposes.

In addition to the historical significance of the Nuneham Park Estate as a classic nineteenth-century English estate, other features can now be preserved, such as the Parrish Oaks. In this part of the country parish boundaries were marked by oak trees that were pollarded at about 12 feet. If this is carried out at the right time in the life of the tree, you get a magnificent tree with many thick stems developing from this point. There is a line of oaks through the meadow marking the boundary between Nuneham Courtenay Parish and The Baldons. These trees are over three hundred years old and need some TLC from a skilled tree-surgeon to give them many more years of life. The maintenance of veteran trees is now well understood.

The grant also enabled us to plant many hundreds of yards of hedges consisting of a mix of native trees and shrubs. The provenance of the plants is important. Wherever possible you want to use plants grown from local genetic stock. Fortunately we have a supplier of native trees and shrubs nearby in west Oxfordshire and so we planted a mixture of eight different species: hawthorn (*Crataegus monogyna*), hazel (*Corylus avellana*), blackthorn (*Prunus spinosa*), dogwood (*Cornus mas*), field maple (*Acer campestre*), dog rose (*Rosa canina*), spindle (*Euonymus europaeus*), hedgerow buckthorn (*Rhamnus cathartica*), and wayfaring tree (*Viburnum lantana*). These plants were chosen because they can be laid. This is an ancient technique where the plants are allowed to grow unhindered for nine years to a height of about 10 to 12 feet. The main stem is then cut part way through near the base and the top is carefully pulled over to an angle of about 30 degrees to the ground. It is then woven through vertical hazel poles that are grown in our coppice elsewhere in the arboretum. A top strand of thinner hazel is then woven along the top at the desired height, in our case four foot six inches.

This is an old skill that is being conserved by the likes of John Savings who has now taught all the arboretum staff how to lay the rest of the hedges. The resulting hedge can then be cut either by hand or more likely by a machine, the hedge being much stronger for being laid. The hedge provides nectar for invertebrates and fruit for birds and small mammals. They in their turn are food for the barn owl that has now taken up residence in the tin barn in the corner of Pylon Meadow. With an estimated only one thousand breeding pairs of barn owls in England, you can see how important small schemes like this can become in a relatively short period of time.

Just as we thought that we were settled into an annual cycle of haymaking and grazing, another neighbouring farmer decided to leave farming and offered to sell us a fifty-acre field known as Palmer's Leys on the south side of Windmill Hill. Sadly we do not yet know who Palmer was. Time was in short supply and so in March 2006 a begging letter was sent out to the members of the Friends of the Botanic Garden and a couple of trusts funds. We needed £185,000. Within three weeks we had £135,000 and an interest-free loan of £50,000, meaning that we could buy the land. The response was extraordinary. It was the most popular appeal that we have ever organized and shows clearly that local people are prepared to invest in the future of biology if they can feel confident that the site is safe in the hands of the new owner. Similar appeals from the local wildlife trust, BBOWT, have been equally successful. People do care enough about nature to get their wallets out when it matters.

The field that became ours in December 2006 had been an arable field of wheat, oilseed rape, or linseed until 2004 but it had been in the set-aside scheme for two years. The site was surveyed in 2007 for its botanical and historical landscape significance. It was decided that the area should be divided into two uneven halves. Twenty acres were planted with native trees and thirty acres would be reverted from arable back to the hay meadow that had existed when the Harcourts had owned the estate. The planting of 13,500 trees was also an acknowledgement of the history of the site because in the 1830s William Vernon Harcourt had been encouraged by botanist Charles Daubeny to plant many acres of oaks and limes. We too planted native trees but this time it was English yew (*Taxus baccata*), small-leaved lime (*Tilia cordata*), oak (*Quercus robur*), ash (*Fraxinus excelsior*), and hornbeam (*Carpinus betulus*).

Planting 13,500 trees is no small undertaking and volunteers were recruited from the Friends of the Oxford Botanic Garden and Harcourt Arboretum; one of them, Keith Holmes, came back day after day. We also invited the local primary school along to help. This is not a new idea. In northwest Ecuador at the Awacachi Biological Corridor the local school children plant thirteen thousand trees each year in this 10,000-hectare (24,000-acre) reserve. If you have planted a tree you will know that you will for ever be connected with that plant in a very simple but deep way. However, not everyone agrees with this type of woodland creation. They would rather the neighboring woodlands were allowed to spread "naturally" into the twenty acres. The problem with this purist view is that the wretched muntjac deer who escaped from a safari park in 1925 will now eat the top off any young tree they come across. It has been estimated that there are in excess of two million of these hoofed hooligans in England and Wales. More shooting is required, partly because they are a good supply of good meat. We now have the benefit of the woodlands planted in this way 180 years ago and they are certainly woodlands and not the plantations that the ecologist fear.

We also created another pond because we want to create a mosaic of habitats to support the fauna. The provision of nectar is one issue. Another is the fact that many species of invertebrate pollinators require plants from more than one habitat to complete their life cycle. For example, brimstone butterflies need buckthorn (*Rhamnus cathartica*) in the hedgerow as well as meadow plants. Different parts of the landscape provide nectar at different times of the year. From February to April the woodland plants are the most important but they are replaced by meadow flowers from May to July. In August and September it is the aquatic pond and marginal plants that are the most important. Finally in October the meadow returns to prominence as the year ends.

So twenty acres were planted with trees and the remaining thirty acres of abandoned arable land were to be reverted to MG5 native grassland. Just like there are opponents of planting woodlands, there are ecologists who do not approve of this assisted restoration. They regard it as reversing the wrong way down a successional gradient, away from the ecological climax endpoint of a mature forest in a temperate ecosystem. We were unconvinced by this argument and decided to proceed to recreate the hay meadow pro-actively. However, before we could start we had to be sure that the vegetation that we had purchased with Palmer's Leys was not special. So in 2007 undergraduate projects by Kat Gourd and Rebecca "Boo" Lewis revealed that while the species numbers were similar on Palmers Leys compared to our Pylon Meadow next door, 45 compared to 54; the number of botanical families was much lower, five in Palmer's Leys versus eleven families in Pylon Meadow. Furthermore

90 percent of the species in Palmer's Leys were in just two families, the Poaceae (grasses) and the Asteraceae (daisies, asters). In places Palmer's Leys was almost a monoculture of the very vigorous Yorkshire fog grass (*Holcus lanatus*). We wanted some Yorkshire fog but not thirty acres of it!

It was decided that rather than trying to over-sow the desired mix of species, we should spray off the existing sward in the summer and then sow into clean soil in the autumn. We did however have a problem with the soil fertility because the legacy of arable farming was still present and the soil was more fertile than we would wish. On a small scale removing fertile top soil is a possibility but not here. An alternative strategy is to use yellow rattle (*Rhinanthus minor*) which is particularly good at subduing Yorkshire fog. Yellow rattle is a plant that many restoration experts see as essential for reversion to hay meadow from both pasture and arable land. It is a annual, semi-parasitic plant whose seeds remain viable in the soil seed bank for just a few years and so it is easy to lose it if you do not provide bare soil for it to grow in. This is why the feet of grazing animals are so important because the large flat seeds will not get into close enough contact with the soil unless an animal stands on them. The parasitic side to its nature means that it can halve the growth rate of vigorous grasses such as Yorkshire fog, cocks foot (*Dactylis glomerata*), and false oat grass (*Arrhenatherum elatius*).

So the reversion starts with two activities. First there is seed collection or acquisition and then there is preparation of the soil for sowing in the autumn. We sought advice from one of the UK's leading meadow restoration experts, Charles Flower. A problem with every restoration or reversion is that each project is slightly different, so you start with a plan but you expect to have to adapt it over the years. Just like the plants in the hedges and the trees in the woodland we wanted seeds of known provenance, and we were better off than many projects because we had our own supply of seeds in Pylon Meadow. However, having collected the seeds from the meadow using a box harvester, we realized that although Pylon Meadow was slightly larger than Palmers Leys, it was only going to give us enough seed to sow one third of Palmer's Leys. As a rule of thumb you need twenty pounds of seed per acre (or 22.5 kg per hectare).

Even though we had our own mixture of species from Pylon Meadow, Charles recommended twelve species that we should add along with the yellow rattle, in part because these species had a range of rooting depths between them and therefore do not compete for the same space and the same water.

Plant Species with Varying Root Depths

SPECIES	MAXIMUM ROOTING DEPTH
GRASSES	10 mm
OX-EYE DAISY*	15 mm
RIBWORT PLANTAIN*	20 mm
COWSLIPS*	
WILD CARROT	25 mm
COMMON SORREL*	
BIRD'S FOOT TREFOIL*	30 mm
LATE KNAPWEED	35 mm
AGRIMONY	40 mm

*These species were among those added to the seeds collected from Pylon Meadow.

The deeper rooting species improve the nutritional value of the hay and so is better for the animals. They also prefer the taste of this hay. The seeds were dried on a mat in a garage and then cleaned though a 10 mm × 10 mm sieve. They were then kept dry for the few months until sowing in the autumn. In some smaller projects the wet hay is spread on the soil straight after cutting in July.

Since we started the restoration of Palmer's Leys the Millennium Seed Bank Project has received a grant of £750,000 from the Esmée Fairburn Foundation to establish a seed bank specifically for restoration projects. It will increase the quality and diversity of seeds available to projects but more importantly the quantity of seeds by getting into partnerships with commercial seed companies, yet another example of the MSBP leading the world.

As in any gardening endeavour, preparation of the soil is critical and in particular the soil seed bank must be reduced to a low enough level so that it does not cause problems for the young seedlings. The soil seed bank is the seeds that have fallen into the soil from plants growing in a patch of land during the past decades and centuries. This can be a problem in restoration projects because the previous plants, which you do not want, keep reappearing and interfering and competing with the plants that you do want. We were lucky that the field had only been abandoned for two years and so the soil seed bank was not too big. If there are many grass seeds in the soil then repeated harrowing and spraying is required until the recruitment of weed seedlings is low enough not to be a problem. If the field being reverted to hay meadow contains the likes of docks, stinging nettles, and creeping thistles, they and their perennating organs must be eliminated before sowing. This may involve several years of work and many sprays of glyphosate. Fortunately these are rarely a problem when you are starting with a former arable field as the farmer will have eliminated these for you.

So in the summer of 2008 we sprayed off the plants that we did not want with glyphosate, and the land was shallow ploughed to turn over the dead plants but to avoid bringing up seeds from further down in the soil. It also removed the risk of bringing fertile soil up to the surface. The seedbed was created using an old chain harrow. If there had been a flush of weed seedlings at this stage we could have applied a second spray of glyphosate at the lowest recommended rate. This was not necessary and two weeks after the seedbed was created the seeds were spread in the autumn of 2008 using an old fertilizer spreader on the back of a tractor. Ten acres seemed like too much to do by hand. We were told that autumn sowing is always best as the soil will be warmer in the autumn than it will be in the spring and so the seeds will germinate quickly to produce seedlings sturdy enough to survive the winter.

Habitats: Soil—The Most Important Part

Restoration ecology is not far removed from very large-scale gardening—and as all good gardeners know, the most important part of any garden is the soil. In some areas of the world, soil is being lost through erosion one hundreds times faster than soil is being deposited. This has obvious implications for both agriculture and the restoration and conservation of habitats. Soil has many functions in addition to being the place where roots hang out. Soil stores carbon, it filters water, and it transforms nutrients into forms that plants can take up. As you might imagine, the rate of loss of soil is unevenly distributed across the earth, but many of the places where the soil is very degraded are biodiversity hotspots. In some cases plant diversity is partly the result of the poor soil, but failing to protect soil is a dangerous game to play because the stakes are high. If you lose your soil and you are back to bare rock, then your ecosystem is put back 470 million years.

The amount of carbon in the soil is very important at a time of rising levels of carbon dioxide in the atmosphere. The carbon is held in the soil's organic matter; globally the soil organic matter contains three times the amount of carbon in either the atmosphere or terrestrial vegetation. Some soil organic matter is stable and persists for thousands of years while other forms decompose quickly and it is largely unknown why this should be. It is not just a question of simple chemistry because the stability of the soil organic matter is also related to the environment and the biology of the region. For example, the thawing of permafrost is significant as is the number and type of organisms living in the soil including the nature and structure of the roots in the soil. Understanding what is going on in soils is important because it forms such a big part of climate-change models. We still have a great deal to learn about how carbon is stored, used, and released in the soil.

Particularly important in the carbon store in soil is fire-derived organic matter, which may be stable for centuries. I have written elsewhere about fire and how the mismanagement of fire can seriously affect the species composition of a habitat. Fire regimes vary around the earth. In some places fires happen every year while in others it may be decades or centuries between fires. Where the fire is annual, you often end up with grassland and less than 1 percent tree cover. Where the frequency is every twelve to twenty years, you can end up with a mega-diverse plant community as is found in the western Cape of South Africa and in southwest Western Australia with a tree cover between 5 and 50 percent. Where the fires occur many decades apart, the vegetation grows into forests with 60 to 100 percent tree cover. The frequency of fire is often in proportion to the precipitation. So there appear to be three basic fire regimes and habitats are locked into these. However, random extreme events could take a habitat from one type to the next and so between grassland and savannah and between savannah and forest there are unstable zones that will be severely altered in some way by changes in climate. Restoration ecologists must remain light on their toes if they are to respond appropriately to changes in fire regimes.

Sure enough the germination in autumn 2008 was excellent and by April 2009 an undergraduate project by Paul Wilkinson started to analyse the species that had germinated. We were helped greatly by the publishing of a new key to the British flora that did not need flowers. The growth of the new sward was extraordinary and so in the summer of 2009 we cut the herbage back to 150 mm to allow light to get to the soil so that late-germinating seeds could germinate. Everything was going to plan and the seeds were again collected from Pylon Meadow in the summer of 2009. The soil was prepared and the seedbed created. Then it started to rain and the soil was never dry enough for the tractor to get on to it. With hindsight we should have sown the second ten acres by hand because we waited until the spring of 2010 and the germination was awful. The middle third looked so different from the first that we almost sprayed it off to start again. Projects by undergraduates Lloyd Crowther and Lucy Capstick showed that a completely different community had germinated in the second third.

However, Charles Flower urged patience and as the summer proceeded more of the desired species appeared and by the second year (2011) the second or middle third was catching up with the first third. In July 2010 we collected the final crop of seeds from Pylon Meadow and prepared the final third of Palmer's Leys. The soils conditions were perfect and sowing took place in autumn 2010 with excellent germination. By the summer of 2012, as I write this, the reversion is well on track and we have the foundations of an MG5 hay meadow.

In six years we have doubled the size of our hay meadow. If every hay meadow in the UK doubled in size every six years, in just thirty-six years we would have replaced the meadows lost in the previous fifty years. On the way we would have contributed to targets 3, 4, 5, 6, 7, 8, 12, 13, 14, 15, and 16 of the Global Strategy for Plant Conservation.

There is no technical reason why any plant species should become extinct. Scientific investigations have given us the knowledge and hence the techniques to repair the damage done to plant communities all over the world. It is gardening on a global scale and the world needs gardeners now more than ever.

What Can You Do? The Science and Practice of Every Gardener's Know-How

My first serious gardening was carried out with my father on the allotments that he rented from the local parish council for the production of vegetables, soft fruits, and later on cut flowers for my mother and the annual village food and flower competition and show. My father was no scientist; he was interested in history and geography, but despite a promising school career, he left school at sixteen to work in the post office. Even though he had no scientific background, he grew

Fire regime interactions

ignition by lightning or human management

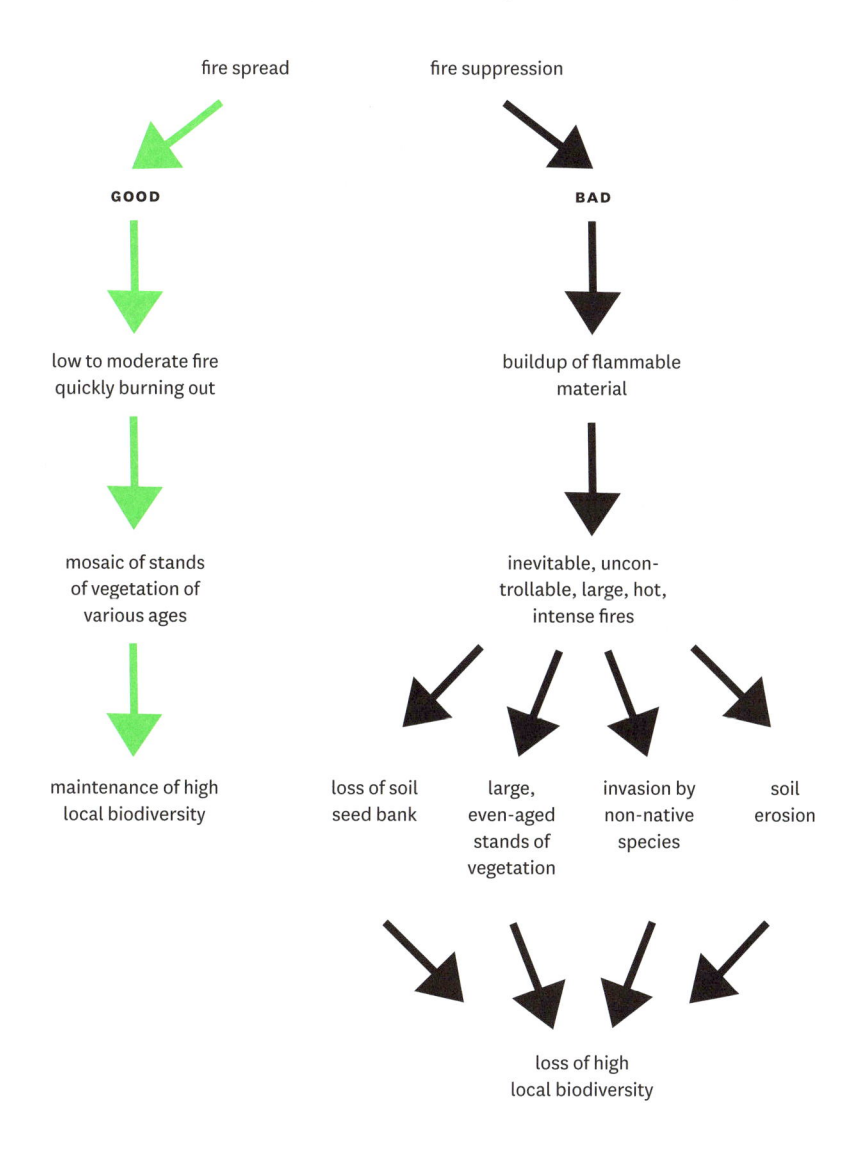

fire spread → **GOOD**

fire suppression → **BAD**

GOOD:
- low to moderate fire quickly burning out
- mosaic of stands of vegetation of various ages
- maintenance of high local biodiversity

BAD:
- buildup of flammable material
- inevitable, uncontrollable, large, hot, intense fires
  - loss of soil seed bank
  - large, even-aged stands of vegetation
  - invasion by non-native species
  - soil erosion

→ loss of high local biodiversity

You, the Gardener, Your Plants, and Our Changing Climate

When there is a change in climate, species are faced with four options. They can stay put and tolerate the new conditions, shift into a new and different habitat, migrate to the same habitat somewhere else, or they can become extinct. To estimate what might happen in the future, data is needed from direct observations, from paleoecological records (pollen and buried stuff), and from experiments. This data can then be fed into models and scenarios can be produced. All the gardeners of the world are important here, since they can provide a huge amount of phenological data about, for example, flowering and fruiting dates. Most countries in the developed world have central databases in which biological records are collated. In the United Kingdom it is the UK Phenology Network. And it is here that gardeners can submit their data and observations.

Scientists try to assess the vulnerability of different species to the negative effects of climate change, with three components to the vulnerability score they can assign: the potential exposure to change, which will be determined by the habitat in which the plant lives; the sensi-

---

his vegetables in a very scientific manner. For him there was no room for intuition; this was an activity, like cricket, with laws and rules that you followed. If you followed the rules, then you would be successful. Sowing dates, distance between rows, fertilizer rates—all were non-negotiable. His methods were based on the advice from scientific experiments carried out by others. Occasionally, based on his own meticulous records and observations, he also worked the science and would alter one of the parameters—but not without good reason. Intuition was not an option, and he grew the best fruit and vegetables and dahlias of anyone I know.

Gardening has been described as the only place where art and science meet on even terms, and perhaps this is one of the reasons why tivity of the species to changes; and finally, the adaptive capacity of the species. Again gardeners have an important role to play here, because when we grow non-native species in our gardens, we are carrying out vulnerability assessments and the plants that we can grow well have a low vulnerability score in this new environment. There is going to be a relationship between these three factors: adaptive capacity will work in the opposite direction to sensitivity.

With the help of your gardening experience and gardener's know-how, climate change modelers can now better define the climate space for a species and can then calculate and map the area that will enjoy this climate space in the future; the climate space for a species might move and it might contract or it might expand. The speed of change of climate will vary between regions, and the ability of species to migrate will vary. There will be areas with a low climate-change velocity, which will become refuges especially for slow-moving species. Of course not all species will lose out. Against all this uncertainty and with so many variables and so many gardeners, we can all take part in a global conservation strategy. Don't despair—repair.

biology is regarded by some scholars (particularly my physicist son) as a soft science when compared with physics or chemistry. However, this opinion is based on a misunderstanding of the true meaning of the word *science*. Science is not a subject; science is a method of working that endeavours to discover the truth about the natural world, and the natural world embraces physics, chemistry and biology. Early scientists such as Theophrastus, the grandfather of botany, were natural philosophers who made very careful observations on the world around them. It is impossible to say who was the first person to go beyond observation but Ibn al-Haytham (a.k.a. Alhazen) must be a strong candidate. Alhazen, a Muslim scholar born in Basra, Iraq (965–c.1040 Cairo), whose specialist area was physics, and in particular optics, is important to my story because he applied the scientific method to his work—a method that backyard and professional gardener alike can follow.

The method is quite simple. First a question has to be asked. It might be very simple such as when is the best time to plant your seed potatoes, or it may be very complicated like how did life begin. The latter question can only answered by breaking it down into many smaller parts, and is not the topic here; the former question, though less complicated, is also addressed by being broken down into individualized queries. Having asked the question, you can come up with a hypothesis, an answer based on your observations. My hypothesis is that 14 April is the date upon which you plant your potatoes if you want to be able to predict the best yield. The next stage is to test this prediction by designing an experiment in which everything is equal except the planting date. So the soil must be the same, the same variety must be used, the same amount of water and fertilizer must be applied, and finally all the crops must be harvested on the same date to compare the yields. You will then analyse the results and weigh the potatoes. The heaviest yield will come from the best sowing date, which according to the prediction will be 14 April. Of course it may not be. You might make the experiment a bit more sophisticated by changing the harvest date in which case you would leave the planting date constant. Alternatively you may choose to test a combination of planting dates and harvesting dates but you must be careful to test every combination. You will then have to compare all of your results over a number of years to check that there are no other variable factors that you have missed.

Thinking Sustainably and Making Necessary Changes: A Conservation Bog

In our capacity as gardeners, we can grow much of our own food and thus reduce our dependence on markets, but there are items that we purchase in order to garden that have a negative impact on finite resources and are therefore unsustainable. The best documented of these is peat, and in particular peat from sphagnum bogs.

Bogs are a beautiful habitat. They are home to not only a special community of plants including in the UK carnivorous sundews, *Drosera* species, but also a fabulous array of birds including snipe, curlews, and skylarks. In the United States there are many areas from Florida across to California and from Washington State to New England where equally wonderful communities live. For example, in Oregon right on US Route 101 in Lane County is the Darlingtonia State Natural Site. You can take a board walk through an awesome stand of *Darlingtonia californica*, or cobra lily. On the East Coast is the immense Okefenokee Swamp.

Bogs are one of Europe's most threatened habitats. In England, less than half of a square mile of raised bog remains untouched (700 hectares, or 1,680 acres). This is the equivalent of one large farm. All of the peat bogs in the United Kingdom contain around 5.5 trillion tons of carbon. That is the same as the amount of carbon held in 50 percent of the trees in Europe (excluding Russia). Harvesting all the peat in the United Kingdom would be the equivalent of cutting down half of Europe's forest and composting the wood. We might actually do this at the current rate because rather than removing the 1 mm that peat bogs "grow" each year, harvesters remove 220 mm. It has been calculated by the UK government that across the country as a whole, peat is being extracted at least fifty times faster than it is regrowing.

In Canada and the United States, gardeners harvest 36,000 acres of peat each year. It is claimed by their producers that at this rate there will be peat for American gardeners for ever. Scientists dispute this because peat bogs take a great deal of time to regrow, and there is not an ecologist in the United Kingdom who believes that peat from the bogs in Britain and Ireland can be supplied to gardeners at a sustainable rate. The environmental impact of harvesting peat is more than just the destruction of a unique habitat and the carbon released as the peat degrades in our gardens. The carbon footprint of the extraction process is the equivalent of an extra 100,000 cars on UK roads. You might wonder therefore why peat is so widely used. Well, it is much easier to produce than good loam, which was the basic component of composts until the 1970s.

Loam was made by slicing the top four inches of soil and turf from a ley, or grass pasture. It was then piled carefully in a loam stack, which was traditionally a yard wide, a yard high, and as long as you needed. You built the stack by placing the turfs upside down and arranged like bricks, overlapping to tie the stack together. You built the walls first and then filled the middle in with broken turfs. Some people added well-rotted farmyard manure between the layers. The pile was left for a few months. When the grass had died you could start cutting into the stack. The loam was put through a sieve with a half-inch mesh and then sterilized. The smell of the electric sterilizer cooking soil in the potting shed at the Botanic Garden is a very evocative smell for me. When the soil had reached the desired temperature the power was switched off and after thirty minutes the loam was released from the base of the machine. It was then left to cool over night before being combined with the other ingredients of our many different compost mixes for the different plants in the collection. Not surprisingly most gardeners were pleased to be able to forego the delights of making potting loam, but I miss it.

Peat is light and so growing plants in containers is easier on the muscles of the growers because they can handle the pots more easily. Peat is clean compared to soil, and it is much less variable. It is sterile and free of weed seeds and diseases which is particularly useful when sowing seeds because seedlings can be especially vulnerable to diseases. In mechanized potting machines it is easier to use peat-based composts than loam so it is attractive to the mass-production market. Furthermore, peat being lighter, peat-grown plants are cheaper to move around the world

Peat only became widely used in the United Kingdom in the 1970s. Nurseries changed from field-grown plants that were sold in the winter when the plants were dormant to container-grown stock that were available all year round. Plants could be sold when in flower rather than dormant. The age of having to have everything available all the time irrespective of season hit gardening like other aspects of our lives.

The arguments against the old soil-based, or loam-based, composts are the reverse of those for peat- based, but there are arguments against peat-based composts too. There is no nutrient to speak of in peat and so all the nutrients have to be added and replenished often because peat does not retain nutrients as loam does. The one area of horticulture where peat was completely misused and tons of the stuff was wasted was when peat was used as a soil improver. It contains no nutrients and it rots down quickly. It has no long-term value as a soil improver whatsoever. When a peat-based compost dries out, it is much more difficult to re-wet than a soil-based compost. The final reason for never using peat in normal gardening is that plants grown in a soil-based compost are more likely to survive in your garden soil than those grown in peat-based composts. Long-term plants perform better in loam-based composts if they are looked after properly.

So why do we still buy plants in peat-based compost? In the United Kingdom the majority of plants are grown in the stuff, so we do not have a choice. However, the UK government is trying to remove peat use from sale to backyard home gardeners by 2020 and to UK nurseries by 2030.

Some nurseries refuse to stop using peat, saying that there is no alternative. There are two points in answer to this. Firstly, when 2030 arrives there will be an alternative because for the previous decade amateurs will have been using the alternative. Secondly, the Botanic Garden in Oxford was founded in 1621 and did not start using peat in any quantity until the 1970s. This means that for three and a half centuries we gardened without peat so to say there is no alternative is nonsense. We shall go back to what we used to use or maybe use some new materials.

One new material is coir fibre, a product of the coconut plantations in the tropics and places like Sri Lanka. There it has been used for making matting, sacks, ropes, brushes, and padding in furniture and mattresses. However, it is a good substitute for peat if handled correctly and if the horticulturist is an observant one who can judge when a plant needs to be watered. This perhaps is the major obstacle to the adoption of new materials. Every compost needs to be handled differently. If you are using a peat-based compost you can firm it really hard and treat it rough and the structure will not be lost. If you treat a loam-based compost in a rough way and firm it into the pot with lots of pressure, it will lose its structure and become water logged and unaerated. Other peat substitutes included composted bark and bracken. Few of these have reached the consistent specifications of peat, but they improve each year and at the Botanic Garden we have found a supplier who can provide a consistent product that our plants like.

There is perhaps just one time when a little bit of sphagnum peat and even sphagnum itself can be justified and that is when you are trying to cultivate carnivorous plants that are so characteristic of the peat bogs. Still there are carnivorous plant growers who have found that the alternatives like coir-based compost do work. Among the most promising alternatives for this niche market is material dredged out of the reservoirs in northern England and other places where the reservoirs are surrounded by moorland. As the water runs into the reservoirs, it takes into the water a mixture of peat, leaf mould, and silt. The water suppliers do not want this in their water and so it is being scraped out, bagged up, and sold.

This reservoir detritus is I think an indicator of where we shall go in the future because it contains leaf mould. Many gardeners used to stack their leaves separately from their compost bins because it makes a mulch that is particularly attractive around ferns. It was also believed that it was always acidic, but this may not be true. There is an appeal to using leaf mould as a peat alternative because in the autumn we are up to our ankles in leaves. The leaves we sweep or hoover up in the autumn in the Botanic Garden do make lovely compost, and talking to gardeners around England I have found that many people make leaf mould, use it in their potting compost, and gladly share their recipes. This is in stark contrast to tales of old head gardeners in England being extremely secretive about the contents of their composts, very much like the recipe for mother's apple pie.

The preferred system is to store it for three years, turning the heap once a year. So you set up four very well drained bins or wooden boxes with no base, no lid, and no front. Then you fill the end one in year 1 and leave it. Before you start sweeping the leaves in year 2 you move the leaves from box 1 to box 2 and fill box 1 with the fresh leaves. In the autumn of year 3 the contents of box 2 are turned into box 3, box 1 into box 2, and the fresh leaves again into box 1. (You may find that box 1 should be bigger than the other boxes because fresh leaves take up more volume than rotting leaves.) You have probably got the hang of this by now and when you turn the contents of box 3 into box 4 in the autumn of year 4 you have leaf mould ready use and all for nothing. My father was wrong when he said that you could never have ought for naught but he was still the best fruit and vegetable grower that I have ever met.

Over the past three decades as a professional gardener I have met thousands of gardeners on five continents. I have found them to be a modest and generous group of people who quietly look after their part of the world for a morsel of eternity because they cherish the biological inheritance with which they share the planet. Most of the gardeners I know are reluctant to acknowledge how knowledgeable they are. And yet, activating and sharing this knowledge is imperative. Within the framework of the GSPC, any gardener can make one or more of the following contributions.

The Botanical Society of the British Isles and other national natural history organizations are always looking for new members who can carry out biodiversity surveys. Most of the organizations offer training for novices and old hands. The recording of botanical data is the foundation stone of conservation. There are many international, regional, and national nongovernmental organizations and local groups that manage nature reserves. All of these need and welcome volunteers who can scrub bash (or as Americans say, clear brush), plant, weed, and generally maintain the vegetation.

Some plant species will be conserved in these nature reserves, but insurance is always a sound investment—you can never have too many backup copies of threatened species. Gardeners are making a significant contribution to this by growing plants, but there is an opportunity to stand up and be counted by creating a national collection under schemes such as the UK Plant Heritage or by joining the US Seed Savers Exchange if your bent is towards fruit and vegetables. There are many schemes around the world where in return for your membership fee you have access to varieties that cannot be purchased anywhere else even though they may be perfect for your plot. By growing our own food we can help to reduce the need for more land to be put under cultivation to feed a growing world population.

When we choose what to grow in our gardens, we now know that we need to be careful not to introduce a plant that might be too happy and move out into the countryside. Gardeners can use their knowledge of what makes a plant a serious weed to reduce the risk of new invasions.

Above all, gardeners must pass on their knowledge. Nearly all gardeners—and every professional gardener that I personally know—have initially acquired their know-how by learning backyard, home gardening from a parent, grandparent, aunt, or uncle. The world needs the skills of all gardeners—now more than ever.

Look out world, here we come.

THE STRATEGY

So Here It Is—Now You Know

If you have reached this point in the book you are either very committed to learning about conservation or you are an insomniac, or you have skipped the previous 75,000 words assuming that the pearls of wisdom are in this final chapter. If the former, then you will have been around the world with me looking into the lives and actions of many thousands, if not millions, of people who have realized that our present lifestyle needs to be modified if we are not to burn out as a species in much less than the average life expectancy of an animal. The fact that so many people are not rushing headlong into the extinction vortex, but are behaving in a sensible and perhaps altruistic way, gives reason for hope.

I am sure that there are many people out there who are cynical about the efforts of conservation biologists in all their many varied guises. The reasons for the cynicism are similarly many and varied, but one of the most common is a feeling that it is too late and that the problems are too large to solve, defeatism set in. This is an unfortunate self-fulfilling prophecy. If NASA had never *tried* to put a man on the moon before the end of the 1960s, Neil Armstrong would never have got there. If we do not even *try* to alter the future of our own species and the many other species whose fate lies in our hands, then we shall never improve the future for our descendants. We shall never even know if we could have succeeded. Another reason to try is that people who know there is a solution have a duty to others. We need all the professions. Our society thrives because of the diversity and specialization of its seven billion human components. In the same way that biological communities acquire resilience, so do human communities. Clearly not all seven billion people are going to become professional or amateur conservation biologists, but plant conservation in particular and the natural world in general are the ultimate cross-cutting issue, impacting on every aspect of our lives.

Even if you never looked at a wildflower, your day-to-day actions may determine the fate of that wildflower. The way in which we all choose to dispose of our income and our talents and how we choose to live our lives will likewise determine the fate of that wildflower. Why worry about one wildflower? This wildflower is a voiceless individual that will not scream with pain if we harm it, nor will it sink its teeth into our calves if we tread on it. This wildflower is a metaphor for all plant conservation in the same way that Neil Armstrong was the metaphor for the incalculable total of human endeavour that went into getting him onto the surface of the moon on 21 July 1969. Likewise, just as no one person got Neil Armstrong to the moon, no one person is going to reverse the decline in biological diversity and save our wildflower. This means that a plan is needed.

The plan that has evolved came out of the joint efforts of just sixteen people who met for two days in a room in a botanic garden on an island in the Atlantic. As a result of their wisdom, experience, and unshakeable belief that there is hope for the plant kingdom, there is now the sixteen-point plan that we have been considering—the Global Strategy for Plant Conservation—that if acted upon can restore Earth to a state that can support our species and the millions of other species that make the third rock from the sun inhabitable. These sixteen men and women and their sixteen targets have given us all the opportunity to make a better world. Defeatism is no longer the default reaction to gloom-and-doom merchants who delight in spreading apathy and malcontent because they personally do not wish to take responsibility and take part in the greatest global endeavour in the short history of *Homo sapiens*.

The GSPC shows how we can all contribute to this endeavour. The goal of this work falls into two broad objectives. The first of these is to protect the soil. This may seem like a strange place to start when at the end of a productive day of gardening we wash the dirt off our hands or take off the gloves that have prevented our hands from coming into contact with the soil in the first place. *Dirt* is itself a pejorative term for a substance that was the prerequisite for the evolution of life in the air, on the dry land. At the beginning of 2013, a controversial article in the scientific journal *Nature* reported that this mysterious stuff may have begun life during the Ediacaran period, 635 to 542 million years ago, before the Cambrian period, known for the eponymous Cambrian Explosion that is thought to have led to the evolution of all the modern groups of animals and plants. What this clearly shows in either case is that soils are at the root of the modern component of Earth's great tree of life.

Soil is a still a poorly understood commodity. It is a beguiling mixture of living animal, vegetable, and mineral. It has taken hundreds of millions of years to accumulate our soils, and yet despite that antiquity it is vulnerable. Take a look at NASA's photographs on the Internet of the clouds of soil being blown off the land, over the seas, and you can see how fragile soil is if the plants are removed. The roots of plants are the curators of the soil; soil provides plants with a place to grow their roots and thereby supply the plant with water, minerals, and other nutrients. In return, the plants hold the soil together and protect it from the dramatic and rapid erosion that can be wrought by wind and rain. Which plants protect the soil in any one given place may be of secondary importance to the fact that at least some plants are doing this.

Clearly the climate in any particular place on Earth will rule out many plants from playing a part. Equally clear is that the floral composition of a community is going to have a huge influence on the animal community. The reverse is also true. This is a tangled web of interactions, a fascinating matrix that is difficult to untangle but which can unravel very fast if there are alterations to the composition of the communities. So we need diverse, dynamic, and stable communities of plants, animals, and fungi that can protect the soils that sustain them.

While the protection of the soil may not depend upon just one possible amalgamation of specific plants, there are occasions when the needs of biology in general and of *Homo sapiens* in particular are species specific. We know, for example, that some orchid and fig species rely on just one species of wasp to pollinate their flowers and thus produce the seeds that will take their genes into another generation. We also know that some species of plants have a unique ability as chemists. So *Catharanthus roseus* produces vincristine for its own protection but also, in a sense, for the protection of another species: it saves the lives of eight out of ten children born with leukemia.

So there are two broad areas of conservation. On the one hand, there is the macro-scale conservation of plant communities that are the green glues that hold the soil in place. On the other hand, there is the micro-scale conservation of specific gene assemblages, called plant species, that provide very specialized services to us and other species. These are hands, the fingers of which can sometimes tightly intertwine. They are also hands that can work independently to play the same tune. To mix our metaphors in a traditional biological tangle, these hands are definitely horns of the same goat going in the same direction. How can we steer or cajole the goat of conservation? This is where the sixteen wise men and women and their sixteen focused targets can give us all parts to play.

The GSPC is a play in sixteen acts and all the world is its stage. All men and women are players and each person may play many parts.

ACT 1: COMPILE AN ONLINE FLORA OF ALL KNOWN PLANTS

The Players Botanists (professional and amateur), database designers, IT managers, geneticists, engineers

Putting Neil Armstrong, Buzz Aldrin, and others on the moon was an extraordinary achievement by any definition of extraordinary. However, no matter how amazing a feat of ingenuity it was to put men on the moon, it was easier than surveying and cataloguing the plant species on Earth around which orbits that moon. We think that we have found and named over 85 percent of the plant species with which we share the planet, but that is only a well-informed guess. There is an ongoing need to continue the work of exploring and mapping the world's vegetation. This is the only way that we can collate the data that will form the basis of all plant biology and in particular plant conservation. For example, how can we talk about rates of extinction if we do not know which species are growing where in the first place?

The way in which the global flora is catalogued is basically the same as ever. Intrepid botanists go out into "the field" and record what they find. They bring back data, photos, bits of plants, seeds, and anything else that they can without compromising the future of that group of plants. The botanists return to their herbaria or to their offices in their homes and they make their dried specimens and then input their data onto their computers. At this point two diametrically opposite professions collide for the greater good. Database designers have given us the powerful communication tools that amalgamate data in a global unified plant library; IT managers and technicians can translate physical data such as 400-year-old dried specimens into digital images that can travel around the world at the speed of 1 gigabit per second.

The way in which we define and identify plant species is constantly being refined and improved. It is hoped that in less than one more lifetime it will be possible to put a species name onto an individual plant by reading one piece of the DNA in the nucleus of its cells. This technique has been nicknamed DNA barcoding because of the similarity between the mechanized identification of plant species and the shop checkout. This will need the joint efforts of geneticists to provide the raw data and engineers to design and build the handheld devices that will replace the need for hand lenses, microscopes, and large books that researchers have had to transport into the field. The scope of DNA barcoding to revolutionize the gathering and sharing of data is immense.

ACT 2: ASSESS THE CONSERVATION STATUS OF ALL KNOWN PLANT SPECIES

The Players Field biologists, amateur naturalists

Only the most pessimistic of botanists would say that all plant species are currently threatened with extinction. Someone with such a gloomy outlook on life would find getting out of bed a pointless exercise. Furthermore, the propagation of such gloomy nonsense would simply demoralize others to the point of inactivity. Most plant species are not currently threatened with extinction in the lifetime of the current generation of schoolchildren. However, 100,000 species may well disappear in that time if nothing is done to prevent the disappearance. Does this matter? I think that it does because ultimately plants give us everything that we need today, and history clearly shows that they have things to give us that we do not yet know that we need.

Take, for example, the yew trees in the forests of the US Pacific Northwest or in the woodlands on the Chiltern Hills in southern England. While cancers have been recognized for more than three thousand years, the treatments were initially invasive and crude. The cures present in yew trees have only been extracted for fifty years. It is impossible to know now what people will be dying from in another thousand years, but we have learned that some species of plants may have synthesized a cure already. If we know which species are currently threatened then we can target the species most in need of our help. In order to know which species are threatened we need observers, professional and amateur, to record and share data on what is growing where, or *not* growing, so that the declining species can be identified.

ACT 3: CARRY OUT RESEARCH TO DEVELOP THE METHODS NECESSARY TO CONSERVE PLANTS
The Players Research scientists, landowners, gardeners, farmers

It is widely accepted by conservation biologists that there is no technical reason why any plant species should become extinct. Every species can be preserved either as a dried and frozen seed, or as a cryopreserved embryo or plant, or as a living individual. However, preservation is not conservation. Preservation is static. Preservation is maintaining the status quo and halting change. Conservation is more dynamic. Conservation is a process that allows for and facilitates change—and reduces the loss of species. While we may have made huge strides in micro-conservation, there is still much for us to learn in macro-conservation.

A range of factors threatens habitats and the plants therein, summarized by the mnemonic HIPPO. Many parts of the world have been transformed over the past seventy thousand years since *Homo sapiens* first migrated out of Africa. The rise of the agricultural systems that have supported an increase in the human population to seven billion is a testament to the ingenuity of our species that is as impressive as putting twelve men on the moon. However, there are areas of the world where habitats have been transformed and where plant communities have been disturbed. The restoration of these communities is an emerging area of biological science, and each year we see expertise increase and thereby improve the chances of conservation successes.

For restoration of habitats to succeed the owners of the land must be committed to the project and able to provide security for the site. There must be research scientists with the right experimental techniques to carry out research to provide meaningful data. Some of the landowners will be farmers who can now combine making a living from the land and providing us all with our essential food with the sustainable management of their land and the biology of that land.

ACT 4: MAKE SAFE 15 PERCENT OF EVERY ECOLOGICAL REGION AND VEGETATION TYPE

The Players Politicians, nongovernmental organizations, reserve managers

To make safe an area of this size, about 8.5 million square miles or the area of the United States, China and India combined, will require a combination of effective management and/or restoration. This is a huge target. It is conservation on a national scale. Nations are (generally) run by governments and all the bureaucratic gubbins that goes with a large organization like a nation. The governments are populated by people, sometimes elected democratically and re-elected at regular intervals. The politicians are advised by other people who do not have to be re-elected at regular intervals but who do need to be qualified to give advice. The power entrusted in politicians makes them potentially very important players in conservation. This does not always sit comfortably with the goals of conservation because the horizons of politicians can be dictated by the next election while conservation needs a longer view to be taken.

Nongovernmental organizations, often charities and not-for-profits, can take this longer view so long as they can continue to attract the support of the people who make donations or volunteer to help with, for example, reserve management. And this type of macro-conservation is happening, with well over 11 percent of the world's total land area made safe. One benefit of focusing on ecological regions and vegetation types is that the rest of the biology—the animals, fungi, and microorganisms— are also conserved. Another benefit is that no country can opt out. No one can claim that their country does not have at least one ecological region and vegetation type that is not unique to that country. The days of blaming all the conservation problems on the destruction of the tropical rain forest are over.

The protection of large areas of land does not have to preclude the removal of natural resources from those areas. In fact people are more likely to protect areas that support them, providing either food or an income. The successful management of reserves requires accurate data and monitoring, and it requires scientifically tested techniques. Thus act 4 is dependent upon the previous three acts.

ACT 5: PROTECT 75 PERCENT OF THE MOST IMPORTANT AREAS FOR PLANT DIVERSITY

The Players Reserve managers, geneticists, politicians, local people

It is a well-accepted fact that biological diversity is not spread evenly on Earth. For example, the land is much more species rich than the seas. Darwin and others have noticed that species diversity tends to increase as you get closer to the equator. There have been several attempts over the years to map the world to show where there are exceptional levels of species diversity, and in particular where there are the largest proportions of unique (or endemic) species. These regions are known as biodiversity hotspots. Without wishing to offend, it is clear that there are areas of the world that have little vegetation. So, while some parts of northern Canada are exceptionally beautiful, they are biologically dull at a species level and so are never featured in the hotspots hit parade. (The same might be said of the moon, a fact that might explain why only twelve men were needed to survey it.)

Through the work of field botanists in acts 1 and 2, we can map where in the world the plant diversity is most dense, more unique, and most threatened. These places can become the priority list. The rich nations can see where best to devote their resources, and they can identify from a biological point of view the poorer nations that deserve the most help. However, help from outside will only be effective if there is the will among the local people to take responsibility for some of the work. If people are too hungry to take on such responsibility, then clearly other problems are more pressing than plant conservation. Very few people are going to starve to death in the interest of plant conservation, the guardians of Nicolai Vavilov's seed bank in St. Petersburg being a heroic and tragic exception to this rule.

At the local level, however, nongovernmental organizations and local people can successfully implement and safeguard areas protected in law by national governments. The myriad of national parks, national nature reserves, sites of special scientific interest, areas of outstanding natural beauty, world heritage sites, and others show clearly that a great deal has been achieved; and the beauty of this system is that it is possible to visit these areas and to have one's life enriched in a way that an image on a flat plasma screen can never emulate.

ACT 6: MANAGE 75 PERCENT OF PRODUCTION LANDS SUSTAINABLY TO CONSERVE GENETIC DIVERSITY

The Players Farmers, foresters, politicians, landowners

The term *production land* may be unfamiliar, but it is a simple concept. It refers to any area of land where biological resources grow and from where they are harvested. At one extreme you have a field of intensively sown wheat or corn, where as a result of high-input agriculture you can grow 7.2 tons per hectare (2.9 tons per acre). At the other extreme are rare regions of tropical woodland where the indigenous population receives no input from the outside, existing entirely on food and other commodities harvested from their woodland. In between these two are such things as the harvesting of bark from the cork oak in Portugal and Spain. Here the removal of the bark every nine years not only supports local incomes but also promotes an understory that is exceptionally rich botanically.

Even where farmers are squeezing every calorie possible from their fields, there is the possibility of governments making subsidies available to allocate some of their land to native species. The creation of unploughed six-yard-wide strips next to the hedges around farmers' fields is a common site in the United Kingdom. Here the native flora and fauna can flourish next to wheat, rape, or whatever crop is being grown. Grants for the planting and maintenance of hedges are also available.

It can be reasonably claimed that everyone's backyard or garden is potential production land. Many gardeners choose to grow their own food so that they can know exactly what pesticides have been used, if any. Home gardeners are not driven solely by economic returns but by the security and satisfaction derived from providing for yourself and your nearest and dearest. Your garden will probably also be feeding the local songbirds, either directly with your bird feeder or indirectly by growing ornamental plants from which the birds can grab a meal for themselves of seeds, fruits, or invertebrates.

ACT 7: CONSERVE 75 PERCENT OF THREATENED SPECIES IN THEIR HABITATS

The Players Landowners, habitat managers, geneticists, ecologists

There are times when macro-conservation and micro-conservation hold hands and work together. In these situations the conservation of one species becomes the raison d'être for the management and conservation of a whole area. In animal conservation there are many well-known examples of these iconic species, such as the giant pandas in China and the spotted owls in the Pacific Northwest. In plant conservation there are also species being conserved in this way, as we have seen with the northern California nature reserve to which visitors go simply for the carnivorous *Darlingtonia californica*. Yet when they get there, they will also see many other plants, from mosses to birch trees.

In the United Kingdom the English bluebell woods are synonymous with the spring. However, in order to provide the bluebells with their perfect habitat, the woodlands must be managed. This management may include the winter removal of other plants that grow over the bluebells during the summer. It may also include the planting of new tree seedlings to ensure that the deciduous tree cover does not all die at once. Management may also be at a much smaller scale. The genetic diversity of a population of plants is important. Repeated inbreeding is not good; inbreeding depression and weak plants will result. Ecological geneticists are needed to carry out assessments of the genetic diversity and determine whether the plants are outbreeding with unrelated plants, which may require the introduction of pollinators, though these can also come in from the headlands of arable fields nearby.

ACT 8: CONSERVE 75 PERCENT OF THREATENED SPECIES AWAY FROM THEIR HABITATS

The Players Horticulturists, seed biologists

There are times when macro-conservation is not an option and micro-conservation alone is the only option. In these situations the conservation is one species at a time. This may sound painfully slow but a great deal can be achieved in several years by one person acting alone. When more people join in, the progress can be quicker, broader, and more resilient. Conservation of one species is conservation on a human scale. A real sense of achievement can be derived in the relatively short life span of one person—and the perfect person to be that one person is a gardener. It is time for gardeners to start making more noise about how important they are as the custodians of the world's plants.

How far from the plant's habitat the species is taken depends on the species concerned. It may be possible to establish a self-supporting population away from the area under threat. A scenario such as this might occur if a road has to be built, or a river diverted, or a mine excavated. It would be nice if plants always took precedent over a road-improvement scheme or a flood-prevention programme or the excavation of millions of dollars of coal, but pragmatism is essential in conservation. Idealism can come later when the risk of extinction has passed or been delayed.

While financial banks may have now acquired a tarnished reputation, the concept of a safe deposit should not be condemned because of the actions of some slippery bankers. The evolution of seeds as a survival capsule makes these little bundles of joy a perfect candidate for long-term preservation of genetic diversity and species. Seven out of every ten species produce seeds that can survive being dried and then stored in a domestic freezer unit. For how long they can survive is unknown, but seeds have survived frozen in Russian tundra for thirty thousand years. Seeds not only provide *Homo sapiens* with his daily bread, they are like manna from heaven for the conservation biologist. We know that a seed consists of an embryo, plus a meal and an overcoat for the embryo, but there is still a great deal to learn about their physiology and especially dormancy and germination. For the three out of ten species that will not tolerate drying or freezing, there are other possibilities such as cryopreservation and plantations.

ACT 9: CONSERVE 70 PERCENT OF THE GENETIC DIVERSITY OF CROPS AND OTHER VALUABLE PLANTS

The Players Agriculturists, horticulturists, seed biologists

The seed banks mentioned in act 8 were originally set up to conserve old varieties of our major crop plants and their wild relatives. A variety may be improved and become seemingly obsolete but it may have hidden talents. All gardeners know that plants survive in our gardens in conditions the like of which they will never see in their current natural habitats. It is inexplicable why plant species from the Azores, where they never experiences frost, will happily survive a frost of 0°F (-18°C). These old varieties may be resistant to new pests and diseases as they evolve. The wild relatives of our current crop plants are also a priceless resource in the biological arms race between crops and their pests and diseases.

Gardeners rarely grow the same varieties of crops as commercial growers. Rarely do we want to harvest the entire crop in one day because we then have to store the produce in the freezer or make it into something like jam. Amateur varieties come and go just like commercial varieties and so there are schemes in the amateur world to continue to cultivate rare and old varieties in the belief that one day they might be life-savers. Food security is becoming one of the most important problems for scientists to solve. We shall need different plants in the future that will tolerate different climates, poorer soils, drier soils, and maybe soils containing toxic levels of minerals.

Nor is it just the edible plants that we need to protect from the loss of genetic diversity from which the cheetahs are currently suffering. The genes of any plant that has a social or economic value are especially worthy of conservation.

ACT 10: PREVENT NEW BIOLOGICAL INVASIONS AND FIGHT CURRENT INVASIONS

The Players Reserve managers, custom officials, plant scientists, volunteers

The threats posed by non-native species running amuck were not identified until it was too late in many cases. It is foolishness of the first order to think that every species is perfectly fitted or designed for its current habitat. Evolution is about *the survival of the slightly less mediocre* and this means that it is perfectly possible that a plant species that has evolved somewhere else will be much better able to survive in a different country and outcompete its new neighbors. One obvious reason for this can be that the foreigner will have left all of its pests, diseases, and predators back home and so its spread is unimpeded by these. Not every foreign species behaves badly. On average only one in a thousand will become a nuisance.

These may not seem to be high odds, but the extent and persistence of the damage that can be perpetrated by these botanical hooligans is very great and almost by definition the damage cannot be contained.

Plant species have become extinct because of the invasions of exotic plants. Water supplies for humans have been affected in some countries. In other areas wildfires have become more common and damaging. Because there is rarely a quick control for these invasions once they have happened despite the valiant efforts of armies of volunteers, prevention is the only solution. Border crossings must be manned and ruthless searches carried out. Sadly plant lovers are the single largest conduit of plant imports. The rule must be until you are confident that you can kill it, do not take a plant where it does not naturally grow.

ACT 11: PREVENT ANY SPECIES FROM BEING ENDANGERED BY INTERNATIONAL TRADE

The Players Civil servants, nursery owners, taxonomists, customs officials

The value of plants is immense and so smuggling is one way of making money from them. It is not only the international trade in narcotic drugs that exercises customs officials. Plants are the start of many commercial processes and overharvesting of these plants from their habitats can put unsustainable pressure on the wild populations. The international trade in herbal remedies can be a powerful destructive force. The same is true of the international trade in animal parts for medicines though in the case of plants they may work.

So laws are passed by politicians based on the advice from experts and civil servants, but it is the customs officials and other law enforcement authorities who are expected to be able to identify the plants whose trade is restricted. In the case of orchids this is extremely difficult if the plants are not in flower. However, the DNA barcoding developed in act 1 comes into its own at this point because many orchid species and varieties can be accurately identified from just a scrap of leaf.

With an improvement in the detection of illegally harvest plants and bits thereof has come the realization in certain countries like the

Philippines and Turkey that there is an honest buck to be made here by setting up commercial nurseries where before none existed. In these countries there was no tradition of commercial ornamental nurseries, but in Turkey, for example, nurseries are growing snowdrops to satisfy the extraordinary demand for snowdrops in Europe that is rivalling the Dutch Tulip Mania of 1636. Fortunately, in addition to dna bar coding, there are also give-away physical signs that a group of plants in a nursery have been grown legitimately. For example, nursery-grown plants tend to be much more uniform than those ripped out of their habitat.

ACT 12: USE ONLY PLANT-BASED PRODUCTS THAT HAVE BEEN HARVESTED SUSTAINABLY

The Players Civil servants, ethical retailers, well-informed consumers

There is no biological credit card. This means that the supplies of those plant-derived products like timber that we need to build our houses, to fashion our furniture, and to manufacture our paper for books like this could run out. Until more has grown we shall just have to go without. It is well known that the energy that we are currently harvesting from fossil fuels like coal are a result of plant-based photosynthesis that took place hundreds of millions of years ago. These are being consumed as if they are savings that were fortuitously put in the bank for us by some evolutionary sugar daddy. Each year we burn fossil fuels that took three million years to accumulate.

Consumers have power. In a recession this is too plain to see as stores put up the shutters for the final time. Under international schemes such as the Forest Stewardship Council standards, when forest products are harvested at a responsible rate that does not endanger the future of the forest, those products are endorsed with a stamp of approval that gives responsible consumers the opportunity to spent their money responsibly and to defeat the forces of unsustainability.

ACT 13: HALT THE LOSS OF LOCAL KNOWLEDGE
The Players Ethnobotanists, lawyers, sociologists

Again knowledge is power. Wherever you travel in the world, you find that the locals have discovered facts about the plants in their region. This is perhaps not surprising since we are all one species with the same needs. The problem with knowledge is that sometimes it is not written down but it is passed down by word of mouth. Oral traditions can be easily lost—in just one generation. How do you recover information from granny when she is six feet underground? There is some fascinating evidence that very early humans cared for the older people so as to preserve their knowledge. How many of us, for example, learned how to grow vegetables from a parent or grandparent? The oral tradition exists everywhere, not just in remote woodland communities.

Intellectual property rights may be a common agenda item at the board meetings of pharmaceutical companies and in the offices of lawyers, but in small communities around the world there are not the same mechanisms for protecting the rights of indigenous people. It seems fair that these communities, who have discovered and passed down the information about the uses of plants, should be able to derive benefit from that knowledge if it is exploited on a global scale. Local knowledge is often vital to support local livelihoods. We therefore need ethnobotanists and ethno-lawyers to gather this information and protect the rights of the owners of the knowledge to ensure that they do not give away their inheritance.

ACT 14: INCORPORATE THE IMPORTANCE OF PLANT CONSERVATION INTO EDUCATION
The Players Teachers, science journalists, broadcasters

Not only are new recipients for knowledge constantly being born, but new knowledge is being discovered and that needs to be disseminated far and wide. Everyone from national decision makers and their advisors to young children going to school for the first time need to know, and deserve to know, how their future can be improved by looking after the herbage around them.

The problem with the information superhighway of the Internet is that there is now far too much information for anyone to keep on top. It is a duty of those who propagate knowledge to disseminate their facts in a form that is digestible by anyone who needs to know those facts. If you cannot explain what you are doing to an interested layman then you yourself do not understand it. When we are talking about awareness of plant diversity and its conservation, everyone needs to know, but how do you compete with other interests in people's lives like sport, music, literature, and most importantly cricket? The simplest way to get plants onto people's list of important things to know is chocolate: show a seven-year old that chocolate comes from a plant and that child will value plants for ever.

The range of ways in which information and knowledge can be passed on have expanded as knowledge and information have expanded. No longer do we have to sit people behind tables and feed them facts like beans and stew. Education has become very diverse from twenty-minute lectures on the Internet by world experts to dramatic reconstructions in botanic gardens. Both of these have provided me with very important messages in a form that makes them instantly burned onto the hard drive that is my memory.

ACT 15: TRAIN SUFFICIENT PEOPLE TO CARRY OUT THE WORK
The Players Teachers, lecturers, students

Plants are not going to be conserved unless somebody does the work. Whether they are going to get involved as professionals or amateurs, training is required by conservation workers. There is neither a shortage of people wanting to teach nor of people wanting to learn. There is a commonly held belief that botany is no longer taught at university. This is nonsense, but the subject has had a name change. Botany conjures up images of Victorian vicarages and Edwardian ladies. Botany is taught in biology, conservation, biogeography, and biodiversity courses the world over.

Gardeners and botanists of a certain age repeatedly express the fear that young people are not interested in plants. Young people are interested in so many things that plants have to compete for attention not only with all the other subjects but also with hormones and not just their own hormones. Perhaps plants are a subject to which people gravitate as they get older in the same way that they tend to stop playing on slides as they get older. As people live longer that actually means that more not fewer people will take up the cause of plants. Many retired people fill their retirement by volunteering to work with nongovernmental organizations in reserves or by working in their own gardens and backyards.

ACT 16: WORK TOGETHER IN NETWORKS SUPPORTING EACH OTHER

The Players The whole cast

The final act is an ensemble piece. We are now able to disseminate and share our experiences and endeavours. In this way mistakes can be avoided and the wheel does not have to be reinvented every time someone wants to conserve a plant or its habitat. The feeling that one is not alone is also of great comfort when the size of the problems starts to get you down. The networks work like ripples spreading out in a pond and then meeting other ripples and reinforcing them.

As this play draws to a close and the players come into the stage, you realize just how many people were involved in putting this show on the road: botanists (professional and amateur), database designers, IT managers, geneticists, engineers, field biologists, amateur naturalists, research scientists, landowners, gardeners, farmers, politicians, nongovernmental organizations, reserve managers, geneticists, local people, foresters, habitat managers, horticulturists, seed biologists, ecologists, agriculturists, customs officials, plant scientists, volunteers, civil servants, nursery owners, taxonomists, ethical retailers, well-informed consumers, ethnobotanists, lawyers, teachers, science journalists, broadcasters, sociologists, lecturers, and students.

When trying to conserve our plant inheritance, we all have a role to play—take a bow.

Further Reading

Anderson, Edgar. 1954. *Plants, Man & Life*. London: John Murray.

Balick, Michael J., and Paul Alan Cox. 1996. *Plants, People, and Culture: The Science of Ethnobotany*. Scientific American Library. New York: W. H. Freeman & Co.

Beerling, David. 2007. *The Emerald Planet: How Plants Changed Earth's History*. Oxford, UK: Oxford University Press.

Chivian, Eric C., and Aaron Bernstein, eds. 2008. *Sustaining Life: How Human Health Depends on Biodiversity*. Oxford, UK: Oxford University Press.

Darwin, Charles. 1859. *On the Origin of Species*. London: John Murray.

Diamond, Jared. 1997. *Guns, Germs, and Steel: The Fates of Human Societies*. New York: W. W. Norton and Company.

Gilbert, Oliver L., and Penny Anderson. 1998. *Habitat Creation and Repair*. Oxford, UK: Oxford University Press.

Hellin, Jon, and Sophie Higman. 2003. *Feeding the Market: South American Farmers, Trade and Globalization*. Sterling, Virginia: Kumarian Press.

Hobhouse, Henry. 2004. *Seeds of Wealth: Four Plants that Made Men Rich*. Washington, D.C.: Shoemaker & Hoard.

Hobhouse, Henry. 1999. *Seeds of Change: Six Plants that Transformed the World*. London: MacMillan Papermac.

Juniper, Barrie E., and David J. Mabberley. 2006. *The Story of the Apple*. Portland, Oregon: Timber Press.

Kingsbury, Noel. 2009. *Hybrid: The History and Science of Plant Breeding*. Chicago: University of Chicago Press.

Leadlay, Etelka, and Stephen Jury, eds. 2006. *Taxonomy and Plant Conservation*. Cambridge, UK: Cambridge University Press.

Lewington, Anna. 2003. *Plants for People*. London: Eden Project Books.

Luisi, Pier Luigi. 2006. *The Emergence of Life: From Chemical Origins to Synthetic Biology*. Cambridge, UK: Cambridge University Press.

Mabberley, David J. 2008. *Mabberley's Plant-book: A Portable Dictionary of Plants, their Classifications, and Uses*. Cambridge, UK: Cambridge University Press.

Mabey Richard. 1997. *Flora Britannica*. London: Sinclair-Stevenson.

Morton, Oliver. 2007. *Eating the Sun: How Plants Power the Planet*. London: 4th Estate.

Motley, Timothy J., Nyree Zerega, and Hugh Cross, eds. 2006. Darwin's Harvest, New Approaches to the Origins, Evolution and Conservation of Crops. New York: Columbia University Press.

Murphy, Denis J. 2007 *People, Plants and Genes: The Story of Crops and Humanity*. New York: Oxford University Press.

Pollan, Michael. 2001. *Botany of Desire: A Plant's-Eye View of the World*. New York: Random House.

Prance, Sir Ghillean, and Mark Nesbitt, eds. 2005. *The Cultural History of Plants*. New York: Routledge.

Prendergast, H. D. V., et al., eds. 1998. Plants for Food and Medicine. Cumbria, UK: Royal Botanic Gardens, Kew.

Smith, Alison M., et al. 2010. *Plant Biology*. New York: Garland Science.

Smith, Bruce D. 1995. *The Emergence of Agriculture*. Scientific American Library. New York: W. H. Freeman & Co.

Southwood Richard. 2003. *The Story of Life* New York: Oxford University Press.

Van Wyk, Ben-Erik, and Michael Wink. 2005. *Food Plants of the World*. Portland, Oregon: Timber Press.

Vaughan, John G., and Catherine A. Geissler. 2009. *The New Oxford Book of Food Plants*. New York: Oxford University Press.

Walker, Gabrielle, and Sir David King. 2008. *The Hot Topic: How to Tackle Global Warming and Still Keep the Lights On*. London: Bloomsbury.

Walker, Timothy. 2012. *Plants: A Very Short Introduction*. Oxford UK: Oxford University Press.

Zohary, Daniel, and Maria Hopf. 2000. *Domestication of Plants in the Old World: The Origin and Spread of Cultivated Plants in West Asia, Europe, and the Nile Valley*. 3rd Edition. Oxford UK: Oxford University Press.

Organization Websites

Bioversity International http://www.bioversityinternational.org/

Botanic Gardens Conservation International
http://www.bgci.org/usa/

The Convention on Biological Diversity
http://www.cbd.int/convention/

The Convention on International Trade in Endangered Species of Wild Fauna and Flora (CITES) http://www.cites.org/

Food and Agriculture Organization of the United Nations (UN FAO) http://www.fao.org/index_en.htm

International Union for Conservation of Nature (IUCN)
http://www.iucn.org/

Plants 2020 http://www.plants2020.net/

Royal Botanic Gardens, Kew http://www.kew.org/

World Wildlife Fund (WWF) http://worldwildlife.org/

Conversion Tables

To convert length:	Multiply by:
Miles to kilometres	1.6
Miles to metres	1609.3
Yards to metres	0.9
Inches to centimetres	2.54
Inches to millimetres	25.4
Feet to centimetres	30.5
Kilometres to miles	0.62
Metres to yards	1.09
Metres to inches	39.4
Centimetres to inches	0.39
Millimetres to inches	0.04

To convert area:	Multiply by:
Square inches to square centimetres	6.45
Square feet to square metres	0.093
Square yards to square metres	0.836
Acres to hectares	0.4
Square miles to square kilometres	2.6
Square centimetres to square inches	0.155
Square metres to square feet	10.8
Square metres to square yards	1.2
Hectare to acres	2.5
Square kilometres to square miles	0.386

Temperatures

°C = 5/9 × (°F−32)

°F = (9/5 × °C) + 32

Index

Abu Hureyra archeological site, Syria, 33
Aburi Medicinal Plant Garden, Ghana, 200–201
Africa, 32, 33, 35, 37, 151, 215, 235, 267. *See also* South Africa
   cotton cultivation, 35
   Flora for East Africa, 50
   food production, 173, 194, 195, 212, 213, 215
   landraces, 173
   medicinal plants, 180–181, 199–201
   RBS used in, 75
   Sub-Saharan, 125, 177, 194, 197, 212
African violet (*Saintpaulia*), 58
agriculture, 32–39. *See also* production lands and management
   arable land, 188
   beverage crops, 41
   China, rice and, 33
   conservation-friendly, 170–171
   conservation goal: conserve 70 percent of the genetic diversity of crops and other valuable plants, 143, 181, 273–274
   fertilizers, 188–190
   food origins and production (map), 212
   food security and, 171–172, 181, 184–185
   forage crops, 214
   four stages of, 38–40
   GM and, 194, 195–196
   Haber process, 188
   habitat destruction and, 217, 230
   human-made and -used fibers from plants, 34–36, 38
   international partnerships, 174–176
   invasive species and, 158
   landraces, 172, 173–174
   Natufian people as first, 33
   no-tillage systems, 174–175
   origins of major crops, 40–41
   percentage of the world's surface, 142–143
   pests and diseases, 193–194
   plant oils, 41, 217
   potato crops, 33, 177–179
   preserving fertility, 145
   production lands and management, 165–171, 270–271
   reliance on cultivars, 171
   seed banks for, 172, 174
   seeds for, 122
   slavery, crops dependent on, 36–37
   sustainable resource use and, 187–197
   sweet potatoes, 177
   UK specialization and, 238–239
   water needs, 190–191, 196
   wild relatives of crop plants, 193, 211–212, 213, 215
agrimony, 246
Albury Botanic Gardens, 88
algae, 22, 24–25
   as biofuel, 193
   invasive species, 158
Alhazen (Ibn al-Haytham), 253–254
angiosperms, 29
aquatic plants, 20, 22, 25, 244
Arbon, Ashley, 222
Archaeanthus linnenbergeri, 79
Arnold Arboretum, Boston, 113
arum family, 201
ash (*Fraxinus excelsior*), 243
assessment of species, 77–81, 266
   IUCN categories and RapidList comparison, 78–79
   players for, 266
   Red List, 74, 77
Asteraceae, 245
Aston Rowant National Nature Reserve, UK, 221, 222
Astralgalus, 74
Australia, 16, 126, 151
   arable land, 188
   Banks and, 126, 127
   Banksia, 126
   Banksia brownii recovery and repatriation, 127–129
   biodiversity hot spot in, 99
   bush die-back threat, 127–129
   endemism in, 99
   farmland degradation in, 188

fire regimes, 249
Gondwana Link project, 233
harvesting of featherflowers, 202
invasive species and, 109, 157, 158, 160, 163
Montane Thicket and Heath community, 127
restoration ecology in, 232–233, 234
seed banks, 124, 130, 138, 139, 140
species recovery projects in, 87–88
translocation in, 87
Australian National Herbarium, 88
Azores, 119, 223
climate, 224
Euphorbia stygiana and, 120–121, 223–229

Bacon, Sir Francis, 180
bananas, 195
Banks, Sir Joseph, 126–127, 128
Banksia, 126
Banksia brownii, 127–129, 140
Banksia solandri, 138, 139
baobab trees, 100
Barnes, Simon, 66
Barnes Reserve of the Wildfowl and Wetlands Trust, 89
Bartram, John and William, 79–80, 111–112, 223
Bauhin, Gaspard, 59–60, 69
Bauhin, Johann, 59
Bauhinia, 59
beans (*Phaseolus*), seed bank, 213
Berkshire, Buckinghamshire, and Oxfordshire Wildlife Trust (BBOWT), 102
Bill and Melinda Gates Foundation, 184, 196
biodiversity, 163
atlases for viewing, 77
biology of islands and, 151
comparing, phylogenies for, 72, 73
concentrations of, 77
conservation goal: conserve 70 percent of the genetic diversity of crops and other valuable plants, 12, 143, 181, 273–274
conservation goal: manage 75 percent of production lands to conserve genetic diversity, 12, 270–271
conservation goal: prevent biological invasions and manage areas invaded, 12, 160
conservation goal: protect 75 percent of the most important areas for plant diversity, 269–270
ecological resilience and, 96
endemic species, 99, 125, 223
ex situ conservation and, 109
50/500 rule, 114
foods crops and dwindling, 171
genetic, 41
goats as threat to, 157
GSPC 2020 objectives, 6, 12, 13, 270–74
hot spots, 52, 99, 125, 204, 233, 269
invasive species and, 158–160
levels of disturbance and, 206–207
Madagascar and, 99, 100–102, 125
number of known species, 15, 22–23
plant mobility and, 152
production-land management and, 168–169
reduction of, as bad, 94–95
as "sacred cow of biology," 94–95
seed banks and, 61–62, 141
Bioversity International (BI), 181
biological keys, 70–71
birch (*Betula pendula*), 205
bird's foot trefoil (*Lotus corniculatus*), 239
black knapweed (*Centaurea nigra*), 239
blackthorn (*Prunus spinosa*), 242
Boart, Jacob, the Younger, 59
bog-bean (*Menyanthes trifoliata*), 169, 239
borage (Boraginaceae), 64
Borlaug, Norman, 169, 171, 195
Borneo, 217–219
clearance for palm oil, 217
Heart of Borneo area, 217–218
illegal logging, 217
Botanical Research and Herbarium Management System (BRAHMS), 75
Botanical Society of the British Isles, 259–260
Botanic Gardens Conservation International (BGCI), 143

bottle gourd (*Lagenaria siceraria*), 32
Brassica oleracea, 31
Brazil, 192, 213
Briza minor, 88
Bromus hordeaceus, 220
Bromus interruptus, 219–222
Brunonia, 127
Brown, Robert, 126–127
Buckland, William, 189
buckthorn (*Rhamnus cathartica*), 244
Burkina Faso, 125
bush die-back (*Phytophthora cinnamomi*), 127–129
buttercup (Ranunculaceae), 131

camellia (Theaceae), 111–112
Cape primrose (*Streptocarpus*), 58
Capstick, Lucy, 250
carbon dioxide
  fixing of, and coal, 27
  fossil fuels and, 42, 191
  sequestration of, plants and, 97
carnivorous sundews (*Drosera*), 255
cassava (*Manihot*), 213–214
  seed bank for, 213–214
  viruses of, 214
catalogue of all known plants (compiling an online Flora), 12, 45–77, 264–265
  accurate and universal names, 45, 53, 56
  in ancient Greece, 54, 55, 58
  classification system for, 47, 56–57
  complexity of, 24
  as conservation goal, 12, 23–24, 46, 264–265
  creating regional Floras, 50–53
  current project, 53
  digital and satellite imaging and, 75
  DNA barcoding and, 66–67, 265
  geographic areas already complete, 48–50
  geographic areas with no or minimal plant inventories, 50
  herbaria, role of, 53, 75
  indigenous populations and, 51
  Internet images and, 53
  known catalogued plant species on earth by evolutionary group, 22
  monographs, 74
  phylogenies (evolutionary trees), 70–73
  plants collected but not classified, 23, 76
  players for, 264–265
  RBS technique, 75
  species already recorded and named, 45, 76
  taxonomic abyss, 23
  time estimate for, 23, 46–47
Caucasus, 99
Caulerpa taxifolia, 158
celery (Apiaceae), 55
Centre for Agricultural Biosciences (CABI), 176
Centre National de Semences Forestieres (CNSF), 125
Cesalpino, Andrea, 57–58
Chamovitz, David, 210
charophytes, 25
Chelsea Physic Garden, London, 111
China, 56
  Emperor Shennong's *Great Herbal*, 54
  ex situ conservation of dawn redwood, 113
  Ginkgo biloba and, 110, 112
  habitat restoration, 230–231
  hemp grown in, 34
  medicinal plants, 54, 80, 198, 199
  phosphate rock for fertilizer in, 190
  plant extinction threats, 80
  potato crops, 177
  production-land management in, 168
  rice domesticated in, 33, 39
  traditional medicine, 198
Chinese fir (*Cunninghamia lanceolata*), 230–231
Christopher, Marina, 225
Cistus, 112, 206
classification of plants, 47. *See also* species
  Darwin on, 69, 70, 73
  European taxa adopted for, 56–57
  genus, 47, 56
  history of systems, 54–69
  Linnaeus's system, 68–69
  monographs, 74, 76
  PhyloCode, 57

INDEX

ranking, current, 56–57
ranking, nineteenth century, 69
ranks below species, 57
Ray's contribution, 62–65
seeds and, 58
size of families, range, 81
taxonomic trees (phylogenies), 70–73
taxonomy, 54, 55, 56–57, 60, 69
climate change, 33, 42, 113, 234
fire regimes and, 249
gardeners and data on, 252–253
HIPPO and, 90
historic, 107
migration and, 163
"natural" states and, 105–106
plant adaptation and, 107, 252, 253
seed dispersal and, 153
spring flowering and, 104–105
threatened plants and, 88
velocity and regions, 104–105
climate space, 253
clover, red (*Trifolium pratense*), 239
clover, white (*Trifolium repens*), 239
cobra lily (*Darlingtonia californica*), 255, 271
cock's foot (*Dactylis glomerata*), 239, 245
Colombia, 213–214
common bent (*Agrostis capillaris*), 238
common sorrel, 246
common spotted orchids (*Dactylorhiza fuchsii*), 238
Conference of the Parties
The Hague, 9
Nagoya, Japan, 9–10, 180
Consortium for the Barcode of Life (CBOL), 67
Consultative Group on International Agricultural Research (CGIAR), 175, 176, 184, 185, 214
Convention on Biological Diversity, 6, 9, 183, 184
Convention on International Trade in Endangered Species (CITES), 116–117, 130
Convolvulus, 76
Cook, Captain James, 126
cork oak (*Quercus suber*), 206, 207
Corrigin grevillea (*Grevillea scapigera*), 87

Costa Rica, 68
Cotswold Wildlife Group, 89
cotton (*Gossypium*), 34, 35–36, 37, 113, 200
Council for Scientific and Industrial Research (CSIR), 180–181
cowpeas (*Vigna unguiculata*), 215
cowslips, 246
creeping marshwort (*Apium repens*), 86, 96, 108
crested dog's tail (*Cynosurus cristatus*), 239
Crick, Francis, 61, 62, 172
crimson spider orchid (*Caladenia concolor*), 88
Crowther, Lloyd, 250
cyads, 116–117
cyanobacterium, 7, 19, 22

Darlingtonia State Natural Site, Oregon, 255, 271
Darwin, Charles, 29, 60–61, 70, 73, 77, 90
on adaptation, 107, 224
on biodiversity hot spots, 269
on the biology of islands, 151
on the "entangled bank," 103
on "foreigners" (invasive plants), 146–147
genetic diversity and, 139
on the isolation of species, 223
on migration, 153, 156, 163
natural selection, 147, 148
principle of divergence, 95
"reproductive assurance," 95
on the struggle for survival, 150
on varieties, 121
Daubeny, Charles, 189, 243
Dawkins, Richard, 142
dawn redwood (*Metasequoia glyptostroboides*), 113, 117
De Materia Medica (Dioscorides), 55, 58
Diamond, Jared, 146
dicots, 62–65
Dines, Trevor, 94
Dioscorides, 55, 58
Dixon, Kingsley, 232–233
DNA, 33, 41, 61, 62, 65, 66, 67, 120, 172
barcoding, 66–68, 265, 275
CIP bank, 178

DNA (*continued*)
  distribution analysis with, 95
  human, "plant-specific" genes in, 210
  seed banks as gene banks, 172, 174
dog rose (*Rosa canina*), 242
dogwood (*Cornus mas*), 242
downy woundwort (*Stachys germanica*), 89, 96
Dryander, Jonas Carlsson, 126, 127
Dryandra, 127
Dunn, Jo, 89

eastern prairie fringed orchid (*Platanthera leucophaea*), 216–219, 221
Ecology of Invasions by Animals and Plants, The (Elton), 146
ecosystems
  bittern recovery programme, 89, 91
  climate change and, 104–105, 107
  conservation goal: protection of at least 15 percent of each ecological region and vegetation type, 12, 89, 91–93, 95–96
  conservation goal: protection of at least 75 percent of the most important regions, 12, 103, 269–270
  damages to, response, 162
  diversity and resilience of, 96
  as "entangled bank," 103
  fire regimes, 159–160
  interdependence of services, 164–165
  invasive species and destruction of, 159
  land sharing vs. land sparing and, 169
  local extinctions and, 95
  pollinator services and, 233–234
  services of, 97–98, 164, 233–234
  value or price of, 98–99
Ecuador, 243
education
  about plant diversity, 13
  botanic gardens and, 237
  incorporating the importance of plant conservation into, 277–278
  at Oxford Botanic Garden, 205
  seed banks and, 140, 142
  USDA NPGS centres and, 215–216
Elston, Charles, 146
Encephalartos ferox, 116–117

endemism, 99, 125
  Azores, 223
  hot spots of biological diversity and, 99
  Madagascar, 99, 125
  Slovakia, 125
  target regions for, 99
English bluebell (*Hyacinthoides non-scripta*), 91, 271–272
English yew (*Taxus baccata*), 197–198, 243, 266
Enquiry into Plants (Theophrastus), 54
Eucalyptus globulus, 158, 206
Eucommia ulmoides, 80, 198
eukaryotes, 19
Euphorbia, 74, 222, 228–229
Euphorbia amygdaloides, 124
Euphorbia characias, 55
Euphorbia dendroides, 119
Euphorbia inermis, 60
Euphorbia mellifera, 119–121
Euphorbia myrsinites, 55
Euphorbia stygiana, 116, 119–121, 223–229
Euphorbia ×pasteurii, 120, 121
European robins (*Erithacus rubecula*), 229
Evenson, Robert, 176
evolution, 15–43
  autotrophs (self-feeders), 19–20
  cyanobacterium, 19, 20, 21
  domestication of seed plants, 27–28, 30
  emergence or origins of life, 16–19
  endosymbiotic event, 7, 20, 21, 24
  of ferns, 26–27
  first plant cells, 20, 21
  green algae and, 24–25
  heterotrophs, 20
  of *homo sapiens*, 15
  invasive species and, 274
  known plant species on earth, catalogued by evolutionary group, 22
  of land plants, 25–26, 42, 150–151
  moon is formed, 16
  native vs. non-native plants and, 150–153
  natural selection and, 147–148
  number of species, 20, 22–23
  oldest fossilized cells, 16

INDEX

oxygen in atmosphere and, 27, 42
photosynthesis, 19, 42
plant classification today and, 70
research and, 130
of seeds, 27
soil, formation of, 26, 42
of trees, 26
ex situ conservation, 106–121
   advantages and disadvantages, 107–109
   conservation goal: conserving 75 percent of threatened species away from their habitats, 272–273
   of cycads, 116–117
   disadvantages
   GSPC Target 8 and, 106
   locations for, 106
   risks of hybridization and, 119–120
   species recovery and, 86, 108, 110–115
extinctions
   in China, 80
   Erica greyi, 125
   "extinct in the wild," 79, 80, 113, 222
   genetic bottlenecks and, 116
   global, 96
   invasive species and, 275
   IUCN categories and RapidList comparison, 78–79
   local, 94, 95, 96
   overcollection and, 80, 86, 112, 275–276
   predictions, 11, 81, 266
   as preventable, 8, 83, 250, 267
   Red List and, 77, 78
   rescue of *Franklinia alatamaha*, 111–113
   rescue of *Ginkgo biloba*, 110, 112
   species endemic to ocean islands, 223
   threatened plants, 80–81

Fabaceae, 214
false oat grass (*Arrhenatherum elatius*), 245
Fay, Michael, 222
faya-tree or fire-tree (*Myrica faya*), 159
featherflowers (*Verticordia species*), 202
feather-leaved banksia (*Banksia brownii*), 127
ferns, 26–27

Ferrula, 54–55
fertilizers, 188–190
field maple (*Acer campestre*), 242
Filer, Denis, 75
fire regimes, 159–160, 206
   interactions, 251
   invasive species and, 160, 275
   soil and, 248–249
   variations of, 249
flax, 34, 38
Flora
   for Britain and Ireland, 23, 48–49, 53
   conservation goal: compiling an online global Flora, 12, 74, 264–265
   of East Africa, 50
   first published, by Ray, 53
   global, 45, 46
   historiae plantarum, 59
   Madagascar, creating, 50–53
   North American species, 46, 49–50
   regional, 46, 50–53
Flora of Cambridgeshire (Ray), 53
Flora of North America, 59
Flora of Tropical East Africa, 50
Flower, Charles, 245, 250
food security, 171–172, 174–176, 274
   genetic resources and, 181, 184–185
   global seed vault and, 182–183
food web, 10
Forest Stewardship Council, 202, 203–205, 276
Fothergill, John, 112
Fourth Global Botanic Gardens Congress, 143
foxglove, 199
Franklinia alatamaha, 11, 79, 80, 108, 111–113
Fuchs, Leonhart, 58
Fuchsia, 58
fuel, 191–193
   from algae, 193
   biodiesel or bioethanol, 192–193
   fossil fuels, 42, 186, 189, 191, 192, 276
   from lignocellulose, 192–193
   water needed to produce biofuel, 192

gardeners, 11, 209–260
   carrying out research to develop conservation methods, 267

gardeners (*continued*)
    choice of plantings, 273–274
    contributions by, within GSPC framework, 259–260
    ex situ conservation and, 108, 109
    garden as production land, 271
    growing food at home, 193–194, 271
    Harcourt Arbortum hay meadow projects and, 237
    hybridization of non-native species caution, 92
    invasive species and, 154
    leaf mould use, 259
    as observers, effects of climate change, 252–253
    peat replacement and bog conservation, 11, 254–259
    plant conservation and, 8, 96, 250–260
    as plant custodians, 110
    scientific method for, 253–254
    species recovery projects and, 87
    training of, for plant conservation, 278–279
gene banks. *See* seed banks
genetic modification (GM), 194, 195–196
germplasm, 215
Gesner, Conrad, 58, 61
Gesneriaceae, 58
Ghana, 199–201
Ghini, Luca, 57–58
giant reed grass (*Arundo donax*), 192
Gilgall, Jordan, 30
Gilpin, William Sawrey, 237
Ginkgo biloba, 110, 112, 130
Gladiolus caryophyllaceous, 109
glaucophytes, 20, 22
Global Crop Diversity Trust (GCDT), 184
Global Strategy for Plant Conservation (GSPC), 2000–2010, 9
    targets hit and missed, 10–11
Global Strategy for Plant Conservation (GSPC), 2011–2020, 6, 10
    five objectives and sixteen targets of, 12–13, 264
    role of lay person, 260–263
    Target 1, 23–24, 74, 264–285
    Target 2, 74, 77, 266
    Target 3, 250, 267
    Target 4, 89, 250, 268–269
    Target 5, 103, 250, 269–270
    Target 6, 168, 250, 270–271
    Target 7, 84, 250, 271–272
    Target 8, 106, 250, 272–273
    Target 9, 143, 181, 273–274
    Target 10, 160, 274–275
    Target 11, 198, 275–276
    Target 12, 198, 250, 276
    Target 13, 211, 250, 277
    Target 14, 211, 250, 277–278
    Target 15, 211, 250, 278–279
    Target 16, 211, 250, 279–280
    vision statement, 6, 163, 210
    writing of, 262
Godfray, Charles, 182–183
Goethe, Wolfgang von, 105, 235
Gollin, Doug, 176
Gourd, Kat, 244
Gray, Asa, 49
Great Herbal (Shennong), 54
Green Revolution, 169, 171
gymnosperms, 29

Haberlea ferdinandii-coburgii, 58
habitat. *See also* ecosystems
    bogs, 254–256
    Borneo, problems of, 217–218
    climate change and, 252
    conservation goal: conserve 15 percent of every ecological region and vegetation type, 12, 89, 250, 268–269
    conservation goal: conserve 75 percent of threatened species in their habitats, 12, 271–272
    conservation goal: manage 75 percent of production lands to conserve genetic diversity, 12, 270–271
    conservation goal: protect 75 percent of the most important areas for plant diversity, 12, 269–270
    destruction of, 11, 86, 88, 90, 91, 146, 217, 230, 267
    ex situ conservation and, 108
    fragmentation of, 102, 233
    Harcourt Arbortum hay meadow projects, 237–247, 249–250
    humankind and carrying capacity of, 164

INDEX

for humans, 98
"natural" states and, 235
plant biodiversity and, 94–95, 96
removing the threat in, 84–86
restoration, 170–171, 216–250
in situ conservation and, 84–106
soil, importance of, 248–249
species loss in, 96
species recovery programmes and, 114
woodland creation, 243–244
woodland destruction, 201–205
woodland management, 271–272
Haldane, J. B. S., 81
Harcourt, Sir Simon, 237
Harcourt, William Vernon, 237, 243
Harris, Stephen, 119
Hawaii, 159
hawthorn (*Crataegus monogyna*), 242
Hawthorne, William, 75
hazel (*Corylus avellana*), 205, 242
hedgerow buckthorn (*Rhamnus cathartica*), 242
el-Hemmeh, Jordan, 39
hemp (*Cannabis sativa*), 34
Henchie, Stewart, 117, 222
Henslow, John Stephens, 189
HIPPO (habitat destruction, invasive species, pollution, population growth, overexploitation), 90–91, 146, 267
Historia Plantarum Universalis (Bauhin), 59
Holme, Robert, 222
Holmes, Keith, 243
honeysuckle, 112
Hoodia, 180–181
hornbeam (*Carpinus betulus*), 243
humankind (*Homo sapiens*), 157
agriculture and, 32–39, 122, 142–143
carrying capacity of habitat and, 164
cooking of food, 28
crops dependent on slave labor, 36–37
domestication of seed plants, 27–28
ecosystems and, 98
food production and, 187–197
food wastage, 194, 197
future food supplies, 169, 171, 180, 181, 184–185, 195, 274
hunter-gatherers and farming, 38–40
maximum population and living within Earth's biological means, 145
plant dispersal and non-native species, 154, 157–158
plant fibers used by, 34–36
plants and survival of, 7, 28, 42, 142–143, 163
"plant-specific" genes in DNA of, 210
population growth, 145, 146, 165, 169, 171, 180, 187, 195
use of fire, 28, 30
Humbolt, Alexander, 146
Humphreys, Helen, 228–229
hybrids
evolution and, 116
ex situ conservation risks of, 119–121
"hybrid vigor," 109, 119
plant mobility and, 153
as potential invasive species, 109
Spanish bluebell and, 91
threatened plants, advantages of, 116

ice plant (*Carpobrotus edulis*), 157
identification of plants
biological keys for, 70–71
DNA and, 62, 66–67
electron microscope and, 62
indigenous populations and, 130, 143
information recorded and, 52
new or existing species, determining, 51–52
type specimen, 52
India, 34, 35, 36, 74, 151
agricultural advances, 174–175
Ayurvedic medicine, 40
groundwater depletion, 190
indigenous populations
biological resources and, 202, 203, 270, 277
conservation goal: maintain and conserve knowledge associated with plant resources, 13, 211, 277
conservation goal: preserve genetic diversity and local knowledge and practice, 12, 143, 181
conservation goal: protect 75 percent of the most important areas for plant diversity and, 269–270
hoodia exploitation and, 180–181

indigenous populations (*continued*)
   medicinal plants and, 40, 180
   naming plants and, 51
   plant collection and, 130
   tropical woodland and, 270
Indonesia, 232
   Harapan Forest project, 232
Inheritors of the Earth, 179
in situ conservation, 84–106, 116
   advantages, 103, 142
   conservation goal: conserve 75 percent of threatened species in their habitats, 12, 271–272
   creeping marshwort, 86
   lady's slipper orchid, 85–86
   problems of, 103–104
   removing the threat and, 84–86
   snake's head fritillary, 85
   translocation, 86, 87–88
Intermountain Flora, 46
International Barcode of Life (iBol) project, 67
International Centre for Tropical Agriculture (CIAT), 213–214
International Institute for Tropical Agriculture (IITA), 215
International Maize and Wheat Improvement Centre (CIMMYT), 174, 175, 182, 211–212
International Potato Centre (CIP), 177–179
International Rice Research Institute (IRRI), 174, 175, 212–213
International Treaty on Plant Genetic Resources for Food and Agriculture (ITPGRFA), 176, 180, 183, 184
International Union for Conservation of Nature (IUCN), 77, 127
   categories and RapidList comparison, 78–79
   extinction categories, 79–80
   threatened categories, 80–81
   World Parks Congress 2003, 100
invasive species, 11, 12, 111, 145, 146–163
   Caulerpa taxifolia, 158
   conservation goal: prevent new biological invasions and fight current invasions, 12, 160, 274–275
   damage by and cost, 158–160

Eucalyptus globulus, 158
faya-tree or fire-tree, 159
Gladiolus caryophyllaceous, 109
history of, 150–153
hybrids as, 109
ice plant, 157
introduced genetic material, 146
invasive non-native species, 146
maritime or cluster pine, 158
Monterey pine, 158
Norway maple, 111
plant conservation and, 161, 162–163
Port Jackson willow, 160, 231–232
predator release and, 156
problematic native species, 146
purple loosestrife, 156
reasons for plant mobility, 154, 157–158
selective advantage of, 156
seven stages of an invasion, 161
soil conservation and, 157
Spanish bluebell, 91
strategic response, 162
study of, first, 146
Tens Rule, 154, 155, 156, 163
Ipomoea, 76
iris (Iridaceae), 56–57

Jadin des Plantes, Paris, 51
Japanese knotweed (*Fallopia japonica*), 160
Jardin Botánico Canario Viera y Clavijo, 9
jatropha (*Jatropha curcas*), 192
Jeans, Julia, 226–227
Jefferson, Thomas, 37
John Bartram Heritage Collection, 223
John Innes Centre, Norwich, UK, 215
Jones, Ben, 134
Jordan, 190
jute (*Corchorus capsularis*), 34, 207

Kelly, Clare, 224
Kidd, John, 189
Killarney fern (*Trichomanes speciosum*), 90–91
Kings Park and Botanic Garden, Perth, 88, 128
Kremen, Claire, 100–101

INDEX

Kruger National Park, South Africa, 68
kudzu vine, 157

lady's slipper orchid (*Cypripedium calceolus*), 85–86, 115
lady's smock (*Cardamine pratensis*), 240
Lamarck, Jean Baptiste, 70–71
land plants, 22, 25–26, 81, 150–151
landraces, 172, 173–174, 179, 211, 215, 216
Lan Su Chinese Garden, Oregon, 154
late knapweed, 246
Lawes, John Bennet, 189–190
legumes, 27
Lewis, Rebecca "Boo," 244
Liebig, Justus von, 189
lignin, 10
Lincoln, Abraham, 37
linen (*Linum usitatissimum*), 34
Linnaeus, Carl, 59, 60, 68–69, 111, 146
linseed oil (*Linum usitatissimum*), 207
liverworts, 25–26
Lyon, John, 112
Lyons, Israel, 126

Mabberley, David, 222
Mabberley's Plant-Book (Mabberley), 222
MacBurney, Susan, 226, 228
Madagascar, 50–53, 151
  biodiversity and, 99, 100–102, 125
  conservation in, priority areas, 101–102
  number of species, 100
  protected areas, 100–102
  Royal Botanic Gardens, Kew and, 125
magnolia, 74, 77
Magnolia denudate, 56
Magnolia liliflora, 56
Mahonia fortunei, 57
maize (corn), 40, 64, 174, 175, 176, 192, 211–212, 213
Manihot esculenta, 213–214
Manihot walkerae, 214
maples, 74
maritime or cluster pine (*Pinus pinaster*), 158, 206
Mattiola, Piers Andrea, 57–58
meadow buttercups (*Ranunculus acris*), 104
meadow clary (*Salvia pratensis*), 94–95

Mead's milkweed (*Asclepias meadii*), 216–219, 221
medicinal plants, 7, 29, 40, 41, 198–199
  China and, 54
  conservation goal: prevent any species from being endangered by international trade, 275–276
  conservation goal: protect from over-collection and source sustainably, 13, 198
  Dioscorides's volumes, 55
  English yew, 197–198, 266
  evolutionary classification and search for, 71–72
  foxglove, 199
  galantamine-producing genus, 72
  Ghana and cultivated plants, 199–201
  hoodia, 180–181
  indigenous populations and, 40
  Neatherthal man using, 41–42
  overcollection and, 198
  Pacific yew, 197, 266
  plant oils, 41
  poisons and, 199
  potato family, 72
  rosy periwinkle, 100, 264
  Strophanthus, 199
  sustainable resource use and, 197–201
Mediterranean region, 153
  as biodiversity hot spot, 99
  climate change and, 234
  dormancy adaptation in, 227
  invasive plants and, 157, 158
Mendel, Gregor, 61
Menyanthes trifoliata, 169
Metrosideros polymorpha, 159
Mexico, 35, 211–212
micropropagation, 115
Millennium Seed Bank Project (MSBP), 86, 124–125, 142, 176
  Banksia brownii in, 128–129, 140
  Banksia solandri in, 138
  Bromus interruptus in, 220
  Esmée Fairburn Foundation grant, 246–247
  euphorbias and, 226
  funding of, 129–130
  percentage of all plant species in, 143
Miller, Philip, 111

mint (Lamiaceae), 126
miscanthus (*Miscanthus*), 192
Missouri Botanical Garden, 8, 43, 143
   Global Flora project, 53
monocots, 62–64
monographs, 74, 76
   on *Convolvulus and Ipomoea*, 76
Monterey pine (*Pinus radiata*), 158
Mora, Camilo, 22
Morison, Robert, 49, 59
mosses, 25–26, 141
mycorrhizal fungi, 103, 141, 190
Myers, Norman, 99, 233

names/naming of plants
   accurate and universal, 45, 53
   binomial system of nomenclature, 59–60
   choice, when duplicate names exist, 53
   duplicate names, 53, 76
   Euphorbia stygiana hybrid, 119, 120
   Eurocentric bias in, 56–57
   history of, 54–61
   indigenous populations and, 51
   lack of central clearing house, 53
   species names, creating, 52
   standardization of, 69
   synonyms, 53, 76, 91
Naming of Names (Pavord), 60
National Fruit Collection at Brogdale, Kent, 216
National Museum of Wales, 67
Natural England, 86
Nelumbo nucifera, 124
Nevali Cori, Turkey, 38
New Flora of Britain and Ireland (Stace), 49
New York Botanical Garden, 154
New Zealand, 151
   biodiversity hot spot in, 99
   invasive species in, 156, 163, 225
Ngalue caves, Mozambique, 28
Nigeria, 213
   global gene bank in, 215
Norway
   Heart of Borneo funding by, 217–218
   Svalbard Global Seed Vault, 182–183, 184
Norway maple (*Acer platanoides*), 111

oak (*Quercus robur*), 74, 243
Ohalo II site, Galilee, 38, 39
oilseed rape, 192
Okefenokee Swamp, 255
On the Origin of Species (Darwin), 60, 69, 73, 103, 146–147, 224
orchids, 48
   Brassia, 48
   DNA barcoding for, 68, 275
   hybrids, 48
   Laelia, 48
   pollinators, 141
   seed germination, 133, 141
   in situ conservation, 85–86, 88
   Sutingara, 48
   wild-harvested, 201
Orwell, George, 148
ox-eye daisy, 246
Oxford Botanic Garden. *See* University of Oxford Botanic Garden
Oxford Preservation Trust, 86
Oxfordshire Rare Plants Group, 86
Oxford University Press (OUP), 59

Pacific yew (*Taxus brevifolia*), 197, 202, 266
palm oil, 192
Parrish oaks, 241
parthenocarpic fruit, 30, 32
partnerships and people for plant conservation, 209–260
   assessing conservation status of all plant species, 266
   Bromus interruptus recovery and, 219–222
   carrying out research to develop conservation methods, 267
   conserve 70 percent of the genetic diversity of crops and other valuable plants, 273–274
   conserving 75 percent of threatened species away from their habitats, 272–273
   conserving 75 percent of threatened species in their habitats, 271–272
   Euphorbia stygiana recovery and, 223–229
   GSPC 2020 strategy and, 210–211, 264–280

INDEX

halting the loss of local knowledge, 277
incorporating the importance of plant conservation into education, 277–278
international cooperation, 211–216
making safe 15 percent of every ecological region and vegetation type, 268–269
online Flora compilation and, 264–265
preventing any species from being endangered by international trade, 275–276
preventing new biological invasions and fighting current invasions, 274–275
protecting 75 percent of the most important areas for plant diversity, 269–270
regional networks and local know-how, 216–250
three North American species, recovery scenarios, 216–219
training of people, 278–279
using only plant-based products that have been harvested sustainably, 276
working in networks, 279–280
Pasteur, George, 119
Pavard, Anna, 60
peas (*Pisum sativum*), 215
peat (sphagnum peat), 255–259
Philippines, 201, 212–213, 276
Phoenix Perennial Plants, 225
photosynthesis, 7, 19, 42, 98, 186
phylogenies (evolutionary trees), 70–73
Phytophthora cinnamomi, 127–129
Picaq Potato Park, Cusco, Peru, 179
pignut (*Conopodium majus*), 238
Pinax Theatri Botanici, 60
Pitcher's thistle (*Cirsium pitcheri*), 216–219, 221
plant conservation, 250–260. *See also specific topics*
agriculture and, 170–171
assessing the status of all known plant species, 12, 74, 77–81, 266
bogs, 254–256
carrying out research to develop conservation methods, 12, 267
compiling an online Flora of all known plants, 12, 45–77, 264–265
of ecosystems, 89, 91–93, 95–96
ecotourism and, 179
education and, 277–278
ex situ, 106–121
funding of, 181, 184–185
gene and seed banking, 61, 122–143, 169–185
bioversity and, 12, 41, 61–62
GSPC 2000–2010, 9, 10–11
GSPC 2011–2020, 6, 10, 11–13
invasive species and, 146–163, 274–275
local scale, 96
macro-conservation, 264, 267, 268, 271, 272
making safe 15 percent of every ecological region and vegetation type, 12, 268–269
of medicinal plants, 40, 198–199
micro-conservation, 264, 267, 271–272 (*see also ex situ* conservation)
native/non-native–natural/unnatural matrix and, 160, 162–163
people as element in, 8, 11, 12, 104, 115, 171, 209–280 (*see also* gardeners; indigenous populations; partnerships and people for plant conservation)
preventing extinction, 8, 11, 84–121
priorities, 73
priority areas, setting, 99, 100–102, 269
production lands and management, 12, 165–171, 270–271
restoration ecology and, 216–250
science of good, 66–68
in situ, 84–106
soil protection and, 262–263
sustainable resource use and, 12, 186–207, 276
training of people and, 13, 278–279
translocation and, 87–88
working in networks for, 279–280
plant distributions, 52
atlases for, 77
data for, 52–53
DNA barcoding and, 67–68
monographs and, 74, 76

plant distributions (*continued*)
  of spreading bellflower, 95
  unequal documentation, geographic and groups, 74
Plant Heritage, UK, 222, 260
  National Plant Collections Scheme, 222–223
Plantlife, 94
plant press, 51
plants
  archaeophytes vs. neophytes, 148–149
  cell, internal structures of, 30
  chloroplasts of, 20, 21
  cuticle of, 25
  decay of, and soil, 26
  defining characteristics, 20, 22
  displacement of native biology, 11
  domestication of, 31, 32
  evolution, 7, 15–43
  evolutionary groups, 22
  flowering, 22–23, 29, 62–64, 71–72, 73
  genes of (see seeds)
  human survival and, 7, 27–28, 42, 98
  micropropagation, 115
  mobility of, 148–149, 152–153
  monocots and dicots, 62–65
  number of species, 22–23
  phloem, 34, 64
  propagation, cuttings vs. seeds, 58, 61
  as renewable, sustainable, 6, 7
  simplest extant, 20
  water cycle and, 97
  wild vs. domesticated crops, 38–39
  xylem, 64
Poaceae, 214, 245
pollen, 25, 42
pollination, 30, 115
pollinators, 103, 112, 165, 241
  brimstone butterflies, 244
  for *Encephalartos ferox*, 116–117
  reestablishment of, 233–234
  seed banks and lack of, 141
  species specific, 264
poplars (*Populus species*), 192
Porley, Ron, 222
Port Jackson willow (*Acacia saligna*), 160, 231–232
Portugal
  cork production, 207, 270

invasive species and, 158
production-land management, 168–169
potato (Solanaceae), 72, 216
  Commonwealth Potato Collection, 216
  cryopreservation, 178
  field-grown gene banks, 178
  gene banks for, 177, 178
  herbarium for, 178
  named cultivars of, 177
  potato park strategy, 178–179
  in vitro conservation, 178
production lands and management, 165–171
  conservation goal: managing 75 percent of production lands to conserve genetic diversity, 12, 168, 270–271
  land sharing vs. sparing and, 169, 170
  Portugal and Spain, 168–169, 270
  in the UK, 165, 168, 270
purple loosestrife (*Lythrum salicaria*), 156
Pyrenean violet (*Ramonda myconii*), 58

Quechua-Aymara Association for Sustainable Communities (ANDES), 179
quinine, 37

Rae Selling Berry Seed Bank, 124
Ramsay, Margaret, 141
rapid botanical surveys (RBS), 75
RapidList, 78
Raven, Peter, 143
Ray, John, 49, 53, 59, 60–65
  six rules for classification, 64
red fescue (*Festuca rubra*), 239
Red List, 74, 77–78, 198
reed canary grass (*Phalaris arundinacea*), 192
restoration ecology, 216–250. *See also* species recovery programmes
  Australia, 232–233
  Borneo, 217–219
  botanic gardens and, 236–247, 250
  China, 230–231
  climate change and, 234
  conservation goal: protect at least 15 percent of each ecological region or vegetation type, 12, 268–269

INDEX

ecosystem services and, 233–234
habitat restoration projects, 229–250
Indonesia, 232
"natural" states and, 235–236
players for, 267
players in, 268–269
seed bank for, 246–247
South Africa, 231–232
species loss and, 234–235
species recovery programmes, 216–229
three North American species, recovery scenarios, 216–219
three principles, 236
what it is, 218
Rhododendron ponticum, 90, 160
rhododendrons, 74, 90
ribwort plantain (*Plantago lanceolata*), 239, 246
rice, 33, 39, 40, 176, 177
African rice (*Oryza glaberrima*), 212
Asian rice (*Oryza sativa*), 212
GM, 195
resistance to yellow stunt virus, 193
seed banks, 174, 175, 182, 212–213
rosin (from *Pinus* spp.), 207
rosy periwinkle (*Catharanthus roseus*), 100, 264
Rothamsted Research Station, 172, 189
GM wheat trials, 195–196
Park Grass Experiment, 189
Royal Botanic Gardens, Edinburgh, Scotland, 220
Royal Botanic Gardens, Kew, England, 43, 50, 142, 220
Encephalartos ferox and, 117
flora of Madagascar and, 125
founding of, 126
Global Flora project, 53
lady's slipper orchid preservation, 86
Millennium Seed Bank Project, 86, 124–125, 128–129, 176
specimens at, 75
Royal Society for the Protection of Birds (RSPB), 102
Ruta Condor Project, 178–179
Rwanda, 172

sainfoin (*Onobrychis viciifolia*), 220
San José de Aymara seed bank, 179
Savings, John, 242
Scotland, Robert, 76
Scottish Crop Research Institute, Invergowrie, Scotland, 216
seed banks (gene banks), 61–62, 106, 118, 122–142
in Australia, 124
choosing species and obtaining permission to collect, 129–130
communal, 179
conservation goal: conserve 75 percent of threatened species away from their habitats, 273
creating a model gene bank, 177–179
for crops and related wild species, 172, 174
dormancy of seeds, 132–133, 138–139
drying and chilling seeds, 136
ex situ conservation and, 115
finding and identifying plants for, 130–131
gene banking and local knowledge, 176, 180–181
as gene banks, 172, 174
genetic diversity and, 139, 141
handling of seeds post-collection, 134, 135–136
how they work, 125
indigenous populations and, 180–181
information recorded upon collection, 134–135
international, 172, 211–216
maintenance of seeds in, 132–133
Millennium Seed Bank Project, 86
Nagoya Protocol and access, 180
oldest, 172
percentage of seeds to collect, 135, 139
potato crops, 177–179
preparing for storage, 136–137
pros and cons, 138–142
quarantine of seeds, 136
recalcitrant seeds and, 140–141
for restoration ecology, 246–247
safeguarding and funding genetic resources, 181, 184–185
seed readiness for collection, 131
in Slovakia, 125
soil and "natural" bank, 122.124
species recovery programmes and, 222

seed banks (*continued*)
   Svalbard Global Seed Vault, 182–185, 211
   testing frequency, 137
   testing viability of seeds, 132, 136–137
   threats to, 184
   in the UK, 124–125, 128, 189
   Vavilov and, 172, 270
   in vitro conservation, 178
seed plants, 22, 29
seeds
   buttercup family (Ranunculaceae), 131
   classification and, 58
   dispersal, 152–153
   domestication of, 27–28
   dormancy, 132–133, 138–139, 227
   evolution of and resilience, 27, 137, 142
   ex situ conservation and, 117
   as food, 27
   gene conservation and, 122–143
   obligate seeders, 127
   oldest germinated, 124, 273
   overcollection and, 117
   preservation of, 172, 173–174
   structure and function of, 123, 273
   unknown elements of, 128
seed stores, 172
Selfish Gene, The (Dawkins), 142
Sibthorp, Humphrey, 126
Silene stenophylla, 124
Silo National des Graines Forestières, 125
Silva, Luis, 223
silviculture, 158, 201–205
   certification for sustainably managed forests, 203–205
   China, 230–231
   forest assessment, 203–204
   using woodland products, 206–207
sisal (*Agave sisalana*), 34, 207
Sixteenth International Botanical Congress (1999), 8–9
sloe or blackthorn (*Prunus spinosa*), 104
Slovakia, 125
Slovak Seed Bank, 125
small-leaved lime (*Tilia cordata*), 243
Smith, Philip, 220, 221
snake's head fritillary (*Fritillaria meleagris*), 85, 91, 96

snowdrops (*Galanthus nivalis*), 72, 104, 276
Socrates, 180
soil
   allelopathy and, 228
   as carbon store, 248
   composts, 256–257, 258
   cowpeas and conservation of, 215
   erosion, 97, 100, 196, 248, 263
   fire-derived organic matter, 248–249
   formation of, 26, 42, 263
   functions, 248
   habitats and, 248–249
   invasive species and conservation measures, 157
   loam, 256
   mesotrophic, 238
   as "natural" seed bank, 122.124
   Park Grass Experiment study, 189
   preparing for meadow restoration, 247
   preserving fertility, 145
   protection of, 262–263
   sequestration of carbon dioxide and, 97
   surface erosion, 175
Solander, Daniel, 126
South Africa, 28, 99, 100, 125
   Cape Peninsula, biodiversity hot spot, 99
   CSIR in, 180
   fire regimes, 249
   invasive species and, 109, 157, 158, 160, 231–32
   Red List, 109
   restoration ecology in, 231–232
South America
   cotton cultivated in, 35
   domestication of seed plants in, 33, 40
   maize crop, 212
   phosphate rock exports, 190
   potato crops and, 178–179
   potato parks, 179
   RBS used in, 75
soybean, 192
Spain, 207, 270
Spanish bluebell (*Hyacinthoides hispanica*), 92
species, 47
   assessment, 77–81, 266

INDEX

collecting, 51
declining, 84, 85
defined, 47–48
DNA of, 66
identification keys and, 70–71
identifying, 51–52
naming of, 52
native vs. non-native, 148, 149
number of, 15
ranks below (var., ssp., cultivar), 57, 121, 153
Ray's definition, 61
recovery programmes, 84–86, 216–250
standardization of names, 69
variation within, 58, 61
Species Plantarum (Linnaeus), 60, 69
species recovery programmes, 84–86, 216–250
backyard gardeners and, 87
Bromus interruptus, 220–222
creeping marshwort, 86, 87
crimson spider orchid, 88
dawn redwood, 113
Euphorbia stygiana, 118–121, 223–229
ex situ programmes, 114–116
lady's slipper orchid, 85–86
snake's head fritillary, 85
three North American species, recovery scenarios, 216–219
spindle (*Euonymus europaeus*), 242
sporopollenin, 25, 42
spreading bellflower (*Campanula patula*), 95
spurge, 55, 124
Sri Lanka, 171, 175
Stace, Clive, 49
stinging nettle (Urticaceae), 126
stoneworts, 25, 26
Strophanthus, 199
sugar (*Saccharum officinarum*), 36–37
sugarcane as biofuel source, 192
sustainable resource use, 13, 186–207
conservation goal: protect wild flora from overcollection and source plant-based products sustainably, 13, 198, 276
economics of biology and, 186

fertilizers, raw materials for, 188–190
food production and, 187–197
food wastage and, 194, 197
forestry and, 201–205
fuel, 186, 191–193, 276
medicinal plants, 197–201
nurseries, 201
peat replacement and bog conservation, 254–259
population growth and, 187, 195
water, 190–191, 192
woodland products in daily use, 206–207
Svalbard Global Seed Vault, 182–183, 184–185, 211
sweet chestnut (*Castanea sativa*), 205
sweet potatoes (*Ipomoea batatas*), 177, 188
sweet sorghum, 192
sweet-vernal grass (*Anthoxanthum odoratum*), 238
switchgrass (*Panicum virgatum*), 192
Syria, 33, 190

taxol, 197
Tennyson, Lord Alfred, 165
Tens Rule, 155, 156, 163
tetrazolium test, 132, 136
Theophrastus, 54, 253
Thomson, Keith, 113
Threatened Flora Seed Centre (TFSC), 124, 130, 139, 140
threatened plants, 80–81. *See also* seed banks
Banksia brownii, 127–128
Banksia solandri, 138, 139
conservation goal: conserve 75 percent of threatened species away from their habitats, 273
conservation goal: conserve 75 percent of threatened species in their habitats, 271–272
conservation goal: protect wild flora from over collection and source plant-based products sustainably, 13, 198, 276
Diamond's evil quartet of threats, 146
ecosystem recovery and, 91–93
ex situ conservation and, 108

threatened plants (*continued*)
　habitat loss, 86, 88
　HIPPO and, 90–91, 146, 267
　hybridization and, 92
　medicinal plants, 198
　overcollection and, 88, 198
　repatriation of, 129
　in situ conservation, 84–88, 89, 91–93
　in Slovakia, 125
　Targets 11 and 12 and, 198
　three North American species, recovery scenarios, 216–219
　types of threats, 88–89, 127–129
Tithymalus cyparissius, 60
toothwort (*Lathraea squamaria*), 239
Torrey, John, 49
translocation, 87–88
Treborth Botanic Garden, Wales, 94
trees, 26, 29, 124. *See also* silviculture
　native British, 243
　planting by schoolchildren, 243
　woodland creation, 243–244
Tripsacum, 212
Turkey, 276
Turner, Ian, 222
type specimen, 52

Uganda, 195
umbellifers, 55
United Kingdom
　agricultural land, 102
　bittern recovery programme, 89, 91
　bogs of, 255
　Bromus interruptus recovery, 219–222
　cotton industry, 37
　Countryside Stewardship, 241
　English bluebell conservation, 91–93, 271–272
　Flora for, 48–49
　fragmentation in conservation areas, 102
　hay meadows, 170–171, 237–247, 250
　hedge species, 242
　invasive species in, 157, 160
　land sharing and organic farms, 169
　medicinal plants used in, 40
　native trees, 243
　peat bogs, 255
　Phenology Network, 252
　plant data in, 130
　plants catalogued in, 23
　plant species of Mesotrophic Grasslands (MG5), 238–239
　plant species with varying root depths, 246
　production lands and management, 165, 168, 270
　seed banks, 124, 129, 172, 189, 215, 216 (*see also* Millennium Seed Bank Project)
　in situ conservation in, 85–86
　species assessment in, 74
　species recovery projects in, 85–86, 88, 89, 90–91, 94–95
　woodland management, 271–272
United States
　biodiversity hot spot in, 99
　bioethanol and biodiesel production, 192
　bogs (swamps) of, 255
　Convention on Biological Diversity and, 183
　endemism in, 99
　food wastage and, 194
　invasive species in, 156, 157, 158
　ITPGRFA and, 183
　seed banks, 124, 215–216
United States Department of Agriculture (USDA): National Plant Germplasm System (NPGS), 215–216
University of Oxford Botanic Garden, 75, 85, 86, 113, 126, 146, 154
　bog-bean (*Menyanthes trifoliata*) at, 169
　Bog Garden, 156
　Bromus interruptus recovery, 219–222
　charcoal making, 207
　Encephalartos ferox and, 117
　euphorbias at, 222
　Euphorbia stygiana and, 119–121, 223–229
　Franklinia alatamaha and, 111–112
　Friends of, 243
　FSC certified timber and, 205
　Harcourt Arbortum, 92–93, 134, 169, 170–171, 205
　Harcourt Arbortum hay meadow projects, 237–247, 249–250

INDEX

IRRI seeds at, 213
Menyanthes trifoliata at, 169
Palmer's Leys, 242–247, 249–250
peat use and alternatives, 257–258
purple loosestrife in, 156
Pylon Meadow, 239–240, 242, 244, 245–246, 249, 250
Windmill Hill meadow, 238–239, 240
woodland creation, 243–244
woodland management, 205–206, 207
Upson, Tim, 222
US Seed Savers Exchange, 260

vascular plants, 22
Vavilov, Nicolai, 172, 270
Venus flytrap (*Dionaea muscipula*), 111

Wales, 67, 94
Walters, Max, 56
Washington state, 74
water
    conserving, ornamental plants and, 191
    crop production and, 190–191
    depletion of groundwater, 190
    invasive species and, 231–232, 275
    management, Sri Lanka, 175
    production of biofuel and, 192
Watson, Hewett Cotterell (H.C.), 120

Watson, James, 61, 62, 172
wayfaring tree (*Viburnum lantana*), 242
wheat, 33, 38, 40, 41, 64, 168, 174, 175, 212
    GM, 196
    Green Revolution agriculture and, 171
wild carrot, 246
wild strawberry trees (*Arbutus unedo*), 206
Wilford, Richard, 222
Wilkinson, Paul, 249
willows (*Salix* species), 192
Wilson, E. O., 146
wood anemones (*Anemone nemorosa*), 104, 131
wood spurge (*Euphorbia amygdaloides*), 124
Working for Water, 231–232
World Conservation Monitoring Centre (WCMC), 81, 200
wrens (*Troglodytes troglodytes*), 229

yams, 215
yellow rattle (*Rhinanthus minor*), 240, 245, 246
Yorkshire fog grass (*Holcus lanatus*), 239, 245

Zimbabwe, 32

About the Author

Timothy Walker has been Director of the University of Oxford Botanic Garden since 1988. He read Botany at Oxford and five years later was awarded a Master of Horticulture by the RHS. He trained at the Oxford Botanic Garden, Savill Gardens, and the Royal Botanic Gardens, Kew, before returning to the Oxford Botanic Garden in 1986 as general foreman. In 1996 he was elected to the post of lecturer in Plant Conservation at Somerville College. Walker is a member of the group of conservation biologists helping to develop the Global Strategy for Plant Conservation and has lectured widely to the public, nationally and regionally. Among his previous books are *Euphorbias* (RHS 2000) and *Plants: A Very Short Introduction* (Oxford University Press 2012).